RICH AND POOR

Perspectives on Tackling Inequality in Ireland

Edited by
Sara Cantillon, Carmel Corrigan,
Peadar Kirby and Joan O'Flynn

Oak Tree Press
Dublin
in association with
Combat Poverty Agency

Oak Tree Press
Merrion Building
Lower Merrion Street
Dublin 2, Ireland
www.oaktreepress.com

© 2001 Combat Poverty Agency

A catalogue record of this book is
available from the British Library.

ISBN 1 86076 211-5

This study forms part of the Combat Poverty Agency's Research Series,
in which it is No. 32. The views expressed in this report are the authors'
own and not necessarily those of the Combat Poverty Agency.
www.cpa.ie

Printed in the Republic of Ireland
by Colour Books Ltd.

Contents

About the Contributors

Peter Archer is a graduate of University College, Cork and is research fellow at the Educational Research Centre, St Patrick's College, Drumcondra. Much of his work focuses on issues of inequality and disadvantage and he has a particular interest in the relationship between research and policymaking. He is currently involved in projects to survey levels of disadvantage in primary schools and other evaluation and development activities.

Sara Cantillon is Co-ordinator of the Equality Studies Centre, University College, Dublin where she lectures on the Economics of Social Policy and Comparative Economic Systems. As Visiting Professor to the World Bank in 1997 she developed poverty training modules and with the UN Economic Commission for Africa lectured on income transfers and public expenditure (Ethiopia, 1997 and South Africa, 1998). Her research areas include non-monetary deprivation indicators, gender and poverty and research methodologies.

Carmel Corrigan is a Social Policy Analyst in the National Economic and Social Council. She has previously worked in a number of organisations including the Combat Poverty Agency, WRC Social and Economic Consultants and the Observatory on National Policies to Combat Social Exclusion.

P.J. Drudy is a Fellow, Associate Professor of Economics and Co-Director of the Centre for Urban and Regional Studies, Trinity College, Dublin. He has published widely on the "regional problem", industrial and urban policy, EU policies and housing. Recent publications include *The Regional Problem: Urban Disadvantage and Development*, Trinity Economics Papers, with Michael Punch and *Housing: A New Approach*, the Report of the Housing Commission, 1999 which he chaired.

Eithne Fitzgerald lectures in the Department of Social Studies, Trinity College, Dublin and before that taught social policy in University College, Dublin. She has worked in the civil service, as a freelance researcher and in the voluntary sector. As Minister of State for Finance and Labour Affairs she enacted the Ethics in Public Office Act and the Freedom of Information Act. She was a member of the Commission on Social Welfare and chaired the Task Force on Violence against Women.

Cecily Kelleher holds the foundation chair of health promotion at the National University of Ireland, Galway. She trained as an epidemiologist and is director of the Centre for Health Promotion Studies which has recently explored the interaction between lifestyle and socioeconomic circumstances among adults and children. With Eamon O'Shea she is a principal investigator in the Health Research Board-funded unit on health status and health gain which explores disadvantage and inequality in Ireland.

Peadar Kirby holds a PhD from the London School of Economics and is a senior lecturer in the School of Communications, Dublin City University. He has worked as a journalist in Peru and with *The Irish Times* and is the author of a number of books on development issues. He is co-editor and a contributor to *Reinventing Ireland: Culture and the Celtic Tiger* and is the author of *Growth with Inequality: The International Political Economy of Ireland's Development in the 1990s,* both to be published in 2001.

Mary Murphy works as National Social Policy Officer with the Society of St Vincent de Paul. Before that she was Assistant Secretary General of the Irish National Organisation of the Unemployed. She has worked in various national policy fora including NESF, NESC and NAPS and was involved in negotiating the Partnership 2000 agreement and the Programme for Prosperity and Fairness.

Joan O'Flynn has been Head of Information with the Combat Poverty Agency since 1994 and is Editor of the quarterly journal *Poverty Today*. She is a graduate of the Equality Studies Centre, University College Dublin. Prior to joining the Combat Poverty Agency, she worked as a Policy and Information Worker with the Action Group for Irish Youth, a London-based charity.

Colm O'Reardon is an Economist with the National Economic and Social Council. He was previously a Combat Poverty Agency Research Fellow while completing a doctoral thesis at Oxford University and was an economic consultant with Indecon while preparing his section of this book. His research interests are political economy and economic inequality

Eamon O'Shea is a statutory lecturer at the National University of Ireland, Galway and is a graduate of University College Dublin and the University of York, receiving his PhD from the University of Leicester. His main research interests are the economics of ageing, health inequalities, social policy and the welfare state.

Michael Punch is a Research Associate in the Centre for Urban and Regional Studies and a Teaching Assistant in the Department of Geography, Trinity College, Dublin. He has recently completed a PhD thesis on uneven development, community organisation and action in Dublin. Recent publications include *The Regional Problem: Urban Disadvantage and Development*, Trinity Economics Papers, with P.J. Drudy and *Housing: A New Approach*, the Report of the Housing Commission, 1999 (Research Officer).

Acknowledgements

This publication has brought together a number of different perspectives to its analysis of inequality between rich and poor in Ireland. Many people were involved in the project including all of the contributors, the editors, Agency Board and staff, anonymous referees and readers. Thanks are extended to each person for their co-operation, patience, interest and expertise. A special word of thanks to the editorial group of Sara Cantillon, Carmel Corrigan, Peadar Kirby and Joan O'Flynn; to Fergus Mulligan who undertook the sub-editing and indexing of the study as well as contributing to the production of the publication, and to the staff at Oak Tree Press for their preparation of the title for publication. Everybody's contribution is highly valued.

Combat Poverty Agency
April 2001

Foreword

Introduction

The aim of the Combat Poverty Agency is to work for the prevention and elimination of poverty and social exclusion in Ireland. The Agency is the government's advisory body on all aspects of economic and social policy relating to poverty. The study arises from the Agency's concern to narrow the gap between rich and poor, through promoting a fairer distribution of resources, services and employment opportunities in favour of people living in poverty (Strategic Plan 1999-2001). In particular it focuses on the role of public policy in addressing imbalances in the distribution of economic and social goods and the implications of this for addressing poverty.

The overall aim of the study is to inform and stimulate debate regarding the manner in which social spending creates, reinforces or reduces inequality and poverty. The study:

- Discusses the link between inequality and poverty ;

- Examines social spending patterns in Ireland;

- Analyses spending in the key policy areas of education, housing, health, taxation and social welfare; and

- Explores options for achieving a more equitable distribution of resources and opportunities in Irish society.

In the first three chapters, contributors discuss theoretical, conceptual and contextual issues that underlie distribution and redistribution patterns in Ireland. Chapter 4 provides an overview of the Irish economy since 1987 and particularly draws attention to changes in the distribution of income and earnings. This leads to Chapters 5-8 where contributors examine to what extent social spending in tax, social welfare, education, housing and health creates or reinforces poverty and inequality. Finally, in Chapter 9, the four editors of the volume, Sara Cantillon, Carmel Corrigan, Peadar Kirby and Joan O'Flynn, draw together key conclusions, advocate a more explicit policy commitment to reducing inequality and eliminating poverty and outline approaches to realise this objective more effectively.

Origins and Rationale for the Study

The Agency commissioned the study in response to the anomalous widening of the gap between rich and poor during a sustained period of rapid economic growth and significant policy consideration of poverty. Overall income inequality increased during the 1990s and Ireland is one of the most unequal countries in the EU. Better-off households are gaining from the economic boom to a greater extent than those who are less well off.[1] The Agency restates its belief that it is government responsibility to control and ameliorate the inequalities arising from economic growth and wealth creation through public policy interventions. The challenge of good governance is to redress imbalances through more redistributive tax and welfare policies and investment in public services[2] and through facilitating enhanced employment opportunities for those most excluded from the labour market.

In commissioning this work, the Agency was interested to examine social spending as an anti-poverty strategy and to use this work to stimulate public debate on the role of public services to prevent poverty and to improve the quality of life for people living in poverty. The Agency advocates the promotion and development of high quality accessible public services. These should be considered as a form of "public wealth" that is

---

[1] Nolan, Brian, Bertrand Maître, Donal O'Neill and Olive Sweetman (2000), *The Distribution of Income in Ireland,* Dublin, Oak Tree Press in association with the Combat Poverty Agency

[2] Ibid.

qualitatively different to the private and individual wealth that generates socioeconomic inequality. This raises the need to explicitly consider both the spending levels required to underwrite public services and for policy to be explicit about the distribution outcomes it pursues. Ireland is a low tax economy and we have the scope to spend much more on public services. The overall burden of tax in the EU is 42.6 per cent of GDP. In Ireland the tax burden is 34.1 per cent[3] of GDP.

This volume complements a significant body of research previously published by the Agency on poverty. Valuable and extensive research on poverty has been carried out on the basis of data collected in the Living in Ireland household surveys undertaken by the Economic and Social Research Institute (ESRI) in 1987, 1994 and subsequently. Based on these surveys, and sponsored by the Department of Social, Community and Family Affairs and the Combat Poverty Agency, Oak Tree Press and the Agency have published several poverty research reports.[4] This research programme continues as work in progress with further reports planned. It is an important resource for understanding the causes, nature and extent of poverty in Ireland and is a significant influence on the debate that shapes anti-poverty policy. Many of the contributors in this study draw on

---

[3] Frazer, Hugh (2000), "Viewpoint" in *Poverty Today* no. 48:3, Dublin, Combat Poverty Agency

[4] Callan, Tim, Brendan J. Whelan, Christopher T. Whelan, James Williams (1996), *Poverty in the 1990s: Evidence from the Living in Ireland Survey*, Dublin, Oak Tree Press in association with Combat Poverty Agency; Nolan Brian, Christopher T. Whelan and James Williams (1998*)*, *Where are Poor Households? The Spatial Distribution of Poverty and Deprivation in Ireland*, Dublin, Oak Tree Press in association with Combat Poverty Agency; Nolan, Brian, Christopher T. Whelan (1999), *Loading the Dice: A Study of Cumulative Disadvantage*, Dublin, Oak Tree Press in association with Combat Poverty Agency; Nolan Brian and Dorothy Watson (1999), *Women and Poverty in Ireland*, Dublin, Oak Tree Press in association with Combat Poverty Agency; Nolan Brian (2000), *Child Poverty in Ireland,* Dublin, Oak Tree Press in association with Combat Poverty Agency; Nolan Brian, Bertrand Maître, Donal O'Neill and Olive Sweetman (2000), *The Distribution of Income in Ireland,* Dublin, Oak Tree Press in association with Combat Poverty Agency; Frawley, James P., Patrick Cummins, *Characteristics and Policies*, Oak Tree Press in association with the Combat Poverty Agency.

the ESRI poverty research, reiterating its importance as an exceptional empirical resource on national poverty trends.

This new study from the Agency seeks to broaden the debate from a more recent focus on income and poverty to revisit and revitalise notions of equality and inequality with a primary interest in the distribution of economic and social goods. The study, however, does not deal substantially with issues of diversity and recognition. The Agency strongly acknowledges that poverty leads to further inequalities. We also recognise that identity-based inequality and unfair discrimination result in poverty and socioeconomic inequalities for many groups such as people with disabilities, Travellers, other minority ethnic groups, women, gay and lesbians, lone parents, homeless people, refugees and asylum seekers, ex-prisoners, older people and others. To successfully address inequalities of distribution, identity-based inequalities must also be tackled. In asserting this, the Agency consciously supports community and voluntary groups working on issues relating to distribution, discrimination and diversity and has also funded and published a number of relevant reports.[5] The Agency is also conscious of the lack of appropriate data on the experiences of people in minority, disadvantaged and excluded groups. We are currently working with relevant interests to establish the feasibility of improving the situation relating to poverty data for groups not currently included in the Living in Ireland and Household Budget Surveys.

Concern with issues of socioeconomic equality, inequality and redistribution is not new in Ireland. Twelve years ago the National Economic and Social Council (NESC) published a comprehensive report on redistribution that examined social expenditure in Ireland from 1973-1980.[6] More recently the ESRI

---

[5] See recent Combat Poverty Agency Annual Reports for a listing of grant-aid to a range of local and national community and voluntary groups working on these issues. The Agency also funds and supports a national programme for national anti-poverty networks including groups working with the unemployed, Travellers, one parent families and other disadvantaged and marginalised groups.

[6] NESC (1988), *Redistribution Through State Social Expenditure in the Republic of Ireland: 1973-1980*, Dublin, Government Publications

published *Bust to Boom?* an extensive inter-disciplinary account of the Irish experience of growth and inequality[7] and Oak Tree Press and the Combat Poverty Agency published *The Distribution of Income in Ireland*.[8] However, the economic context has changed dramatically from economic depression in the 1980s to current economic buoyancy.

Why Tackling Inequality Matters

Poverty is not inevitable, and poverty and inequality are not necessarily one and the same thing. Unjust distribution of wealth and resources and structures and procedures that confer unequal economic, social, political and cultural benefits on different sections of the population embed inequality and generate poverty. This view emphasises the structural causes of poverty and the extent to which inequality causes and perpetuates poverty. It avoids the conceptualisation of poor people as a "problem" and locates the solutions to poverty in the systems and structures that society maintains and develops. Visible manifestations of poverty and inequality such as homelessness, drug-use and crime by young people can become scapegoat issues without the structural analysis that poverty is created by the unequal distribution of resources, opportunities and power in society. An unequal society maintains systems and structures that sustain the winners from that system — the rich and the powerful. The structures of society, particularly the class structure, greatly influence life-chances. A working-class or poor child is less likely to benefit as much from, for example, the educational system as a middle-class or better-off child.

Poverty in Irish public policy is generally understood in the way described in the National Anti-Poverty Strategy, *Sharing in Progress* (Government of Ireland, 1997):

---

[7] Nolan, Brian, Philip J. O'Connell and Christopher T. Whelan, eds (2000), *Bust to Boom? The Irish Experience of Growth and Inequality*. Dublin, Institute of Public Administration

[8] Nolan, Brian, Bertrand Maître, Donal O'Neill and Olive Sweetman (2000), *The Distribution of Income in Ireland*, Dublin, Oak Tree Press in association with the Combat Poverty Agency

> People are living in poverty if their income and resources,
> (material, cultural and social) are so inadequate as to pre-
> clude them from having a standard of living which is re-
> garded as acceptable by Irish society generally. As a result
> of inadequate income and resources people may be ex-
> cluded and marginalised from participating in activities
> which are considered the norm for other people in society
> (p.3).

This definition describes poverty as a concept that is relative to wider social standards. To experience poverty is to experience unjust inequality in the distribution of material, cultural and social goods, to experience inequality in living standards and inequality in social participation. For an Agency concerned with combating poverty, tackling inequality matters because:

- Poverty leads to and can arise from unjust inequalities.

- Unjust inequalities deny access to basic human rights, undermine full citizenship and thus contribute to the production and reproduction of poverty;

- There is a fundamental link between poverty and income
  inequality, social inequality and political inequality;

- Inequality and unfair discrimination based on social characteristics such as age, ethnicity, disability, gender and
  sexual orientation lead to poverty;

- A very unequal society is unlikely to have sufficient social solidarity necessary to support measures to eliminate poverty.

A range of links between poverty and inequality are described above. While poverty and inequality are not necessarily the same, they can produce similar social and economic impacts:

- The loss of human potential is a major impact of poverty and
  inequality. They both hinder human development in a holistic sense and diminish the quality of life available to people.

- The dissatisfaction of excluded groups who do not benefit
  significantly and fairly from the wealth creation of society
  threatens social cohesion and the overall level of "well-
  being" in a society and generates social division.

- The supply of labour and consumer demand contribute to the maintenance of economic growth and Irish competitiveness in a global economy. From these perspectives poverty and inequality cost the economy because they restrict both the supply and quality of labour and constrain consumer demand.

- Poverty and inequality also generate other costs to the economy. The government loses revenue through lost tax on both income and expenditure taxes such as VAT and through social insurance. Paying for poverty and inequality through the cost of providing income maintenance support, social services support and other supports may also be higher. This is not to advocate cuts in social expenditure but to suggest that public expenditure should be considered as investment in the human, social and economic infrastructure to create a new "public wealth" and to foster a more just distribution of resources and opportunities.

- Efforts to tackle poverty through targeted programmes alone without reducing serious inequalities will only have limited success and will not address the structural causes of poverty.

- There is a relationship between greater inequality levels and poor health standards. Ill health increases the risk of poverty.

Policy Context for Social Change

At local, national and international levels, an extremely positive context now exists for transforming our unequal and divided society.

In Ireland, the context includes a growing economy and revenue buoyancy and very low levels of unemployment. There is a strong anti-poverty infrastructure that includes the current national agreement a Programme for Prosperity and Fairness, the National Anti-Poverty Strategy, the National Development Plan, National Drugs Strategy, National Children's Strategy, poverty-proofing of public policy and the integration of local government and local development. The recently established

Equality Authority and the emerging Human Rights Commissions in both the Republic and the North and new political institutions on the island to embed the peace process are also important developments with great potential to contribute to ending poverty, inequality and discrimination.

It is vital to acknowledge the important steps forward in policy. A ten year National Anti-Poverty Strategy (NAPS) is in place and currently under review, along with several other strategies mentioned above. A national sustainable development strategy is in place and a spatial strategy is also currently in development. Public expenditure has increased in many areas such as educational disadvantage, social welfare, health, child care, housing and disability services. However many of these increases have been from a low starting base and the quality of our public services in some areas is still not commensurate with other EU member states. In addition, the scale of services is not commensurate with provision elsewhere or with the more generous possibilities that now exist arising from our new found wealth.

The Agency strongly supports the range of policy efforts in recent times concerned with tackling poverty. Space does not allow for the detail here. However, the Annual Reports of the Inter-Departmental Policy Committee on Social Inclusion document these comprehensively.[9] Work currently in progress provides a critical opportunity for strengthening the policy and research focus on poverty and inequality. For example, under the review of the National Anti-Poverty Strategy, emerging issues such as racism have been identified. The Combat Poverty Agency is supporting new research on poverty and racism and new work on poverty reduction indicators is underway. Nationally as part of the review of the Anti-Poverty Strategy, a series of working groups will consider new poverty reduction targets under the themes of child poverty, women's poverty, older

---

[9] Interdepartmental Policy Committee (1999) Social Inclusion Strategy, Annual Report of the Interdepartmental Policy Committee, Dublin, The Stationery Office; Interdepartmental Policy Committee (2000) Social Inclusion Strategy, Annual Report of the Interdepartmental Policy Committee, Dublin, The Stationery Office

people, health and housing/accommodation. A new Indexation Group, established under the Partnership for Prosperity and Fairness will examine the issue of the adequacy of social welfare payments for adults and children.

At EU level, Article 137 of the Treaty of Amsterdam now allows action to combat poverty at an EU level. A new article, Article 13, allows the Union to "take appropriate action to combat discrimination based on sex, racial or ethnic origin, religion or belief, disability, age or sexual orientation". As a result EU leaders finalised a first ever European strategy to fight poverty and social exclusion at the Nice Summit in December 2000 and agreed clear objectives in this regard. There are also new structures such as the European Social Action Programme and the European Social Protection Committee. Significantly, each EU member state is required to develop a National Action Plan against poverty and social exclusion (NAP incl) by June 2001.

Globally, the UN World Summit for Social Development in Geneva in June 2000 reaffirmed the commitment to eradicate poverty, to foster social development that reduces wealth inequalities and to distribute the fruits of economic growth more equally. The Political Declaration at the conclusion of the Summit provided very clear direction that:

> social development requires not only economic activity, but also reduction in inequality in the distribution of wealth and more equitable distribution of the benefits of economic growth within and among nations, including, inter alia, realisation of an open, equitable, secure, non-discriminatory, predictable, transparent and multilateral rule-based international trading system, maximising opportunities and guaranteeing social justice, recognising the inter-relationship between social development and economic growth.

Social Spending Policies, Trends and Impacts

The volume examines social spending patterns in Ireland and analyses spending in the key policy areas of education, housing, health, taxation and social welfare. The Agency reports

below the key points from the original material in the chapters
of this volume.

Social Expenditure

Trends in gross social expenditure in Ireland, as a percentage
of GNP, have varied in recent decades from around one quarter
in the late 1970s and the latter half of the 1990s to one third in
the first half of the 1980s. After the fiscal adjustment of the late
1980s, social expenditure fell from 33 per cent of GNP in 1986 to
24 per cent of GNP in 1990. The ratio of social expenditure to
GNP rose again in the first half of the 1990s to 26 per cent in
1995. It is now close to the 1990 share of 24 per cent of GNP, reflecting the improvement in the economy. The critical question is
not the optimal scale of expenditure on inequalities but whether
spending is in line with prosperity levels as measured by GNP
per head. In the early 1990s, on the basis of per capita income,
social spending was higher than might have been expected.
Given the economic growth in the second half of the 1990s and
the slower social spending growth, it is unlikely this is still the
case. A welfare state classification in 1997 placed Ireland in the
low-spending social expenditure category.

A large percentage of the Irish population receives some
form of social transfer. These transfers are concentrated on
people with a low standard of living. There is a significant redistributive effect, measured by the impact of social transfers
on the distribution of income. However it is equally clear that
considerable inequalities remain even after the transfers. This
is not because the welfare state is any less effective than elsewhere but because of the considerable and increasing inequality in market incomes.

Tax and Social Welfare

Ireland's tax and welfare systems redistribute a relatively
smaller share of income than in other developed countries, reflecting the type of welfare system we have chosen and our low
tax burden. Our modestly progressive income tax system is
largely counterbalanced by the regressive nature of expenditure taxes. The result is a broadly neutral overall pattern of re-

distribution over the tax system as a whole. Thus it is the welfare system rather than the tax system that carries the primary role of redistributing income. In international terms Ireland's welfare payment and tax levels are both relatively low so the level of re-distribution effected through both systems is also low. A result is that Ireland's disposable incomes are among the most unequal in the developed world.

Income tax reductions since 1987 have mainly reduced tax rates and have disproportionately benefited the better off. Substantial reductions in taxes on profits, capital gains and property transfers favour the accumulation and concentration of capital. The absence of any property or wealth tax, the halving of capital gains tax and the erosion of capital acquisitions tax leaves Ireland with one of the most lenient capital tax regimes in Europe.

Social welfare incomes have risen faster than inflation but slower than incomes elsewhere in the economy, therefore the relative position of welfare recipients has deteriorated. The generous treatment of capital wealth is in contrast to the decline experienced in welfare payments relative to other incomes. The scale of welfare improvements relative to earnings has a key role in determining whether the poorest households hold their relative position or disimprove. In the longer-term if the current policy of setting welfare increases above price increases but below earnings growth continues, the gap between rich and poor will further widen.

Social partnership with its core trade-off between modest pay rises and tax cuts has leaned more towards lower taxes than higher welfare spending. The ratio between announced allocations on Budget day to extra tax cuts and welfare increases show that, from 1987 to 1997, the cost of income tax packages ranged between the same scale as the welfare packages, to twice the welfare package. In 1998 the tax package was almost three times the welfare package; in 1999 and 2000, around five times the welfare package.

During the 1990s the evidence suggests that the tax and welfare systems widened rather than narrowed the inequality gap during this time. While prosperity alters the distribution of

income and wealth, the scale of revenue generated also offers
unprecedented possibilities for change. In a near-zero growth
environment, redistribution to the poor is at a cost to the non-
poor. When growth is abundant, redistributing its fruits offers
quite a painless way to achieve a more egalitarian result.

Education

Increasing investment in education in an undifferentiated or
universalistic way to increase participation levels, as occurred
in Ireland, is unlikely to have a major impact on inequality.
There are a number of reasons for this. In particular, the main
beneficiaries of increased spending e.g. through abolishing
fees, are families who would otherwise have paid for their children's education. Increased participation in education only has
an impact on inequality after advantaged groups have already
attained full participation.

Despite efforts to pursue a policy of targeting resources in
education since the 1980s, spending on education remains regressive and genuine positive discrimination towards disadvantaged groups is rare. Spending is regressive because the
state spends much more on the education of better off young
people who stay in the education system than it does on young
people from poorer families who tend to leave the system
early. In 1999, per capita expenditure on a third level student
(IR£4,000) was over two and a half times the expenditure on a
primary student (IR£1,900) and almost 70 per cent higher than a
second level student (IR£2,900). Young people from poorer
backgrounds are grossly under-represented in third level institutions. Approximately 20 per cent of students from lower
working class backgrounds participate in third level compared
to 80 per cent of students from upper middle class backgrounds. Even though regressivity remains, since 1990 there
has been an important policy shift in this funding inequity. The
ratio of per capita third level expenditure to primary level expenditure has dropped from 3.9:1 to 2.2:1. An examination of
total expenditure over the 1990s reinforces the trend in regressivity. Between 1990 and 1998 expenditure at primary level increased by 71 per cent; 88 per cent at second level and 134 per

cent at third level. Pressure to increase third level places in response to demographic demands while protecting primary spending from falling enrolments and thereby increasing per capita spending seems to underlie this trend. Teachers' salaries and superannuation accounted for almost 80 per cent of extra money spent on primary education in the 1990s. With the recruitment of extra teachers, further improvements in average class sizes at primary level occurred during the 1990s when average class size fell from 30.8 to 26.1.

Along with a number of other initiatives, designation of schools has been a central part of government policy to combat disadvantage since 1984. The main conclusion from designation efforts at primary level is that until 1993, they did not result in genuine positive discrimination. They did however succeed in bringing the income and resources of schools in disadvantaged areas up to the level of those in non-designated areas. In 1997, the European Social Fund estimated that the annual cost of a number of specific schemes to tackle disadvantage was about 2 per cent of total educational expenditure. Such targeted expenditure had been rising steadily since the early 1990s.

If tackling poverty and removing inequality are priority issues spending needs to be targeted at those who benefit least from the present educational system. However one of its limitations is the extent to which advantaged groups can maintain their advantage by expanding their expenditure on their children's education. A further limitation is that there are systemic reasons for educational inequalities such as aspects of curriculum, assessment and selection and streaming procedures. Finally, any action to tackle inequality in education must link with efforts to address structural inequality in wider society.

Housing

Housing policy has interpreted and promoted housing as a commodity rather than a "social good" or right, thus generating housing inequalities. The changing trends in the social class of house buyers indicate that those from the professional classes make up an increasing proportion of house buyers as evidenced by the occupations of those receiving loan approvals.

The proportion of new house buyers who are already owner-occupiers has increased significantly between 1994 and 1998 — from 36 to 50 per cent of the total. This indicates that housing is considered an investment opportunity. There are significant differences between building costs and the price of housing suggesting that supernormal profits are being made by developers. Many of the tax reliefs provided to investors are regressive because people on low incomes are unable to benefit. They do not incur tax liability nor do they have the necessary capital to invest in property development in designated areas. Home owners in Ireland have no housing cost, effectively receiving a state subsidy, often called imputed income (the rent the occupant would otherwise have to pay). Applying an equity principle, taxation would apply to imputed income. There is more favourable treatment for home owners than private rented tenants who must pay rent and receive a minimal tax allowance. Cash grants by the state to first time buyers of residential property is also a manifestation of inequality between sectors within housing. The discount on the sale of local authority housing to tenants is further evidence of the favourable treatment of home ownership above other tenures. While popular, the discount is a substantial subsidy towards the privatisation of social housing.

Housing can no longer be treated solely as a market commodity if current inequalities are to be addressed. A considerable re-orientation of current policy, which is both inefficient and inequitable, is required to reduce the highly favourable treatment of owner-occupation in comparison with other tenures in Ireland. A balanced approach to housing policy would involve an expanded role for the non-market production and allocation of housing and a fair deal for households, whether they own or rent their homes.

Health

There has been little effort to shift the focus in health policy to support the less advantaged or to create targets that narrow inequality beyond more general rhetoric about issues of equity and access. This prevails although class differentials in mortality and morbidity patterns and lifestyle behaviours are known to exist. Health promotion strategies to tackle common disease patterns also demonstrate a graduated pattern of effectiveness. International research, though contested, suggests that countries with less income inequality enjoy better health. Health differences between countries reflect, not differences in wealth, but differences in income distribution. Inequality is bad for the health of populations regardless of the country's absolute standard of living. Societies with more income equality will have better health.

In Ireland, a lack of data at individual, ecological and health service utilisation levels has contributed to official inertia in dealing with both the causes and consequences of health inequalities. Two recent data sets are now available to examine important socioeconomic relationships in health in Ireland. These are the National Health and Lifestyle Surveys commissioned by the Department of Health and reported on in 1999. This data shows that medical card holders do worse than noncard holders from health care need and utilisation through to smoking and drinking. The health inequality debate is less advanced in Ireland than in other European countries. Carrying out a substantial research agenda is necessary before an integrated strategy dealing with health inequalities is formulated and implemented. Although the importance of equity is acknowledged in policy formulation, the fact is that little has been achieved in the implementation of policies that might address the serious equity problems existing in both health status in itself and health care provision in this country.

Investment in material conditions, as a response to health inequalities, can improve the living standards of poor and impoverished communities within the framework of full political and economic participation. Investment to enhance social relations is also important as cultural processes matter. More unequal societies are less likely to generate and foster supportive social environments, which in turn contribute to higher levels of health inequality.

A Future Agenda

This volume seeks to stimulate debate about the performance of public policy in addressing imbalances in the distribution of economic and social goods and the implications of this for tackling poverty. There are different views and approaches on how best to tackle inequality. The Agency, however, is of no doubt on the basis of the work in this study and other reports it and others have published that efforts to combat poverty that do not set out to very significantly reduce economic, social, cultural and political inequalities will be unsuccessful. While there are of course many other arguments for reducing inequalities, the goal of ending poverty requires that reducing inequalities should be a central goal of public policy. Drawing from themes identified in the study the following sets out below the Agency's perspective on key issues to be addressed in the future for social expenditure to be strengthened as a strategy to reduce inequality and so eliminate poverty.

Devising Explicit Policy Objectives to Tackle Inequality and Poverty

A dominant theme recurring throughout the volume is the challenge to policy to move towards more robust equality objectives. It is one of the dominant themes of this volume. The Agency agrees with this. As we see in Ireland, economic growth generates and resides alongside increasing income inequality. It is important now to question the purpose of economic growth. While the extent of growth is important so too is the quality and distribution of the benefits of such growth.

Our economic model is based on competitiveness and selection. If left to its own devices, this model creates exclusion for those who, for whatever reason, are unable to meet the competitiveness criteria. There is a need to address this by putting in place policies and procedures that will defuse this impact and instead ensure that the benefits of economic growth are redistributed to bring about greater social change. This means that the values and knowledge that influence the shaping of public policy would reflect stronger equality objectives.

Growth and development should serve social ends — to eradicate, but at a minimum to prevent and reduce poverty and inequality — thereby maximising equality and human welfare levels for all. This means clearly setting out explicit social objectives that should include the reduction of inequalities and poverty, establishing strong strategies towards reaching these objectives and identifying appropriate performance indicators. An objective to reduce inequality through a more equal distribution of wealth and of the benefits of economic growth suggests that policymakers should be seeking to look for the most socially optimal resource allocation. This reinforces the necessity of the state's interventionist role in resource allocation and is an affirmation of national strategies to tackle poverty and social exclusion. However it also suggests that in implementing these strategies, the balance in the efficiency/equity trade-off is carefully reconsidered to ensure that equity is a primary rather than a residual concern.

The concept of social quality could also be examined further for its capacity to integrate the economic and social policymaking. Social quality rejects the view that economic growth and development are likely to be undermined by progress in the social sphere and that economic progress does not necessarily mean social progress. Economic and social programmes would be evaluated for their contribution to enhancing social quality. Programmes would be assessed for their impact on social relations, people's self-respect and capabilities and on maximising economic and social participation, thus expanding the "horizons of equality beyond income transfers and social provision" (Cantillon and O'Shea, Chapter 3).

Making Economic and Social Rights an Irish Reality

Social and economic rights are a theme also raised by various contributors and are a concern for the Agency for a number of years. In May 1999 the United Nations Committee on Economic, Social and Cultural Rights specifically recommended the inclusion of justiciable economic, social and cultural rights in the Irish Constitution. It also urged the expansion of the NAPS and the integration of a human rights approach to the NAPS Strategy. The Agency endorses these sentiments and is working to support the application of a rights approach to the Anti-Poverty Strategy.

A social rights approach involves a contract between the state and the citizen. One of the strengths of this understanding of rights is that it "protect[s] the weak from the strong and make[s] all equal".[10] A rights perspective, properly understood and applied, includes a corresponding emphasis on duties, not only of service providers, but of beneficiaries and claim holders.[11] At a European level, it is disappointing that the new Fundamental Charter on Rights will not have a legislative status. Many member states, including Ireland, were reluctant to grant the Charter this authority. Even without a legally binding Charter, Ireland continues to have international legal obligations under the United Nations Conventions on Economic, Social and Cultural Rights and on the Rights of the Child. The Council of Europe's social charter is also relevant.

These responsibilities suggest that Irish policymaking should be more explicit in framing its policies and actions from a rights perspective. For example, the working groups set up under the NAPS to consider new targets and the revision of existing targets should examine how their deliberations can take account of economic, social and cultural rights. Final decisions on the NAPS targets should also consider this. New legislation such as the Disabilities Bill similarly should take account of this approach.

Existing examples of a rights approach are evident in the Constitution, current legislation and social expenditure. These include social welfare, health and housing legislation, policies and provision and the constitutional right to primary education. In the future, the developing peace process may have an influence on the rights debate in the Republic. In particular, the establishment of a Human Rights Commission in both parts of the

---

[10] Cox, Robert Henry (1998), "The Consequences of Welfare Reform: How Social Rights are Changing", *Journal of Social Policy*, Vol. 27, 1, 1-16

[11] Connolly, J. (2000), *Economic Social and Cultural Rights and the Review of the National Anti-Poverty Strategy*, unpublished paper produced for the Combat Poverty Agency

island and of a joint committee of representatives from both Commissions will be relevant. This provides for the potential to develop all-island protocols and strategies and to harmonise policies and measures. A strong focus on economic, social and cultural rights in either jurisdiction is an impetus for the same in the second jurisdiction. The Bill of Rights currently in development for Northern Ireland may contain rights relating to the distribution of resources and services. This will have implications for the Republic as a joint committee of representatives from both Human Rights Commissions is required to work on an All Ireland Charter of Human Rights. The EU Peace and Reconciliation Programme in the twelve border counties can also influence and act as a resource for the debate on a rights approach.

Creating Greater Equality — The Challenge for Social Partnership

In each social partnership agreement since 1987, the link between growth, improved living standards and social equity has been emphasised to varying degrees. Maintaining economic competitiveness and agreement on public finances have characterised many of these agreements. As illustrated in this volume, this period generated increased prosperity for the majority of Irish people. Despite this, high levels of inequality, particularly income inequality, still persist. Several contributors point out that the Irish model of social partnership, as a way of organising our political and economic affairs, needs to find a way of addressing and breaking the pattern of growth with inequality. Stronger acknowledgement of the interdependency between economic competitiveness and social inclusion can potentially redirect priorities away from an over emphasis on economic growth and market-friendliness to greater social concern and more balanced and equitable social development. It is critical that this emphasis is adopted at a time of economic buoyancy. There is danger that if growth slows down there will be less political will and strong resistance from the vested interests of wealth and power holders to be concerned with redistribution issues.

The Agency strongly supports the involvement of people experiencing poverty in policy decisions that affect them. As the national resource agency on community development we are responsible for developing and supporting initiatives whereby people who are marginalised and excluded can join with others to participate in actions to influence change and to exert control over the social, political and economic issues that affect their lives. This is an integral part of the social change advocated by the contributors to this study and is one that the Agency strongly endorses.

Opportunities at a local level for engagement in partnership work have existed before in area-based partnership companies. They now expand to include opportunities at a local government level as part of the reform of local government and the integration of local development and local government. The recently established Community Fora at county council and corporation level and the developing programme of work by the Agency and the Departments of Environment and Social, Community and Family Affairs to extend the National Anti-Poverty Strategy to local government can provide for an intensification of community involvement in policy relating to poverty, disadvantage and inequality.

Strengthening the Information Base

To devise strategies for a fairer and more equal society it is vitally important to know the distributive patterns, including patterns of power, within Irish society. We have a strong information base to build on but several contributors here have also identified serious gaps in our knowledge, acutely in the case of health.

Addressing data gaps is an essential strategy for better policy formulation and for understanding how we live. Public policy has a role in providing the necessary financial and other supports to enhance the research infrastructure concerned with poverty and inequality issues. Some of the key research questions for the future concern the relationship between wealth, poverty and inequality in Ireland. In the context of significant employment growth, to what extent does generating wealth by earning equity via the housing market or the stock market impact on the reproduction of poverty and inequality? To what extent do class, gender, race, disability and other variables structure people's access to income and wealth and other economic and social goods? To what extent does powerlessness, as a condition of being poor in Ireland, restrict people to partial participation in society?[12] To what extent are poor people more than a data source and are genuinely empowered and included in work that develops research and policy approaches on poverty and inequality? These are fundamental questions for organisations that commission research on poverty and inequality. The commitment in the Programme for Prosperity and Fairness to examine the underlying methodology of the NAPS provides a useful framework for debate and analysis of these issues in the future.

Conclusion

This volume crystallises a fundamental question about the future of Irish society. Do we want the future to deliver more or less equality? Contributors have argued in an unambiguous way for more robust equality objectives in Irish social policy. The Agency's position is clear. Our mission statement, to work for a fairer and more just society through the prevention and elimination of poverty, is unambiguous. Inequalities that are unfair undermine democratic society and cause and perpetuate poverty. A commitment to social justice demands that we work to promote greater equality as a strategy for eliminating poverty. This means:

- Reducing the class divisions in Irish society;

- Halting and reversing the escalation of income inequalities;

- Working for more equal distribution of wealth;

---

[12] For example, non-skilled manual respondents with less than a Leaving Certificate are twice as likely as those from the professional and managerial class who have enjoyed a third level education to perceive themselves as politically powerless: Hardiman, Niamh and Christopher T. Whelan, 1994, "Politics and Democratic Values" in *Values and Social Change in Ireland*, Christopher T. Whelan (ed.), Dublin, Gill and Macmillan

- Reducing employment, health, housing, educational and other social and cultural inequalities so they are not an impediment to the realisation of people's full potential and participation in society;

- Working for the elimination of discrimination;

- Promoting and celebrating diversity in all its forms.

Combat Poverty Agency
April 2001

Introduction

Inequality is one of the hallmarks of Irish society. Our recent prosperity has not benefited all but has, in fact, marginalised and excluded a sizeable part of our population including the long-term unemployed, single parents, Travellers, early school-leavers, small farmers and the elderly.

Rich and Poor sets out to analyse the causes and extent of social and economic divisions in Ireland and to answer a number of fundamental questions. Why is it that despite greater national prosperity a sizeable sector of our people struggle to survive on an inadequate income? Why do these groups tend to remain on the margins when it comes to jobs, education, health care, housing? And how can policymakers be encouraged to make the decisions that will break this cycle of inter-generational poverty?

The purpose of this book is to stimulate and inform debate on the ways that social spending policies create or reinforce inequality and poverty. For the first time in our history, the government has massive resources generated by our buoyant economy available for redistribution. In the context of the National Anti-Poverty Strategy and other policy initiatives such as recent equality legislation, the National Development Plan and the developing Spatial Strategy, we can choose to share those resources in a more just and equal way or continue to restrict them so they benefit only a limited group.

Rich and Poor attempts to chart a course for a fairer, more equitable society. The authors approach the many aspects of inequality from a number of different perspectives. In Chapter 1, Peadar Kirby clarifies the differences between poverty and inequality and shows how poverty reduction has replaced greater wealth and income equality as a policy objective. He then examines the different views of society which equality and poverty reduction imply, drawing on the work of Amartya Sen to show the implications for society of choosing one objective over the other. He goes on to question the absolute distinction between poverty reduction and equality, arguing that poverty reduction is more accurately seen as a weak formulation of the state's distributional objective and equality as a demanding one. Kirby questions whether this weak formulation is realisable on its own or whether it demands attention to socioeconomic issues also. He applies this argument to Irish social policy, tracing the change in distributional objectives from the 1970s to 2000.

Joan O'Flynn and Mary Murphy in Chapter 2 focus on vertical distribution or the extent to which policy results in redistribution from the well-off to the less well-off. They define redistribution and show the close link between power and the distribution of income and resources. They go on to examine the relationship between a number of ideologies and distribution, how ideology is reflected in economic policy, such as the trade-off between equity and efficiency, and measuring progress in achieving more equal outcomes. The chapter then discusses conventional redistribution tools and other potential routes to more equal distribution outcomes, assessing a rights approach and national policy planning trends. The authors advocate a rights approach and a clearer understanding of the inter-relationship between social inclusion, equality and competitiveness. Combined with more participatory decision-making this framework can achieve more equitable outcomes.

Sara Cantillon and Eamon O'Shea examine the relationship of social expenditure, redistribution and participation and their potential relevance in an Irish context in Chapter 3. They consider various definitions of social expenditure and review the literature on its distributional impact in Ireland, comparing it with other EU states. They reaffirm its positive impact on income inequality and show that the narrowing of income inequalities through social transfers is higher in Ireland than most EU countries. The chapter concludes with a broad discussion on the effectiveness of social expenditure beyond simple redistribution measures and effects. It focuses on the qualitative impact of a lack of broader support services to independent living, drawing on two examples, disability and ageing, to show what could be achieved with a more comprehensive, social quality-oriented approach to goalsetting in social provision.

The implications of economic change in Ireland are covered by Colm O'Reardon in Chapter 4 who traces this change at a macroeconomic level for income distribution. He describes post-1987 economic successes and the model of social partnership which underpinned them. The chapter also reviews research results on income distribution and poverty in this period, relating macroeconomic changes to the income distribution data. He contends poverty and income distribution are major challenges to the model, despite the achievements of social partnership. The author concludes with a discussion of a number of policy implications, particularly those arising from a tightening labour market.

In Chapter 5 Eithne Fitzgerald shows that the Irish welfare and tax systems redistribute a smaller share of income than other developed countries. Social welfare incomes have risen faster than inflation but well below other incomes so that the relative position of social welfare recipients has deteriorated. Tax cuts have disproportionately benefited the well-off and social partnership, with its trade-off between modest pay increases and tax cuts, has leaned more towards lower tax than higher welfare spending, she suggests. The recent economic boom offers a relatively painless opportunity for redistribution but the evidence suggests that the Irish tax and welfare systems have widened the inequality gap.

The impact of educational public spending on inequality is covered by Peter Archer in Chapter 6. Using different definitions of inequality he considers the extent to which educational policy can have an impact without dealing with wider social inequality. He shows that children from poor families do not progress as well as others in school and with few educational qualifications they remain poor as adults. Greater undifferentiated investment has done little to reduce inequality and despite efforts to target resources, education spending remains regressive and instances of genuinely positive discrimination are rare.

Does housing, a basic human need, contribute to levels of inequality? This is a core theme in Chapter 7 by P.J. Drudy and Michael Punch. There has been significant government intervention in housing but this has been biased mainly towards owner-occupiers. This has caused serious difficulties: higher rents and prices, long waiting lists for social housing, and little regulation and a great deal of tenant insecurity in the private rented sector. The authors call for fundamental policy changes to address the inherent inequalities of housing: the introduction of residential property tax; capital gains tax on the sale of the principal residence; public land banking and control of land prices; rent regulation and security of tenure for private tenants; and a reorientation of social housing to broaden its base and effectiveness.

Chapter 8 by Eamon O'Shea and Cecily Kelleher deals with some of the critical issues in the health inequalities debate. Genetic or constitutional factors, lifestyle and behaviour, the influence of the wider social, cultural and economic environment and access to health services can explain variations in health status. The focus of resources and debate has been on access to services but, the authors contend, most analysts believe the contribution of health care to morbidity and mortality is marginal compared to other influences. There has been more research on the nature and causes of health inequalities in industrialised nations, focusing on understanding the neomaterial and psychosocial impact of relative poverty and a lifecourse approach to the health of individuals. In Ireland, inadequate data has contributed to official inertia in tackling the causes and consequences of health inequalities. The authors conclude that while the importance of equity is acknowledged in policy discussion, there has been little progress in implementing multisectoral policies in health status and health care provision. This is vital to avoid unnecessary deaths in the future.

Bearing in mind the authors' varied approaches to the topic of inequality it is clear that Ireland's strong economic performance provides a unique opportunity to address the systemic inequalities which affect so many citizens. *Rich and Poor* is an attempt to stimulate debate on these issues, to examine the reasons for this inequality and to encourage policymakers and those who hold power to begin creating a more inclusive, egalitarian society. This is not an impossible goal; in fact it is stated explicitly in the Constitution: "The State pledges itself to safeguard with especial care the economic interests of the weaker sections of the community. . . ." (*Bunreacht na hÉireann*, Art.45.4.1). The resources are there, what is needed is the will to make this pledge a high priority in Irish social and economic policy.

Chapter 1

Inequality and Poverty in Ireland: Clarifying Social Objectives*

Peadar Kirby

If real incomes are rising rapidly — as they are — those whose incomes do not rise as rapidly will, by definition fall behind, even if their own living standards are also improving. Does it matter? If everybody is better off, should we be concerned that some — the majority indeed — are more better off than others, so long as everybody gets something? — Brendan Keenan, *Irish Independent*, 7 October 1999

1.1 INTRODUCTION

Brendan Keenan highlights the reality that, as real incomes rise during a period of high economic growth, there is a danger that the gap between the well-off and the poor can grow. This can happen even while the income of the poor increases in real terms. The question he asks is an extremely important one and relates to the central distributional objective of social policy: namely, whether it is to reduce poverty or to narrow the gap between the rich and the poor. This chapter explores some bases for answering this question.

At the heart of the issue is the difference between poverty and inequality. Though the terms are often used interchangea-

---

* A special word of thanks to John Baker, Department of Politics, UCD, whose detailed comments on an earlier draft were extremely valuable to the author and have helped improve the chapter greatly.

bly, there are important distinctions between them which require clarification. Thus, a country could have high levels of poverty but low levels of inequality. Bangladesh or Sri Lanka are examples of this as they have greater equality of income distribution than in many developed countries but have high levels of poverty (see World Bank, 1999: Table 5). The opposite can also be true as countries combine declining poverty with growing inequality. Brazil in the 1990s is a good example, as the percentage of households below the poverty line fell from 41 per cent to 29 per cent between 1990 and 1996 while inequality continued to rise.[1] Though, until recently, we have had far less regular distributional data on Ireland than we have on many Latin American countries, we now know that in the 1990s income inequality in Ireland has increased while poverty (defined in terms of the "consistently poor") has decreased (Callan et al., 1999; Nolan and Maître, 2000). Furthermore, as Table 1.1 shows, Ireland has, in comparative terms, a serious problem of socioeconomic inequality. This table groups 25 countries according to an inequality ratio (IR) derived from the ratio of the income of the top 20 per cent to that of the bottom 20 per cent of the income distribution. The countries include those of the OECD but also some newly industrialising countries (NICs) since Ireland's late industrialisation makes it more comparable to these countries (Kirby, 2000: 36-39). Ireland is found to be close to the bottom of the list of OECD countries and behind a number of East Asian NICs in its level of socioeconomic inequality.

---

[1] Between 1990 and 1996, the poorest 40 per cent of the urban population in Brazil saw their share of the national income grow from 10.3 to 10.5 per cent while the richest 10 per cent saw their share grow from 41.8 to 44.3 per cent. Rural income showed similar trends. The Gini coefficient (an international measure of inequality) for urban household income grew from 0.528 to 0.538 over the same period (CEPAL, 1999 and 2000).

Table 1.1: Income Inequality: Ireland, OECD Countries and NICs

Country	IR	Rank	Country	IR	Rank
Austria	3.2	1	Britain	5.6	14
Norway	3.5	2	Korea	5.7	15
Finland	3.6	3	Australia	5.8	16
Denmark	3.6	4	Canada	7.2	17
Sweden	3.6	4	**Ireland**	**8.0**	**18**
Belgium	3.6	6	Hong Kong	8.7	19
Germany	4.1	7	United States	9.4	20
Japan	4.3	8	Singapore	9.6	21
Netherlands	4.9	9	Costa Rica	12.9	22
Italy	5.1	10	Mexico	13.5	23
Taiwan	5.2	11	Chile	17.4	24
Spain	5.3	12	Brazil	25.7	25
France	5.6	13			

Sources: *World Development Report 1998/99*, Table 5, p.198; Jong-Il You, 1999, Table 1, p 40; Irish data updated for 1994 from Callan and Nolan, 1999, Table 8.3, p.173.

Hence the importance of Keenan's question since it challenges us to decide whether it matters or not that inequality increases while poverty is decreasing.

Taking Keenan's distinction that poverty and inequality can be separate policy objectives, the discussion begins by clarifying the principal difference between them. The section then traces how the objective of greater equality in people's income and wealth has been replaced by one of poverty reduction while equality has come to take on an altogether new meaning, namely an equality of opportunity for women and minority groups. The context in which these changes took place is also outlined. The next section examines the different views of society which the terms equality and poverty reduction imply and draws on the work of Nobel economics laureate Amartya Sen to make explicit the implications for society of adopting either one

or the other as the objective of public policy. In the following
section, Keenan's absolute distinction between the two terms is
questioned and it is argued that, instead of being presented as
discrete objectives, poverty reduction is more accurately seen
as a weak formulation of the state's distributional objective and
equality as a demanding one. In the light of this, it is asked
whether the weak formulation, namely poverty reduction, is a
realisable objective on its own or whether it requires attending
to issues of socioeconomic inequality also. The argument is applied to Irish social policy in the next section, tracing the
change in its distributional objectives from the 1970s to 2000.
The final section draws conclusions.

1.2 POVERTY OR INEQUALITY?

There can be few widely used social concepts that generate
such passionate debate as poverty and inequality. The difference between them has already been illustrated and this can be
summarised as follows. A concern with poverty leads to a focus
on groups in society defined usually in terms of their low income, and it devotes attention to increasing the income of these
groups. The concern can be with absolute poverty (often expressed in terms of a minimum necessary for survival) or with
relative poverty (expressed in terms of how the income of the
poorest compares with average incomes in society). In contrast,
a concern with inequality focuses on the disparities within society as a whole, particularly between the highest income or
wealth holders and the lowest (for example, comparisons of the
income of the top and the bottom 20 per cent of income earners
are common within this approach). Attention is devoted to reducing these disparities by trying to ensure both that the incomes of those at the top are in some way controlled (through
redistributive taxation, for example) and that the incomes of
those at the bottom increase in ratios greater than do those at
the top. The objective of such policies is to narrow the gap between the incomes of the richest and poorest.

If we hold, with Keenan, that poverty reduction and economic equality are separate objectives, the latter tended to be
given priority by policy makers in Western states during the

"golden era" of welfare capitalism from the 1950s to the late 1970s. These years saw a marked decline in socioeconomic inequality throughout the OECD; as Corry and Glyn (1994: 208) put it referring to this period: "Inequality of household income generally fell, quite strongly (USA, Japan, Sweden, France) or more modestly (UK, Germany, Netherlands)". For example, writing in 1979, the historian Ernest Gellner could describe equality as "the pervasive spirit of our age" and he listed 14 elements which he regarded as being among the social roots of this egalitarianism, such as social mobility, uniform training and socialisation, deliberate equalisation from above and the positive philosophical endorsement of equality (Gellner, 1979). This is not to deny that, at this time, poverty reduction was also a policy objective in some countries such as the United States, where President Johnson launched a war on poverty in the 1960s.

However, from the late 1970s onwards poverty reduction began to replace equality as the principal distributional objective of public policy, especially in the United States and Britain. While this shift is associated with the crusading conservative governments of Ronald Reagan (1981-89) and Margaret Thatcher (1979-90), it also reflected a major change in the dominant political ideology. As Glyn and Miliband put it:

> While parties of the Right have traditionally defended inequality and hierarchy in the name of tradition and order, the neo-liberal analysis and prescription of the 1970s and 1980s provided a revived economic and ethical justification for increased inequality. The famous 'trickle-down' effect was adduced to support the idea that by making the rich richer, the poor would be made richer too (Glyn and Miliband, 1994: 6).

Meghnad Desai summed up the significance of this change. Referring to most of the 20th century up to then, he said that egalitarianism was accepted as a crusading philosophy:

> Those who did not agree with egalitarian distribution were on the defensive and even when their arguments were incisive their impact on policy or political debate was limited. Those

who were against egalitarianism were *conservative*. It was
only in the 1960s and 1970s that a *radical* defence of inequality emerged. . . . (Desai, 1995: 3; emphasis in original).

This radical defence was elaborated by various political theorists, collectively known as the anti-egalitarians. These denied
that there exists, either in nature or in social organisation, any
basis for the claim that human beings are equal. They furthermore claimed that the objective of equality is inherently contradictory (for example, if the state seeks to make people equal
in one regard such as incomes they will still be unequal in others such as educational qualifications or wealth holdings) and
that the attempt to achieve it could only result in tyranny since it
would interfere with people's basic freedoms. The essential
force of the argument is summarised by William Letwin:

> Egalitarians of all shades are pursuing a will-of-the-wisp.
> They are deluded by loose thinking and utopian fantasies.
> Their conviction that equality is the highest good or at least
> one among the highest goods rests on incoherent intellec-
> tual foundations, suffers from internal contradictions, and
> takes its departure from an exaggerated estimate of how
> much inequality exists. They are grotesquely optimistic in
> supposing that equality will bring in its train all the other
> great goods such as liberty, fraternity, wealth, justice and
> general virtue. Even worse, they ignore the likelihood that,
> if they have their way, the ultimate outcome will be a de-
> cline into widespread poverty and tyranny (Letwin, 1983:
> 69-70).

The anti-egalitarian attack formed part of a wider change in
economic thinking, often called the neo-classical counter-
revolution (Toye, 1993). This criticised the distorting effects of
state interference on the market and on its ability to allocate
resources efficiently. The emphasis on market-led approaches
to economic growth and the slimming down of the state led, in
turn, to new approaches to social policy characterised by such
elements as the targeting of resources on the poorest, the selective privatisation of state services and the use of social policy
to integrate the marginalised into the market. This approach to
poverty reduction was seen as a more responsible use of state

resources since it targeted spending on those most in need and did so without threatening the macroeconomic fiscal disciplines and confidence on which growth depends in a liberalised and globalised economy (Mishra, 1999).

This wider context helps explain the widespread move by states away from socioeconomic equality as an objective of policy, what Anne Phillips calls "the retreat from economic egalitarianism" (Phillips, 1999: 13). The causal connections between economic restructuring and distributional policy can be identified as follows. Enhanced global competition severely constrains nation states in their ability to guarantee minimum social standards to their citizens; it thus resituates the state making it more responsive to the imperatives of global capital than to the needs of its citizens (Falk, 1996). In a bid to remain globally competitive, states are liberalising their labour markets which is resulting in a downward pressure on wages and a worsening of working conditions. They are also prioritising taxation reduction and conservative fiscal management over adequate social protection, resulting in what has been called "the hollowing out of the welfare state" (Mishra, 1999: 36). As a result, the commitment of states to socioeconomic equality, and their ability to deliver it, have been severely eroded.

Wider political and cultural changes have further spurred the move away from the aspiration to equalise people's living conditions and resulted in a radically new understanding of equality. The apparent demise of the socialist option as an alternative to capitalism weakened the aspiration towards socioeconomic equality as this had been a central goal of the socialist project. Alongside this, the emergence of the women's movement, the movement towards racial equality and the gay rights movement resulted in radically redefining the meaning of equality, from a focus on reducing the gaps between people's income and wealth to one which recognises cultural and gender differences and gives them legal protection. This is done, for example, through anti-discrimination legislation or affirmative action policies. While such policies seek to ensure that people are not excluded from jobs or social benefits for reasons of gender, ethnic origins, political or religious beliefs, sexual orientation or disabilities, they do not aspire to reduce

the socioeconomic inequalities that exist in society. Their understanding of equality, therefore, is limited to offering equal
opportunities to all. Baker outlines the limitations of this view:

> [T]he whole point of these principles is to regulate the com-
> petition for advantage. All that differs is who ends up on top
> — people from privileged backgrounds, or people with the
> best natural talents, or a representative sample of talented
> men and women, black and white. The choice between
> them decides who will benefit from inequalities but doesn't
> change the inequalities themselves (Baker, 1987: 46).

This change in the understanding of what equality means is well
illustrated in Ireland's Equality Authority whose functions are
entirely limited to the latter understanding of equality.[2] The
move in Irish social policy from the aspiration to greater socioeconomic equality to an equality of opportunity for women and
minority groups is documented later in this chapter.

As a result of this changed understanding of equality in the
social debates of the 1980s and 1990s, Anne Phillips finds that
socioeconomic equality is "no longer valued even as an ideal"
(1999: 50). Instead:

> The majority of theorists say that inequalities are justified
> when they arise from individual ambition and choice; or that
> we should be ensuring people a sufficiency rather than wor-
> rying about whether they have equal amounts; or that
> money inequalities are irrelevant so long as money cannot
> purchase all the other good things in life (ibid.: 51).

This new understanding of equality is therefore consistent with
poverty reduction being made the principal distributional objective of public policy, an objective which, as Phillips puts it, is
limited to ensuring people have a sufficiency of material goods
rather than equal amounts of them.

The move away from the more demanding goal of greater
equality in people's socioeconomic conditions and the emer-

---

[2] The Equality Authority's name in Irish, An tÚdarás Comhionannais, makes
this clear since "comhionannas" refers exclusively to identity. The word "co-
throime" is the word for equality in a socioeconomic sense.

gence, in its place, of poverty reduction as the main distributional goal of public policy can be seen therefore as part of the move from a more state-directed model of development to a more market-driven one, widely labelled neoliberalism (Gray, 1999). Providing this context may help explain why poverty reduction has replaced socioeconomic equality as the principal distributional goal of public policy, but it does not provide the basis for answering Keenan's question as to whether this really matters. For this, one needs to make explicit the normative assumptions on which these policy objectives rest, in particular assumptions about what constitutes human well-being, about the relationship between the individual and society, and about the sources of social cohesion.

1.3 VIEWS OF SOCIETY: INCOME OR WELL-BEING?

A useful starting point for examining these normative assumptions is Amartya Sen's identification of "two implicit programmes" which inform discussion of issues of poverty and inequality, one based on social welfare and the other on social justice (Sen, 1992: 95). The social welfare view tends to treat poverty reduction as its main distributional objective and to restrict its focus to that section of society which it defines as poor whereas the social justice view shows a concern with inequalities within society as a whole and how to reduce them. Bill Jordan identifies the first as a liberal, Anglo-Saxon approach and the latter as a continental European approach (Jordan, 1996: 3-4) and Robert Erikson suggests that "poverty is the main welfare problem for social liberalism, while inequality is the main problem for social democracy" (Erikson, 1993: 80).

These views rest on assumptions about what constitutes individual and social well-being, assumptions that are all too often left unexamined. In the influential utilitarian view of human well-being, Sen identifies the tendency to reduce it to comparing people's real incomes, or what he calls "the commodity basis of utility" (1999: 69). This approach predominates within welfare economics (O'Shea and Kennelly, 1995: 1) and, in the

Irish case, finds expression in the ESRI's research on poverty.[3]
Yet, as Sen points out, income is not the same as well-being and
he identifies five reasons why there is a variation in the well-
being that people derive from their incomes. These are:

- Personal heterogeneities, such as physical characteristics
  like disability, illness or old age;

- Environmental diversities such as climate or prevalence of
  disease;

- Social climate such as levels of crime, provision of education or presence of pollution;

- Differences in relational perspectives, by which he means
  the public standards expected of individuals in different societies (thus, being relatively poor in a rich country may result in a worse quality of life than being much poorer in a
  poor country); and

- Distribution within the family which can benefit or disadvantage particular family members (such as girls) (ibid.: 70-
  72).

Sen concludes:

> These different sources of variation in the relation between
> income and well-being make opulence — in the sense of
> high real income — a limited guide to welfare and the qual-
> ity of life (ibid.: 71).

While Sen acknowledges that income is an important element
of well-being, he focuses attention on the ability of people to
translate this into things like an adequate diet or access to
medical care (1992: 114-115). In other words, what has to be
evaluated is the actual quality of living that people manage to
achieve, particularly "our capability to lead the kind of lives we
have reason to value" (1999: 285). This takes exclusive attention

---

[3] The ESRI research measures poverty based on two measures, both of them
related to commodities. The first is income and the second a list of items regarded as essential for living in Irish society. See footnote 12 of this chapter
for further discussion of these "deprivation indicators".

away from material resources and emphasises people's freedom to function as they choose in society. It also involves a shift
in focus from the individual (in terms of the amount of income a
person receives) to the wider community in which the individual lives. Sen makes much of the fact that, though African
American men may well be far richer in terms of income than
are men in countries like China, Sri Lanka, Costa Rica, Jamaica
or the Indian state of Kerala, they have a far lower chance of
reaching an advanced age than do men in these countries and
this gap is widening rather than narrowing (ibid.: 96). Obvi-
ously this difference cannot be explained in terms of differences in income but requires attention to "social arrangements
and community relations such as medical coverage, public
health care, school education, law and order, prevalence of
violence and so on" (ibid.: 22-23). This establishes that rising
income levels are not sufficient as a basis for judging that people are better off, despite what Keenan seems to suggest in his
question with which this chapter opened. To make a judgement
on well-being, we need to examine how capable people are of
functioning as they wish to in a particular society.

Any adequate view of human well-being, therefore, must include a focus on the individual's relationship to society. It must
firstly assess the material dimensions of this relationship, including the adequacy and equitable distribution of such public
goods as education, health care or policing to allow all citizens
develop and express their capabilities as they might wish to.
For example, observation would lead one to conclude that the
quality of education and health care available to many people
living in deprived areas in Ireland has deteriorated over the
past two decades. Improving these people's income (through
access to employment, for example) may still leave them less
capable of functioning in society as they might wish. Therefore,
as Sen emphasises, assessment must go beyond material dimensions to examine people's status in society. Quoting Adam
Smith, he points to the requirement that people have the ability
to appear in public without shame. Going further, he refers to
the view of the philosopher John Rawls that self-respect is "perhaps the most important primary good" (quoted in Sen 1999:

136). Sen believes that any theory of justice as fairness has to ensure the social basis of such self-respect.

These concerns give us more rigorous grounds for establishing what might constitute both individual and social well-being, grounds that derive from a social justice view of society. Since they move us beyond the income of the poor to the relationship of the poor to society, they inevitably touch on issues of equality. This they do in at least two ways: firstly, they raise concerns about equality of access for all to public goods such as education or health care and, secondly, they raise the thorny issue of how people's status is related to their material standard of living. In other words, they force consideration of whether people's equal worth, in their own eyes and in the eyes of society, can be maintained in a society in which the gap between the incomes and wealth of the richest and poorest becomes ever greater. Anne Phillips highlights the challenge posed for the material distribution of goods in society:

> The key question has always been whether it makes sense to talk of equality of respect between groups whose material conditions are so markedly different. Equality might not mean sameness, but can it be compatible with such an extraordinary imbalance in income, life-chances and power? (1999: 128).

She goes on:

> A society that condones excesses of poverty in the midst of wealth, or arbitrarily rewards one skill with one hundred times the wages of another, is not recognising its citizens as of equal human worth. On the contrary, it is making it harder than ever for the members of that society to keep up their pretence that they consider their fellow citizens their equals (ibid.: 131).

These concerns found fullest expression in the developed social democratic welfare states, particularly in Scandinavia. As Gøsta Esping-Andersen describes them:

> Rather than tolerate a dualism between state and market, between working class and middle class, the social demo-

crats pursued a welfare state that would promote an equality of the highest standards, not an equality of minimal needs as was pursued elsewhere. This implied, first, that services and benefits be upgraded to levels commensurate with even the most discriminating tastes of the new middle classes; and, second, that equality be furnished by guaranteeing workers full participation in the quality of rights enjoyed by the better-off (1990: 27).

Even though economic restructuring has weakened states' ability to foster the robust equality to which these welfare states aspired, theorists continue to draw attention to the importance of the underlying aspiration that motivated them. As articulated by David Miller, this is "the idea of a society in which people regard and treat one another as equals, and together form a single community without divisions of social class" (Miller, 1997: 83). Unlike the social welfare view which focuses attention only on the poorest and tends to equate their welfare with increased income, this social justice view sees the aspiration towards equality as fundamental to the well-being of individuals, and of society.

But what might such a principle of equality mean in practice? It means, at least, that the issue of income distribution and the distance between the incomes of the highest and the lowest income earners is of major concern. Miller believes that "where income differences are very large, this will almost inevitably create a segregated society in which people live very different styles of life and associate socially almost entirely with those on similar incomes". He adds that "we have to tackle the issue of income distribution, but on the basis of reducing differentials to a size that is not destructive of social equality rather than on the basis of attempting to reduce them to zero" (96). The guideline he gives is that the relation of the top to the bottom income might be in the region of IR£80,000 to IR£10,000. Brian Barry adopts a slightly more rigorous ratio of six to one (Barry, 1998: 23).

In the light of these it is interesting to attempt some estimate of the ratio of highest to lowest incomes in Ireland in the late

1990s.[4] For the year 1997 we can find out the incomes of top income earners from the Irish Management Institute's "Executive
Salaries in Ireland" annual survey. This shows that the average
income of the upper quartile of chief executives in companies
with a turnover of over IR£150 million was IR£160,475; from the
Census of Industrial Production 1997 (the latest available at the
time of writing) we find that average annual earnings in the
lowest wage manufacturing industries were IR£6,950. This,
then, gives us a ratio of 23:1, an enormous gap compared to that
recommended by both Miller and Barry. Calculating the income of social welfare recipients further widens the gap. Most
long-term social assistance benefits were raised to IR£67.50 a
week in June 1997, giving an annual income of IR£3,510. This
widens the ratio between the highest earners and social welfare
recipients to 45.7:1. The dangers of this situation are highlighted by John Sheahan:

> Inequality does not foster solidarity; it fosters mutual de-
> struction. Before societies can achieve the solidarity neces-
> sary to make sustained progress, it may be essential to
> break the existing pattern by giving priority to reducing
> inequality (1992: 40).

The discussion in this section has made explicit some key assumptions underlying the view of individual and social well-
being espoused by those promoting poverty reduction and
those promoting greater socioeconomic equality, what we have
called a social welfare view and a social justice view. It therefore offers a basis — derived from different ethical values[5] — on
which to judge whether it matters that inequality might grow
while poverty is being reduced. However, there are other
grounds on which Keenan's question could be answered. To
these we now turn.

---

[4] The examples here use gross incomes both because that is what Miller and
Barry appear to be referring to and also because calculating disposable income from gross income is far from straightforward.

[5] These values rest on different ontologies or views of the human person, and
on different theories of society.

1.4 LINKS: CAN POVERTY BE REDUCED WHILE INEQUALITY RISES?

Up to now the discussion has accepted Keenan's view of poverty and inequality as two discrete concepts. In this view it is possible, at least in principle, to reduce poverty while inequality is increasing and it remains simply a matter of empirical investigation to find out whether this is, indeed, happening. It has been argued in the previous section, however, that this view rests upon assumptions about how income translates into well-being and the discussion there raises questions as to the adequacy of poverty reduction as an objective to counter disadvantage in any substantial way. This section moves beyond a conception of poverty and inequality as discrete concepts, arguing that they are more accurately seen as different formulations of the principal distributional objectives of public policy. It argues that, both conceptually and empirically, poverty reduction cannot be divorced from fostering equality. For those not convinced by the arguments based on ethical values in the previous section, an argument based on realising distributional objectives effectively may prove more compelling.

Up to this point, our treatment of poverty and inequality as discrete concepts has avoided the disagreement that exists among experts on what the terms mean. On poverty, for example, Trinity College economist Seán Barrett has described as "outlandish and spurious" claims that a third of the nation lives in poverty (*The Irish Times*, 4 October 1999) even though ESRI figures show that, in 1997, 36.2 per cent of households fell below a poverty line based on 60 per cent of average income, an increase from 33.4 per cent in 1994 (Callan et al., 1999: Table 3.2, p 20).[6] At issue here are different understandings of what constitutes poverty, reflecting widespread international debates on the subject. In one survey, Paul Spicker identified "*at least* eleven discrete senses" in which poverty is understood in the social sciences (Spicker, 1999: 150-162; emphasis in origi-

---

[6] The debate on the meaning of poverty between Barrett and the ESRI poverty researchers goes back to the late 1980s. See the articles on the topic in the issue of *The Economic and Social Review*, Vol. 20, No. 4, 1989.

nal) [7] while Simon Maxwell, in listing nine different definitions, speaks of "the bewildering ambiguity with which the term 'poverty' is used" (Maxwell, 1999: 1). Similar difficulties arise when discussing inequality. In understanding the term, equality theorists identify a spectrum which runs from a weak version involving equal rights, through a liberal version involving equal opportunities to much more demanding versions requiring equality in people's socioeconomic conditions (Baker, 1998; Lynch, 1999). As Caroline Daniel put it:

> The problem is that although most people want equality of something, there is no consensus about what should be equalised (1997: 11).

These disagreements alert us to the fact that the range of meanings given to the terms "poverty" and "inequality" make the distinction between them harder to uphold. This can be illustrated by looking at the debate about the distinction between absolute and relative poverty. While attempts have been made to establish criteria to measure absolute poverty (the World Bank's poverty line of a dollar a day is probably the best known), many poverty researchers hold that poverty can only be assessed in relation to the living standards of each society. In this view, poverty is a relative concept. Discussing variations in what constitutes deprivation in different societies, Sen puts the point strongly:

> We could, of course, debate about the exact ways in which normative judgements should take note of such social variations, but the primary exercise of diagnosing deprivation cannot but be sensitive to the way various types of hardships are viewed in the society in question. To deny that connection is not so much to be super-objective but to be super-dense (1992: 108).

Understanding poverty as a relative concept has been central to Irish anti-poverty research and is the basis of the definition of

---

[7] Spicker's eleven definitions are: need; standard of living; limited resources; lack of basic security; lack of entitlement; multiple deprivation; exclusion; inequality; class; dependency; and unacceptable hardship.

poverty in the National Anti-Poverty Strategy (NAPS, 1997: 30). In moving from an absolute to a relative definition of poverty, however, it becomes impossible to sustain the view that poverty is distinct from inequality. Since relative poverty is a measure of how far people fall below average incomes, it is conceptually closer to a measure of inequality.

A second debate concerns the difference between means and ends. Most anti-poverty research is directed to identifying those in a society on low incomes, usually through measuring the percentages of the population falling below a specified poverty line or whose income is insufficient to buy a specified bundle of goods regarded as essential for survival. However, these approaches identify poverty with income deprivation and, as has been argued in the previous section, run the risk of treating an increase in income as an end in itself rather than as a means to improving quality of life. Yet, it is clear that improving income is by no means sufficient to guarantee a better quality of life. For example, in Chile's booming economy for most of the 1990s, people's incomes had risen and poverty had declined dramatically. Yet, during research there in 1996 the author was given accounts of families with multiple incomes in which the nutrition of the children had worsened despite the household's improved income. This was because of the changed culture of consumption in which expenditure on modern electrical goods (like CD players and walkmans) took precedence over expenditure on a balanced diet. This new pattern of expenditure was helped by the pervasive use of consumer credit cards (Kirby, 1996: 38). To those who use mainstream forms of poverty evaluation, these Chileans are better off than they were previously; this is how the World Bank and the Chilean government see the situation. However, it is only possible to draw this conclusion if improved incomes are seen as an end in themselves. Any adequate evaluation of their contribution to people's well-being involves consideration of how these incomes impact on people's lives. As is clear from the example here, this is difficult to do without straying into issues of equality. For example, how can we understand the forces driving Chilean families to prioritise electrical goods over an adequate diet if we fail to take into account wider social pressures and consumption practices?[8] These pressures and practices are intimately related to issues of social status and self-respect.

The distinctions between absolute and relative poverty and between ends and means, therefore, make it impossible to treat poverty as a discrete concept, divorced from how income, wealth, resources and power are distributed in society. In the light of this, a more adequate way of conceptualising the relationship between poverty and inequality would be to see them as lying along a distributional spectrum running from quite minimalist conceptions at one end to much more demanding ones at the other. Thus, simply insuring that no one in society fell below a minimum income necessary for survival, while being unconcerned about how wide the gap between rich and poor became, could be formulated as a minimalist distributional objective. This would constitute the poverty-reduction end of the spectrum of distributional possibilities. At the other end might be an objective to reduce the disparities in wealth and income between the richest and the poorest, perhaps fixing some maximum ratio beyond which they should not be allowed to widen. This would constitute a demanding egalitarian distributional objective. However, formulating the relationship between poverty and inequality in this way does not get us very far towards an answer to Keenan's question. All it does is highlight that the minimalist objective cannot be blind to issues of equality if it is concerned about really improving the lives of the poor.

We now turn to examine these issues empirically to find out if, in practice, the attempt to reduce poverty can be successful without seeking also to reduce inequality. A good place to begin is the claim that economic growth results in poverty reduction. For example, a major World Bank-sponsored study of growth and its social impact in 21 developing countries over the period 1950-85 found a "clear positive correlation between income growth per capita and poverty redressal" though it

---

[8] Baker gives another example from Britain in the 1980s. He examines the paradox that official statistics showed the real incomes of the poorest households were rising yet evidence showed higher levels of hardship in terms of rising numbers lacking heat, shelter and even food. He concluded: "Economic hardship is the result of excessive inequality" (Baker, 1991: 58).

found an extremely mixed picture when examining the impact of growth on inequality (Lal and Myint, 1996: 39-41). However, the definition of poverty they used was "the numbers below a fixed national poverty line corresponding to the real income per capita of the bottom 20 per cent in the base year (1950)", a minimalist definition that virtually ensured that growth must result in poverty reduction (ibid.: 31). What impact such growth had on the well-being of the poorest is, however, an entirely different question since the definition of poverty used is not related to average living standards and how they changed over the period in question. It therefore provides no basis for deciding whether the lives of the poor have improved in any substantial way.

Few states, however, leave the fate of the poor entirely to economic growth. Perhaps the clearest means widely used today to ensure that growth benefits the poor is to target social spending on them. This, however, ignores what is happening to inequality. Acknowledging that the case for targeting is, in principle "quite strong and cogent", Sen however draws attention to its "messiness and disincentive effects" (Sen, 1999: 135, 137). Among these are:

- Information distortion, namely that mistakes will inevitably be made, benefiting the cheats and disqualifying the needy;

- Incentive distortion, whereby those likely to lose their benefit will, for example, forego employment or stay in low-paid employment to keep the benefit;

- Disutility and stigma, which essentially undermine a person's self-respect;

- Administrative costs, namely that such schemes involve extensive bureaucracies to operate; and,

- Political sustainability and quality, drawing attention to the weak political position of the poor to ensure the schemes continue and remain adequately funded (ibid.: 135-136).

While Sen believes these problems can be overcome, they place severe question marks over the effectiveness of attempts to reduce poverty while neglecting inequality. Korpi and Palme point out that social scientists have become increasingly critical of the effectiveness of targeting just as support for it has increased among policymakers in Western countries (1998: 663). They explain the apparent paradox that more universal welfare regimes are more effective in reducing poverty by pointing to the effects targeting can have on widespread social support for welfare spending:

> The targeted model . . . tends to drive a wedge between the short-term material interests of the poor and those of the rest of the population, which must rely on private insurance. It gives the better-off categories no rational basis for including the poor, and leaves the poor to trust in the altruism of the more fortunate (672).[9]

This points therefore to the difficulties that arise in practice when an attempt is made to reduce poverty without also addressing inequality. On Korpi and Palme's evidence, the more effective way to reduce poverty is in the context of reducing inequality.

Another important piece of evidence that links poverty reduction and equality comes from the United Nations Development Programme (UNDP). As part of its annual *Human Development Report*, the UNDP has developed the concept of pro-poor growth, to specify under what conditions economic growth reduces poverty. Among the findings is that income poverty is reduced more quickly where equality is greater:

> Recent studies have estimated that annual per capita GDP growth of 10 per cent would reduce the incidence of income poverty by 30 per cent in relatively egalitarian societies, with a Gini coefficient of 0.25, and by only 10 per cent in less equal societies, with a Gini coefficient of 0.50 (UNDP, 1997: 73).

---

[9] In the Irish case, O'Connell and Rottman have argued that universal welfare schemes tend to benefit the middle classes more than the poor, since the former can supplement the minimal levels of universal entitlement through private spending in areas such as education, pensions or health care (1992: 224–225). However, Korpi and Palme point out that, in Scandinavia, quality public benefits and high levels of middle class taxation discourage the resort to private spending to supplement public benefits (1998).

The Gini coefficient is a widely used international measure of income or wealth inequality in which the closer the coefficient is to 1, the greater the inequality. In countries such as Indonesia, South Korea and Malaysia, where economic growth has brought big gains in poverty reduction, the UNDP identifies the following reasons for the outcome:

> Their growth strategies expanded economic opportunities for poor people, with relatively equitable distribution of financial and physical capital, including land. And the resources generated by economic growth were heavily channelled into human development, especially into improving health, education and skills (1997: 74).

Thus, empirically, evidence points to the fact that a surer way to reduce poverty is in the context of egalitarian policies. Believing that poverty is declining while inequality is growing suggests that a very restrictive definition of poverty is being used which overlooks the impact on the quality of life of the poor, particularly poor people's capability to function in society. This, then, gives us a stronger answer to Keenan's question, namely that it does matter that inequality might be growing while poverty is declining. It matters firstly because the assertion that poverty is declining rests, in the context of growing inequality, on a very restrictive view of poverty which tells nothing about whether the quality of life of the poor is improving or disimproving. It matters secondly because the evidence points to the fact that the surest and most sustainable way to reduce poverty is as part of egalitarian policies. It matters thirdly because an increase in inequality may in time undermine the ability of the poor to function as equals in society and is also likely to undermine the cohesion of society itself.

The argument thus far has been couched in general terms. It might be claimed that this does not apply to Ireland. Therefore, the next section examines whether any of these considerations might apply to the distributional objectives of Irish social policy.

1.5 IRISH SOCIAL POLICY: FROM EQUALITY TO POVERTY REDUCTION

A general change, between the 1970s and the 1990s, in the distributional objective of social policy under the impact of neo-liberal economic policies has already been noted. In Ireland, this shift can be clearly traced to the re-discovery of poverty in 1971 (Nolan and Callan, 1994: 22). In a paper to a conference organised by the Catholic bishops' Council for Social Welfare that year, Ó Cinnéide concluded that "*at least* 24 per cent of the population have a personal income below the poverty line" which he based on social security or income maintenance rates of payment in Ireland, North and South (Ó Cinnéide, 1972: 397; emphasis in original). This led to a succession of studies which sought to measure the percentage of the population living in poverty, in particular the major studies by ESRI poverty researchers which gathered extensive survey-based data in 1987 and 1994 (with the 1994 cohort surveyed again in 1995, 1996 and 1997) allowing a stream of studies to be published on the extent of poverty in Ireland (see especially, Nolan and Callan, 1994; Callan et al., 1996, and Callan et al., 1999). These studies, says Frederick W. Powell, "played an important part in promoting an awareness that augmented living standards resulting from economic expansion have not benefited all sections of the population equally" (Powell, 1992: 290). In doing so, however, they also subtly changed the focus of social policy from equality in income and wealth distribution to poverty reduction, a focus shared by bodies such as the Combat Poverty Agency which commissions some of this work.

In the absence of a coherent official expression of the principles underlying social policy, the reports of the National Economic and Social Council (NESC) offer a source for identifying the principles which the social partners (among them the Government) believe should inform social policy, thus providing a guide to official thinking. The emphasis on growing equality in income distribution as the principal aim of social policy is noteworthy in the early NESC reports. For example, in Report 8 entitled "An Approach to Social Policy", the Council endorses and publishes a report by David Donnison which sees equality in the distribution of resources, social status, power and security as the central issues of social policy (NESC, 1975b). It followed this with a report on income distribution (NESC, 1975a) and in 1981 in a statement on its priorities for the future development of Irish social policies, it laid down six aims of which the first two are:

- The reduction of inequalities of income and wealth by transferring resources to those in need and by equitably distributing the burden of such support;

- The elimination of inequalities of opportunity which arise from inherited social and economic differences (NESC, 1981: 15).

The other four aims relate to the provision of employment and access to specified services for all, the development of services for the disadvantaged and the development of "responsible citizenship" (15, 16). It went on to clarify that "the substantial reduction of inequality is thus the main aim of social policy and the redistributive activities by which it is expressed" (17). In its comments on a report on redistribution through state social expenditure which it published in 1988, the Council reiterates that it sees equality as the aim of social policy (Rottman and Reidy, 1988: 6-7).

The fate of this aim can be charted in the series of comprehensive strategy documents on economic and social policy over subsequent years (NESC, 1986, 1990, 1993, 1996, 1999). This finds a substantial weakening of the principle (indeed its virtual disappearance) in a number of the reports before it reappears in a substantial way in the 1996 and 1999 reports but in a radically changed formulation, reflecting the new understanding of equality outlined above. Some of the themes of the anti-egalitarians appear in the 1986 report[10] though the aim of more equitable social policies, largely through reforming social

---

[10] For example, in discussing redistribution it says that "the goal of 'equality' with which 'redistribution' is associated may have different and possibly conflicting meanings (equality of opportunity, equality of conditions, equality of outcomes etc)" (NESC, 1986: 200). The issues raised in this paragraph are not considered elsewhere in the lengthy report.

services to make them more effective and redistributive, is kept. The aim of equality has virtually disappeared from the 1990 report except in relation to the educational system (NESC, 1990: 314-16). Instead attention is focused on the extent of poverty and the adequacy and effectiveness of social welfare payments. Equality re-enters in the 1993 report as it repeats the aims of social policy from its 1981 report, but drops entirely and without explanation the first aim (the reduction of inequalities in income and wealth) while adding that, in relation to the aims it does repeat (aims 2, 3, 4 and 5), these objectives "should be pursued so as to have regard to inequalities of income and wealth" (NESC, 1993: 411, 412). Addressing what it sees as a trade-off between efficiency and equity, the Council states that it "sees social inequalities being narrowed through a restructuring of policies, services and subsidies rather than through increased public expenditure" (414) though its extensive treatment of social welfare, health, education and housing hardly mentions the objective of equality.

Having substantially weakened its commitment to social equality over the previous decade, the Council in its 1996 report acknowledges a serious problem has emerged of uneven distribution of Ireland's increased social resources and capacities over recent decades:

> There have been many forms of such mal-distribution, but social class inequalities have been especially important, in particular, those associated with the emergence of a pervasively marginalised segment of the working class. The growth of this group in the 1980s not only damaged the life chances of those directly involved. It amounted to the main social-structural weakness in Irish society and exacted costs on all segments of the population (NESC, 1996: 29).

In two subsequent chapters, the report offers its prescriptions for this "major challenge for future development" (ibid.: 51). The first (Chapter 8) details action on unemployment and social exclusion, referring to the "significant deprivation of resources, including income and other material assets (wealth), or less tangible resources such as educational attainment" as these factors "usually set the conditions for participation in the normal life of the community or determine the capacity of people to function as citizens and members of society" (ibid.: 173, 174). It sees exclusion as a dynamic and cumulative process and as being multidimensional (including such elements as poor housing, poor educational attainment, low income, lack of employment, varying family circumstances, and lack of local infrastructure, services or community associations) (ibid.: 176) and it sees the aim of policy as being "to support self-generating social inclusion" (ibid.: 178). Chapter 9 of the NESC report details the elements of what it calls "the modern equality focus" among them gender equality and a broader equality paradigm with particular reference to such groups as disabled people and Travellers (ibid.: 207–213), thus reflecting the new understanding of equality based on the recognition of gender, ethnic and other differences. However, it excludes all mention of equality in income distribution as a goal of social policy, neglecting evidence that inequality in income distribution in Ireland was among the worst in the OECD.[11]

NESC's 1999 report further develops this understanding of equality. Its main addition is to advocate a rights-based approach to social inclusion (NESC, 1999: 76-78). (This approach is discussed in Chapters 2 and 9 below.) It treats equality as an element of social inclusion and outlines an understanding of equality based upon anti-discrimination and equal opportunity measures (69-74). In a brief section, it mentions questions "about the contribution of inequality of condition to inequality of outcome" (75) and acknowledges, in a footnote, that "radical equality theorists . . . argue that the focus of policy should be on how to eliminate major inequalities and hierarchies" (footnote 20, p 75). However, apart from this brief mention, the report fails entirely to address the issue of socioeconomic inequality. Significantly, in the list of benchmarks it gives to evaluate progress on its equality agenda, it lists standards of health, education, housing, training, social protection and social services but does not mention either the distribution of these services nor

---

[11] This evidence is contained in a report on income distribution in the OECD published by the organisation in 1995 and so available to NESC when compiling its 1996 report (Atkinson et al., 1995).

income/wealth distribution (76). Finally, the NESC expresses its concern about increased relative poverty but it stops short of advocating that relative poverty be substituted for the "consistently poor" as the main poverty target in the National Anti-Poverty Strategy (402-405). Acknowledging that income inequality is growing, it concludes that this can be expected to be a temporary phenomenon if welfare payments are linked to overall incomes rather than to inflation and that childcare and other policies ensure that all who wish to work can do so (402).

The distributional objectives that inform Irish social policy at the beginning of the 21st century are best summarised in two sets of documents. The first is the National Anti-Poverty Strategy which has been described as "arguably the most significant social policy document ever published by government" (Curry, 1998: 46). It defines poverty as follows:

> People are living in poverty, if their income and resources (material, cultural and social) are so inadequate as to preclude them from having a standard of living which is regarded as acceptable by Irish society generally. As a result of inadequate income and resources people may be excluded and marginalised from participating in activities which are considered the norm for other people in society (NAPS, 1997: 3).

Though defining poverty in relative terms and involving marginalisation from participation in society (a definition based far more on concerns about inequality), the NAPS goes on to elaborate a global target for reducing the number of the "consistently poor" from 9-15 per cent to less than 5-10 per cent by 2007 (NAPS, 1997: 9). Despite setting targets and policy actions in five areas — educational disadvantage, unemployment, income adequacy, disadvantaged urban areas and rural poverty, the target for reducing the "consistently poor" has become the key yardstick for the strategy. But here the definition of poverty is far more restricted since it refers only to those below average incomes (those whose income is below 40 per cent, 50 per cent or 60 per cent of average income) who also lack items from a list of goods regarded as necessities (Callan, et al., 1999:

Chapter 5).[12] Figures from the ESRI relating to 1997 showed the global target to be almost met and so it was revised to reducing consistent poverty to below 5 per cent by 2004 (Inter-Departmental Policy Committee, 1999: 3). However, a consequence of choosing a minimalist measure has been to overlook the sharp increases in relative poverty that occurred between 1994 and 1997 (Callan et al., 1999: Chapter 3). Furthermore, in revising the target in 1999, the government opted to overlook the call of the ESRI researchers for "a set of tiered and inter-related poverty reduction targets" which would explicitly include reductions in relative income poverty (ibid.: 75). Ireland's anti-poverty strategy therefore has focused exclusively on reducing poverty while being apparently indifferent to the sharp rise in income inequality (measured by relative poverty and income distribution data).

If the NAPS fails to address the growing socioeconomic inequality in Irish society, this failure may derive from the understanding of equality which informs Irish social policy. This is well illustrated in documents of the National Economic and Social Forum (NESF) recommending equality objectives for public policy (NESF, 1997, 1996). Despite some general references to wealth and income inequalities, reduction of such inequalities is entirely absent from the NESF's recommendations and the documents equate equality objectives with anti-discrimination and equality of opportunity measures for women and minority groups.[13] The Programme for Prosperity and Fairness (2000),

---

[12] The deprivation indicators used by the ESRI to measure the "consistently poor" all relate to the absence of purchasable material goods or services (such as a dry, damp-free dwelling, a colour TV, a refrigerator, a car, central heating, two pairs of strong shoes, a week's annual holiday away from home, Callan et al., 1999: 36). They exclude any indicators that might measure inequalities of participation in society such as levels of health and mobility, levels of education, security of life and property, and participation in public life through voting and/or membership of voluntary groups, as have been included, for example, in the Swedish Level of Living surveys (Erikson, 1993: 68). What they measure, therefore, is levels of poverty based on the absence of material goods while avoiding any attempt to measure how such material goods might translate into people's ability to function as equals in society.

[13] Although a four-paragraph section in the 1996 NESF report on "Equality Proofing Issues" recognises the importance of society moving towards "the equalisation of wealth, income, working conditions, power and privileges for

negotiated between the social partners in early 2000, reflects this understanding of inequality and, it has been argued, will further increase the gap between rich and poor (Kirby and Zappone, 2000).

It is fair to conclude therefore that Irish social policy, despite displaying an understanding of the multidimensional nature of social exclusion and the damage it is doing to the cohesion of society, has adopted in practice a relatively minimalist distributional objective, namely to reduce the numbers of those who are "consistently poor". It pays virtually no attention to evidence of growing socioeconomic inequality and therefore gives the impression that this is of no concern. It adopts no benchmarks to assess whether socioeconomic inequality is improving or disimproving. While using the vocabulary of social exclusion/inclusion, it fails to realise that growing economic inequality is a central cause of social exclusion and that any commitment to social inclusion must include adopting policies to narrow the gap between rich and poor. Indeed, so confused is the rhetoric on social exclusion that a government minister can claim Ireland is becoming a more inclusive society even while evidence shows growing socioeconomic inequality (Ahern, 2000). Thus Brian Barry's verdict seems to apply:

> [A] government professing itself concerned with social exclusion but indifferent to inequality is, to put it charitably, suffering from a certain amount of confusion (1998: 23).

Drawing on the argument earlier in this chapter, it can be stated that the Irish state believes that it is possible to reduce poverty while socioeconomic inequality is growing. It does this by adopting a minimalist measurement of poverty and by neglecting the links between poverty and inequality.

Some implications of failing to sort out this confusion and adopt a more demanding set of egalitarian social objectives can be illustrated by returning to some of the issues highlighted by David Donnison in his report for the NESC (NESC: 1975b). For

---

all" (NESF, 1996: 17), this objective receives no mention elsewhere in the document and does not form part of the NESF's recommended equality objectives (ibid.: 37).

example, he drew attention to the fact that "Irish fiscal traditions . . . tend to take proportionately more from the poor than the rich" (ibid.: 53). If Irish social policy had maintained equality as a consistent aim over the intervening two decades, it is unlikely that researchers could report in 1998 that the percentage of earnings paid in direct taxes by the bottom 10 per cent of the population had increased from 3.14 per cent in 1987 to 11 per cent in 1994/95 whereas the percentage paid by the top 10 per cent had fallen from 28.62 per cent to 27.66 per cent. This happened in a period when the proportion of earnings paid in direct taxation on average fell from 22.96 per cent to 20.15 per cent (Collins and Kavanagh, 1998: 182). Similarly, if the focus of research on income distribution issues over the past two decades had been on equality rather than on the numbers in poverty, it is likely that more attention might have been paid to the challenge posed by Donnison:

> . . . for the replacement of stigmatising selectivity now operating at the bottom of the social scale by other forms of selectivity concentrated more often at the top of the scale to ensure that those best able to pay bear a larger share of tax burdens and get no exorbitant share of social benefits (NESC, 1975b: 67-68).

However, with the focus of research being on the poor, the data on the situation of the rich, and particularly on the distribution of wealth in Irish society, remain very deficient. This is more than 20 years after the NESC drew attention to the need for reliable and adequate data on the extent of the main inequalities in Irish society (NESC, 1975b: 15).

Keenan's question can, therefore, be said to reflect the changed emphasis in Irish social policy over the past two decades and the distributional objective which informs the NAPS. Thus, his question reflects not just current priorities but a longer historical trend. It can be seen as perhaps the single most important question about the distributional objectives of Irish society and among the most important questions facing Irish social policy.

1.6 CONCLUSIONS

This chapter has provided some bases for deciding whether it matters or not that inequality might be increasing while poverty is declining. The first conclusion that can be drawn is that the question raised by Keenan does matter; indeed, it forces consideration of the kind of society we want. A second conclusion is that Keenan's firm distinction between poverty and inequality has been found, both on conceptual and empirical grounds, to be untenable. Instead, it has been argued that the objectives of poverty reduction and socioeconomic equality are more adequately seen as lying along a spectrum of distributional objectives, from relatively minimalist ones to more demanding ones. The central point of the argument has been that considerations of individual and social well-being require serious attention being devoted to egalitarian objectives and, furthermore, that poverty is more effectively reduced in the context of attempts to share income, wealth and resources more equitably throughout society. Finally, in looking at Irish social policy, it was found that, despite some fine rhetoric about social inclusion, the distributional objectives of policy are to reduce poverty while showing scant concern about the fact that socioeconomic inequality is increasing.

Alongside evidence about the extent of inequality in Ireland (see Table 1:1), some partial Irish evidence can be cited suggesting widespread support for reducing income disparities. This comes from a nationwide survey of subjective social indicators, the findings of which "would tend to favour economic policies which aim to distribute incomes and wealth more evenly and which try to avoid great income disparities" (Davis and Fine-Davis, 1991: 342). This alerts us the fact that, in making a choice between relatively minimalist distributional objectives or more demanding and egalitarian ones, we know very little about what the citizens of this state might choose.

Finally, the issues discussed in this chapter reflect some key international concerns — both empirical and conceptual — as we enter a new century. The disturbing growth of inequality worldwide over recent decades has been charted by the United

Nations Development Programme (UNDP) in its annual *Human Development Reports*. For example, the 1999 report stated:

> Gaps in income between the poorest and richest people and countries have continued to widen. In 1960 20 per cent of the world's people in the richest countries had 30 times the income of the poorest 20 per cent — in 1997, 74 times as much (UNDP, 1999: 36; see also Figure 1.6, pp 38-39).

Furthermore, poverty reduction as the principal distributional objective of policy can be seen as an attempt to formulate a distributional objective consistent with neoliberal approaches to governance. Since these approaches give priority to capital accumulation, the adoption of minimalist objectives for social policy ensures that the needs of society are made subservient to the needs of the economy.

The issues discussed in this chapter touch therefore on central challenges for the new millennium, challenges about the relationship between the economy and society, about wealth and well-being, about the individual and society. Indeed they touch on the nature of capitalism itself since, as a social system, it has always been characterised by a tension between the imperatives of accumulation and the satisfaction of social needs (Wallerstein, 1998).

References

Ahern, Dermot (2000), "Government policies have linked social and economic objectives", *The Irish Times*, 20 May

Atkinson, Anthony B., Lee Rainwater and Timothy M. Smeeding (1995), "Income Distribution in the OECD Countries: Evidence from the Luxembourg Income Study", Paris, OECD

Baker, John (1991), "The Paradox of Rising Incomes and Increasing Hardship" in *Policy and Politics*, Vol.19, No.1, pp.49-60

Baker, John (1987), *Arguing for Equality*, London, Verso

Baker, John (1998), "Equality" in Seán Healy and Brigid Reynolds, eds, *Social Policy in Ireland: Principles, Practice and Problems*, Dublin, Oak Tree Press, pp.21-42

Barry, Brian (1998), "Social Exclusion, Social Isolation and the Distribution of Income", Case Paper 12, Centre for Analysis of Social Exclusion, London, LSE

Callan, Tim and Brian Nolan (1999), "Income Inequality in Ireland in the 1980s and 1990s" in Frank Barry, ed., *Understanding Ireland's Economic Growth*, Basingstoke, Macmillan, pp.167-92

Callan, Tim, Brian Nolan, Brendan J. Whelan, Christopher T. Whelan and James Williams (1996), *Poverty in the 1990s: Evidence from the 1994 Living in Ireland Survey*, Dublin, Oak Tree Press with the Combat Poverty Agency

Callan, Tim, Richard Layte, Brian Nolan, Dorothy Watson, Christopher T. Whelan, James Williams and Bertrand Maître (1999), *Monitoring Poverty Trends*, Dublin, ESRI, the Department of Social, Community and Family Affairs and Combat Poverty Agency

CEPAL (2000), *Panorama Social de America Latina 1999-2000*, Santiago, CEPAL

CEPAL (1999), *Social Panorama of Latin America 1998*, Santiago, CEPAL

Collins, Michael L. and Catherine Kavanagh (1998), "For Richer, For Poorer: The Changing Distribution of Household Income in Ireland, 1973-94" in Seán Healy and Brigid Reynolds, eds., *Social Policy in Ireland: Principles, Practice and Problems*, Dublin, Oak Tree Press, pp.163-92

Corry, Dan and Andrew Glyn (1994), "The Macroeconomics of Equality, Stability and Growth" in Andrew Glyn and David Miliband, eds, *Paying for Inequality: The Economic Cost of Social Injustice*, London, IPPR/Rivers Oram Press, pp/205-16

Curry, John (1998), *Irish Social Services*, Dublin, IPA

Daniel, Caroline (1997), "Socialists and Equality" in Jane Franklin, ed., *Inequality*, London, Institute for Public Policy Research, pp.11-27

Davis, Earl E. and Margret Fine-Davis (1991), "Social Indicators of Living Conditions in Ireland with European Comparisons" in *Social Indicators Research*, Vol.25, Nos 2-3, pp.103-365

Desai, Meghnad (1995), "Introduction" in Meghnad Desai, ed: *LSE on Equality*, London, LSE Books, pp.1-9

Erikson, Robert (1993), "Descriptions of Inequality: the Swedish Approach to Welfare Research" in Martha Nussbaum and Amartya Sen, eds, *The Quality of Life*, Oxford, Clarendon Press, pp.67-83

Esping-Andersen, Gøsta (1990), *The Three Worlds of Welfare Capitalism*, Cambridge, Polity Press

Falk, Richard (1996), "An Inquiry into the Political Economy of World Order" in *New Political Economy*, Vol.1, No.1, pp.13-26

Gellner, Ernest (1979), "The Social Roots of Egalitarianism" in *Dialectics and Humanism*, No.4, pp.27-43

Glyn, Andrew and David Miliband (1994), "Introduction" in Andrew Glyn and David Miliband, eds, *Paying for Inequality: The Economic Cost of Social Injustice*, London, IPPR/Rivers Oram Press, pp.1-23

Government of Ireland (2000), "Programme for Prosperity and Fairness", Dublin, Stationery Office

Gray, John (1999), *False Dawn: The Delusions of Global Capitalism*, London, Granta Books

IMI (1998), *Executive Salaries in Ireland 1998*, Dublin, Irish Management Institute

Inter-Departmental Policy Committee (1999), "Social Inclusion Strategy", Dublin, Stationery Office

Jordan, Bill (1996), *A Theory of Poverty and Social Exclusion*, Cambridge, Polity Press

Kirby, Peadar (2000), "Growth with Inequality: The International Political Economy of Ireland's Development in the 1990s", unpublished doctoral dissertation, London, London School of Economics

Kirby, Peadar (1996), "The Impact of Neo-liberalism on Chilean Society", unpublished report, Dublin, Trócaire

Kirby, Peadar and Katherine Zappone (2000), "PPF will not narrow the growing gap between rich and poor", *The Irish Times*, 13 March

Korpi, Walter and Joakim Palme (1998), "The Paradox of Redistribution and Strategies of Equality: Welfare State Institutions, Inequality, and Poverty in Western Countries" in *American Sociological Review*, Vol.63, No.5, October, pp.661-87

Lal, Deepak and H. Myint (1996), *The Political Economy of Poverty, Equity, and Growth: A Comparative Study*, Oxford, Clarendon Press

Letwin, William (1983), "The Case Against Equality" in William Letwin, ed. *Against Equality: Readings on Economic and Social Policy*, Basingstoke, Macmillan, pp.1-70

Lynch, Kathleen (1999), *Equality in Education*, Dublin, Gill & Macmillan

Maxwell, Simon (1999), "The Meaning and Measurement of Poverty", ODI Poverty Briefing, London, Overseas Development Institute

Miller, David (1997), "What Kind of Equality Should the Left Pursue" in Jane Franklin, ed., *Inequality*, London, Institute for Public Policy Research, pp.83-9

Mishra, Ramesh (1999), *Globalization and the Welfare State*, Cheltenham, Edward Elgar

NAPS (1997), *Sharing in Progress: National Anti-Poverty Strategy,* Dublin, Stationery Office

NESC (1975a), *Income Distribution: A Preliminary Report*, Report No.11, Dublin, NESC

NESC (1975b), *An Approach to Social Policy*, Report No.8, Dublin, NESC

NESC (1981), *Irish Social Policies: Priorities for Future Development*, Report No.61, Dublin, NESC

NESC (1986), *A Strategy for Development 1986-1990*, Report No.83, Dublin, NESC

NESC (1990), *A Strategy for the Nineties: Economic Stability and Structural Change*, Report No.89, Dublin, NESC

NESC (1993), *A Strategy for Competitiveness, Growth and Employment*, Report No. 96, Dublin, NESC

NESC (1996), *Strategy into the 21st Century*, Report No.99, Dublin, NESC

NESC (1999), *Opportunities, Challenges and Capacities for Choice*, Report No.105, Dublin, NESC

NESF (1996), *Equality Proofing Issues*, Forum Report No.10, Dublin, NESF

NESF (1997), *Partnership 2000: Development of the Equality Provisions*, Forum Opinion No.1, Dublin, NESF

Nolan, Brian and Christopher T. Whelan (1996), *Resources, Deprivation, and Poverty*, Oxford, Clarendon Press

Nolan, Brian and Tim Callan, eds (1994), *Poverty and Policy in Ireland*, Dublin, Gill & Macmillan

Nolan, Brian and Bertrand Maître (2000), "A Comparative Perspective on Trends in Income Inequality in Ireland", paper presented to the Irish Economic Association annual conference, Waterford, April

Ó Cinnéide, Séamus (1972), "The Extent of Poverty in Ireland" in *Social Studies*, Vol.1, No.4, pp.381-400

O'Connell, Philip J. and David B. Rottman (1992), "The Irish Welfare State in Comparative Perspective" in J.H. Goldthorpe and C.T. Whelan, eds, *The Development of Industrial Society in Ireland*, Oxford, Oxford University Press, pp.205-39

O'Shea, Eamon and Brendan Kennelly (1995), "Caring and Theories of Welfare Economics", Working Paper No.7, Department of Economics, Galway, University College, November

Phillips, Anne (1999), *Which Equalities Matter?*, Cambridge, Polity Press

Powell, Frederick W. (1992), *The Politics of Irish Social Policy 1600-1990*, The Edwin Mellen Press

Rottman, David B. and Mairéad Reidy (1988), *Redistribution through State Social Expenditure in the Republic of Ireland 1973-80*, Report No.85, Dublin, NESC

Sen, Amartya (1987), *On Ethics and Economics*, Oxford, Blackwell

Sen, Amartya (1992), *Inequality Reexamined*, Oxford, Clarendon Press

Sen, Amartya (1997), *On Economic Inequality*, expanded edition with a substantial annexe by James E. Foster and Amartya Sen, Oxford, Clarendon Press

Sen, Amartya (1999), *Development as Freedom*, Oxford, Oxford University Press

Sheahan, John (1992), "Development Dichotomies and Economic Strategy" in Simón Teitel, ed., *Towards a New Development Strategy for Latin America*, Washington DC, Inter-American Development Bank, pp.21-45

Spicker, Paul (1999), "Definitions of Poverty: Eleven Clusters of Meaning" in David Gordon and Paul Spicker, eds, *The International Glossary on Poverty*, London, Zed Books, pp.150-62

Teague, Paul (1998), "Monetary Union and Social Europe" in *Journal of European Social Policy*, Vol.8, No.2, pp.117-37

Toye, John (1993), *Dilemmas of Development*, second edition, Oxford, Basil Blackwell

UNDP (1997), *Human Development Report 1997*, Oxford, Oxford University Press

UNDP (1999), *Human Development Report 1999*, Oxford, Oxford University Press

World Bank (1998), *World Development Report 1998/1999*, Oxford, Oxford University Press

World Bank (1999), *Entering the 21st Century: World Development Report 1999/2000*, Oxford, Oxford University Press

You, Jong-Il (1999), "Income Distribution and Growth in East Asia" in Yilmaz Akyüz, ed., *East Asian Development: New Perspectives*, London, Frank Cass, pp.37-65

Wallerstein, Immanuel (1998), *Historical Capitalism with Capitalist Civilization*, London, Verso

Chapter 2

The Politics of Redistribution[*]

Joan O'Flynn[†] and Mary Murphy

2.1 INTRODUCTION

This chapter examines links between the distribution of income and resources and the distribution of decision-making power in a society. It also critically examines the potential for redistribution through the National Anti-Poverty Strategy, social partnership and a social rights approach. It supports a rights approach and argues for a clearer understanding of the interdependent relationship between social inclusion, equality and competitiveness. Combined with more participatory models of decision-making this new framework has the potential to achieve more equitable outcomes for people.

The chapter is concerned with vertical redistribution, i.e. the extent to which policies result in individuals and groups on higher incomes or wealth distributing to those on lower incomes or wealth. Section 2.2 defines redistribution and demonstrates the inextricable link between power and the distribution of income and resources. The next section (2.3) illustrates key characteristics of a number of political ideologies, including liberalism, radical egalitarianism and the Third Way, and the relationship between them and distribution. The fourth section

[*] Thanks to the referee, editors and readers for their insights and assistance with drafts of this chapter.

[†] The views expressed here are the author's own and do not necessarily reflect the views of the Combat Poverty Agency.

illustrates how ideology is particularly reflected in aspects of economic policy such as the trade-off between equity and efficiency. It also discusses issues relating to the measurement of progress in achieving more equal outcomes.

Section 2.5 discusses the conventional tools used to redistribute income and wealth and section six explores other potential routes to more equal distribution outcomes. These include an assessment of a rights approach and some trends within national policy planning.

2.2 DEFINING REDISTRIBUTION

People's access to resources such as income, wealth, goods and services is central to determining their living standards. Economic growth, the growth in output of an economy over time, is relied on as the principal means to improve living standards for all. In a capitalist society like Ireland the market place is considered the main mechanism for both generating and allocating these resources. In the market, people sell the resources they own to generate their income. As Le Grand et al. (1992: 196) point out, the income to be derived from the market depends on the "amount and type of capital (resources) they own and the price they can get for it". Put simply, people with resources that command a high market price will have high incomes, people with resources that command a low price will have low incomes. Saleable resources include property, land and financial assets such as investments, stocks and shares. A person's human capital, which commonly refers to education and training, is a most significant asset for many people through which they sell their labour within the market place in exchange for a wage or salary.

In many capitalist economies, levels of unemployment, poverty, educational disadvantage, ill-health, homelessness and other indicators of disadvantage prove that all do not benefit equally from these market processes. In Ireland there is ample evidence of inequality and poverty (for example, Callan et al., 1996; Callan et al., 1999; UNDP, 1999; UNDP, 2000). Other inequalities include wage and income differentials: women continue to earn only 70 per cent of men's earnings and there is a growing income gap between those dependent on social welfare income and those with waged income. The extent and nature of other inequalities are discussed further in this book, particularly in Chapters 4, 5, 6,7 and 8.

The market produces unequal shares of income, wealth, goods and services. Redistribution emerges then as a political response to the failure of the original market processes to produce fair and just outcomes. It can be motivated by a desire for more social cohesion, more stability and control and/or a desire for equality and justice. The notion of what is fair or equitable is contested. Arising from this Le Grand et al. (1992) see four possible types of objectives for redistribution policy. The first is a minimum standards approach concerned only with those at the lowest end of the income distribution scale, people in poverty. With this approach the elimination of poverty is the limit of any redistribution policy. The second approach suggests that income is distributed according to need. The third suggests that merit (desert) should be the basis. The idea of equality of opportunity reflects this idea of merit so that the income distribution profile that emerges, when everyone has the same opportunities available to them to be rich or poor, is considered a fair one. A fourth approach is more extensive and seeks total equality where every member of society should have the same income. Le Grand et al. (1992, 203) conclude that "the goal of full equality is highly unlikely to be met by a market system . . . full equality would only arise if there was equality in resource ownership — for which there is no mechanism in a market system".

Redistribution then typically refers to intervention by government or others to readjust unequal market distribution outcomes. Policy structures redistribution through a wide range of measures such as programmes, services, fiscal systems, laws, regulations, rights and entitlements. Policy relates to actions that "deliberately or accidentally effect the distribution of resources, status, opportunities and life chances among social groups and categories of people within a country, and thus help shape the general character and equity of social relations" (Conroy, 1999). Decisions on which redistribution outcomes are considered desirable influence which policies are formulated and implemented. This process is influenced by the ideologies guiding the different actors in the political system. The relationship between political ideology and redistribution is discussed further in sections 2.3 and 2.5 below.

Townsend argues against a narrow interpretation of redistribution. He suggests that research concerned with redistribution must do more than "deal only with the minimum benefits and services available to the poor. Redistribution takes place in the context of the entire structure of wage and wealth disparities, including those which govern top earnings, bonuses and wealth accumulation and the corresponding structure of social relations" (Walker and Walker, 1997: 267). This intimates an interdependency between social, political and economic structures and processes and the need to reflect on the inherent power struggle between the "haves" and the "have-nots" and the reflection of the dominant power interests in policy. Goldthorpe judges that "Strategies grossly misjudge the resistance that the class structure can offer to attempts to change it. There is a serious underestimation of the forces maintaining the situation in which change is sought relative to the force of the measures through which it is supposed change can be implemented" (Le Grand 1992). Commenting on Irish policy choices, Breen et al. (1990, 215) somewhat in sympathy with this, suggest that the state underpins the class structure and opposition to policy change is minimised in Irish politics by "obfuscating the full class implications of policy changes". Poverty proofing discussed in section 6 below has potential to make the full class implications of policy changes more transparent.

Unequal distribution of decision-making power in a society is central to maintaining the unequal distribution of income, wealth and opportunity (Crompton, 1993: 57). For Weber, structured inequality is created by the social relations of exchange. For Marx it is created by production relationships. Thus for Weber, class and status are the bases of power in society while for Marx the class structure is the origin of every other social structure including power. Class and status confer differential capacities on individuals and groups in society resulting in economic inequality. These capacities manifest themselves in locating individuals and groups in differential positions in society: social inequality. These positions are characterised by unequal social relationships, in turn characterised by power differentials: political inequality. The relationship between these different inequalities is reinforcing rather than linear and the structure of inequality is maintained and continues. Westergaard and Resler suggest that "power is visible only through its consequences" (Haralambos and Holborn, 1991). This refers to the "winners and losers" of decisions, very often heard in political rhetoric, especially in budget day speeches by various Ministers for Finance. A Marxist perspective suggests that the non-decision-making aspect of power maintains the status quo as only safe decisions are made. This means certain issues are prevented from being discussed or decisions being taken in respect of them. The Marxist concept of ideological domination is relevant here as it produces an acceptance of capitalism and its associated inequalities as the dominant belief system. Section 2.6 below discusses how the process of policy planning and social partnership in Ireland may dilute ideological debate.

Parkin (Haralambos and Holborn, 1991: 188) comments that:

> Egalitarianism requires a political system in which the state
> is able to hold in check social and occupational groups who
> because of their skills or education or personal attributes
> might otherwise gain a disproportionate share of society's
> rewards.

However, Weber doubted the capacity of political parties to achieve this. While legal and political structures can modify the role of property and market relations to decide the structure of society, political structures work to the advantage of their instigators. Further, the class antagonism of political parties is diluted because they represent a number of groups in society (Parkin, 1993: 74; Morrisson, 1995: 243).

The challenge then is as much about the redistribution of power as it is about the redistribution of income, wealth and opportunities. However, what Dahrendorf (1999) calls the "internationalisation of decisions and activities" resets that challenge within a wider context of global free trade. Further, technological change will also be a new factor in determining equality of opportunity and distribution outcomes.

The global distribution of economic power and its impact on the capacity of nation states, institutions and economic actors to make effective choices in relation to national economic and social life are relevant here. The emergence and growing importance of transnational corporations (TNCs) lies in the concentration of economic power in "private" hands and not in the hands of either local communities or national governments. One of the implications of this is the reduced bargaining power of workers around wages. Capital has increased capacity to relocate to economies where there are lower labour and production costs and local workforces experience greater employment insecurity. Profit maximisation is the raison d'être of capitalism. In reality, much trade remains regional. Few TNCs do more business outside rather than inside their home regions (Dahrendorf et al., 1995: 3). But as Giddens (2000: 30) points out, there is a full global economy in the financial markets. This is linked to the "communications revolution and the spread of information technology". One of the implications of the financial services technological revolution is an expansion in productivity and growth levels but with less employment (Dahrendorf et al., 1995: 11). Expanding information technology reduces demand for unqualified workers. Reductions in job opportunities and wages follow. People who are equipped to take these opportunities benefit greatly and a widening income gap emerges. In this context, the distribution of work and power is important. Rather than making the nation-state and government obsolete, Giddens (2000: 31) argues that governance rather than government (meaning the national government) better describes some of the administration and regulatory capacities available under this new order and this concept also allows for the inclusion of non-governmental organisations.

Even within expanding globalisation, some commentators argue that the capacity of national governments to influence more equal distribution outcomes remains strong and vitally important. Dahrendorf et al. (1995) suggest that this is "because it is understood that the norms that govern the public domain differ from the norms and principles of the market and of private relations". This results in key areas of policy and public provision such as health care, education and social protection from unemployment, sickness, old age remaining somewhat protected from internationalisation and not fully exposed to the international marketplace. Nonetheless concerns about public spending levels may mean that education, health and social welfare often face pressure to cut costs and increase productivity to maintain national competitiveness. The fiscal criteria as part of the preparation for European Monetary Union is an example of this. If this is so, the structure of say the welfare, education and health systems and their capacity to deliver more equal income and wealth distribution outcomes, reflects values, social objectives and influences that are shared nationally, if not also internationally.

2.3 POLITICAL IDEOLOGIES AND REDISTRIBUTION

Many factors influence the degree to which any society creates and tolerates an unequal distribution of resources or, alternatively, strives for a society where there is a greater sharing of resources. These include the dominant political ideologies and their related economic systems. Here we review a number of political ideologies and how they influence the concept of redistribution and impact on actual policy. This, of course, is not a detailed exposition but seeks to frame the redistribution debate in the context of three main political ideologies presented as aspects of a political spectrum. These are liberalism, radical egalitarianism and the relatively new Third Way. The theories underlying these ideologies are key to their perspectives on redistribution. There are many other ideological traditions such as feminism, ecologism, nationalism, conservatism, facism that impact on decisions and processes relating to redistribution incomes but these are not reviewed here.

2.3.1 Liberalism

Liberalism embraces three core ideas that underpin individual rights (Held, 1987: 74). These are the constitutional state, private property and the competitive market economy. These core ideas are reflected in the Irish Constitution. All liberal ideologies are characterised by the individual right to pursue one's well-being and self-development. This emphasis on individual rights ignores pre-existing social hierarchies and inequalities and assumes that inequalities of income, status and power will always prevail. Liberals believe that the market is the most efficient allocator of resources. Because liberalism is based on a consensus-based process, redistribution requires the agreement of the minority, i.e. the wealth, status and power holders. Effectively they hold a veto and the status quo is usually upheld. Civil, political and social rights are endorsed by liberals as a means by which the state guarantees the formal equality of individuals and the freedom to pursue their own ends without interference.

For classical liberals or libertarians, state intervention to redistribute is morally wrong because it will reduce total market efficiency. Individual rights require minimal state intervention. A free market operating without state intervention is the libertarians' preferred mechanism for ensuring individual well-being. Taxation is perceived as state interference and a violation of the basic right of autonomy. Welfare is seen as paternalistic, generating dependency and undermining individual freedom. Such a "nanny state" also imposes a burden on taxpayers and capital. Neo-liberalism is the contemporary labelling of this version of liberalism whose advocates include Nozick and Hayek (Barr, 1994: 6; Plant, 1995: 122-135). Redistribution for social justice purposes is generally rejected as it requires state intervention through forcing some people to relinquish their income or wealth resources — such as earnings or inheritance — through taxation. More recently the New Right has embraced these core beliefs and married them with conservative ideals.

The roots of liberalism lie in the challenges to secular and ecclesiastical hierarchies from the seventeenth century on. Individual rights emerge as an alternative to the paternalism of feudal society and as a cornerstone of the new capitalist economic order. Two hundred years later at the end of the nineteenth century, there was a growing acknowledgement that individual freedom was now constrained by the competitive nature of capitalism. This led to a new strand of liberalism that advocated political intervention in the economy to tackle unemployment and low wages and to provide basic goods such as health and welfare. This was premised on the notion of "positive liberty" where society is reinterpreted as a collection of mutually dependent individuals. The public good transcends the private interests of a minority of wealth-holders and the active intervention of the state was necessary to enjoy the right to equal citizenship. Inequality and poverty were an impediment to this freedom and so the state had a new role to play.

Rawls, a liberal egalitarian, reflects this. Egalitarian liberals believe that not everybody gains equally from the structures and systems of society which provide advantages to some and disadvantages to others. One of Rawls' principles is that social and economic opportunities should be equal and goods distributed equally unless everyone, including the least well-off, benefit from unequal distribution. This acknowledges the need for redistribution to improve the position of the least well-off. It allows the state to collect and redistribute goods, although the protection of individual liberty remains primary. Rawls (1972: 7) points out that "the choice of a political constitution and the main elements of the economic and social system" require, first, the application of social justice principles. The Irish Constitution reflects this idea. Article 45 and its sub-articles provide for a competitive market economy, one of the key characteristics of liberalism. The articles acknowledge the possibility of unequal outcomes in the operation of private enterprise by suggesting in Article 45.3.2 the need to protect others from "unjust exploitation". Article 45.4.1 provides a commitment by the state to "safeguard with especial care the economic interests of the weaker sections of the community". These clearly promote state intervention arising from a concern with the way the market distributes goods and services.

2.3.2 The Radical Perspective

The liberal understanding of equality of opportunity of access to goods and services is step one for the radical egalitarian. Equality in the living conditions of all citizens is the aim and this is characterised as:

> . . . equality of respect and social status, universal provision for basic needs, substantial economic equality including a narrowing of the inequalities of income, wealth and economic power, substantial political equality including a democratisation of society, and the participation and inclusion of all social groups (Baker, 1996).

The achievement of equality of condition requires working for equality in, for example, wealth distribution, income, working conditions, participation and power in society and for the equal development of the potential of each individual. Mechanisms to reduce or at least neutralise the reproduction of privilege and class power are central to more equal power relations. To equalise political power the fundamental inequalities of condition that cause structural inequalities must be tackled. In contrast to the liberal emphasis on individual rights, the radical perspective is concerned with social relations and structures. This, in turn, also means a concern with relationships between groups in society.

Radical perspectives promote and support state intervention for greater equality in the distribution of goods and services. Capitalism and the free market are seen as fundamentally unequal systems that generate divided societies. State intervention is a legitimate measure of distributive justice. Taxation, therefore, is a "social good". It is understood as a way to collect and transfer income and wealth from individual taxpayers to the government for subsequent redistribution. From the radical egalitarian perspective, the ultimate economic objective must be to serve social ends — to maximise equality and human welfare levels for all.

2.3.3 THE THIRD WAY

Social democracy as a political belief system seeks to strike a balance between free market economies and state socialism or centralised economic models; between market individualism and planned state-led approaches. Accepting capitalism, it seeks to humanise it. This middle way featured in much of post-War Europe through centre-left governments since the 1940s until the end of the 1970s. Progressive taxation; strong state involvement in economic and social life; welfare support systems; public power through the democratic will of the people; collective decision-making involving government, business, trade unions; full employment; a confined role for markets and a mixed economy and a strong commitment to egalitarianism are central characteristics of social democracy (Giddens, 2000). By the late 1970s the social democratic consensus was beginning to fray. As Novak (1988) describes it:

> It is a form of politics which sought to reconcile the conflicting interests of capital and labour, which used the power of the state in the attempt to maintain social harmony, but which left the fundamental structures and institutions of capitalism intact.

Drawing on the UK experience, he concludes that the social democratic approach was unequal to growing demands from the labour movement, the emergence of consciousness and organisation amongst the poor, black people and women and crisis in the performance of the capitalist economy. By the late 1990s however, centre-left parties or coalitions were again in power in much of western Europe including the UK and Germany. Their prime ministers, Blair and Schroeder, are key proponents of a new form of thinking called the Third Way that reflects the impact of the globalisation of markets on political philosophies. The Clinton administration in the US has also been associated with its development.

Proponents of the Third Way argue that the core social democratic values of fairness and social justice, liberty and equality of opportunity, solidarity and responsibility to others need to be adapted to the challenges of the 21st century. Giddens (1999) summarises the Third Way approach as embracing a positive attitude towards globalisation; being concerned with a dynamic concept of inequality and as such interested in equality, pluralism and exclusion; being responsive to changing patterns of inequality; accepting that welfare systems and the broader structure of the state are the source of problems, not only the means of resolving them. The Third Way is the renewal of social democracy. Theoretically, democracy must mean more than voting. The Third Way is one where there is an active civil society and decision-making from the bottom up. Local communities are involved in the social and material regeneration of their areas and no permanent boundaries between government and civil society prevail. Government and state reform is a basic tenet of the Third Way with greater efficiency and more transparent processes. Existing welfare institutions require modernisation to reflect the demands of the global market place and to emphasise education and employability. Active welfare policies are coupled with labour market reform. As Blair and Schroeder (1999) put it: "Modern social democrats want to transform the safety net of entitlements into a springboard to personal responsibility". Increasing taxes that "take from the rich and give to the poor . . . isn't the simple and soverign solution it seems to be on the surface" (Giddens, 2000b: 96). While retaining a commitment to progressive taxation as a means of economic redistribution, tax cuts can contribute to social justice through increasing investment, profit and disposable income and lower tax rates may generate more tax revenue. Taxes that inhibit effort or enterprise should be avoided. Building up the tax base through employment creation is a "key emphasis of third way politics" and a substantial tax base can keep economic inequality under control (Giddens, 2000b: 100). Wealth tax, especially inheritance tax should be retained and new taxes such as green taxes and moving taxes to consumption as well as income are other ways of building up the tax base.

In political discourse in western societies, the above perspectives are accommodated to varying degrees in the traditions of neo-liberalism/market fundamentalism or social democracy. In Ireland, for instance, it has been recently claimed that "Fianna Fáil has believed in a Third Way long before such a concept was articulated" (Ahern, 2001). Neo-liberalism confines itself to equality of opportunity with an emphasis on individual-oriented approaches while social democracy is concerned with reducing inequality of outcome through collectivist or redistribution approaches characterised by a high taxation and high public expenditure economy.

2.4 ECONOMICS, IDEOLOGY AND REDISTRIBUTION

Political ideology is translated into the design and structure of our economic and social policy decision-making systems. One of the key manifestations of this is the degree of primacy of efficiency over equity, reflecting the supremacy of liberalism over more explicit social justice objectives. The trade-off between these and the implications for redistribution policy are discussed. This trade-off is a policy input as it influences policy design and formulation. Issues relating to the measurement of outcomes are discussed in the second part of this section.

2.4.1 Equity and Efficiency

Equity and efficiency are the two primary concerns regarding the best system for the distribution of material resources and goods in any economy and society. Equity relates to the most socially just allocation of any good. Political ideologies influence the extent to which equity is a consideration in final policy decisions. Optimal economic efficiency seeks to produce the optimal allocation of any good to maximise output, taking account of efficiency in production, product mix and consumption.

In the liberal tradition, economic efficiency is primary. State intervention to regulate the distribution of goods through a financial mechanism such as taxes or subsidies on incomes and/or prices is only justifiable in certain conditions. These include market failure or the failure of perfect competition or perfect information. Otherwise the market is the best provider in an economically efficient manner and the state is a provider of last resort. Equity is seen as a desirable economic or social outcome for its own sake but secondary to efficiency. On the other hand, a radical perspective acknowledges there are prior inequalities that influence the unequal rewards provided by the market. It therefore may be more accepting of a high efficiency cost as the means to a more just distribution of goods. The resolution of these tensions is commonly referred to as the efficiency and equity "trade-off".

The efficiency/equity trade-off in taxation policy is concerned with the impact of taxation on both the incentive to work and invest. Efficiency proponents argue that taxes should be kept low and that economic growth can only be generated through increased investment, productivity and labour force activity. The primacy of efficiency is reflected in social welfare policy when the level of welfare payment is kept relatively low to maintain the incentive to work. By contrast, a dominant equity perspective is concerned to ensure that social welfare payments are at least adequate to provide for a decent standard of living relative to average incomes. An equity dominated taxation policy is concerned with more equal sharing of the tax burden.

This economic growth/efficiency theory is not universally accepted. For example, Kenworthy (1995: 119, 225-254) suggests that greater equality may promote investment as investors anticipate a better financial return because of increased consumer demand generated by greater equality in income distribution. Considering a comparative study of 17 industrialised democracies her central tenet is there is no empirical evidence that more equality has a negative impact on investment or work effect. Further, a review of inequality in the US demonstrates that economic inequality stifles economic growth while other studies suggest that greater equality is better for growth. Some of the reasons put forward for this include greater productivity because of improved health and education outcomes, greater entrepreneurship because of enhanced profit-sharing or wages and reduced social costs because of less poverty (Lynch, 1998: 42).

The EU is currently exploring the relationship between social protection and economic growth in work on social protection as a factor of productivity. In Ireland similar discussions on the complex relationship between economic efficiency or competitiveness and social inclusion is recently found in National Economic and Social Council Strategy (NESC, 1999). In reality the relationship between equity and efficiency is far more interdependent than a simple "trade-off" analysis would suggest and is taken up again in section 2.7.

2.4.2 Measuring Outcomes

For those promoting equity objectives, the income and wealth distribution outcomes of policy are important. The ability to measure progress in achieving more equitable outcomes and to understand the relationship between specific policies and outcomes are key challenges for those seeking more social justice. A number of issues relating to the measurement of outcomes are discussed briefly below.

GNP is the commonly used measure of a country's general economic prosperity while GNP per head measures the average monetary standard of living of the population. The more an economy grows the greater its GNP and its prosperity levels. The influence of liberalism is evident in the use of the GNP indicator. The overuse of the per capita measurement reflects an ideology dominated by economic rather than social concerns. The economic growth approach is only concerned with the expansion of income. However as Haq (Martinussen, 1996: 303) points out, the *distribution* of growth is as important as the quantity of growth. If redistribution policy has social objectives then it is also in some way concerned with improving the quality of people's lives. Indicators need to be able to capture the outcomes of redistribution policy such as income and wealth distribution and inform on regional, gender, race or class imbalances within overall income distribution trends. As well as telling us about people's economic well-being, social and cultural well-being are equally important. A further gap in measuring policy outcomes is the capacity to assess and measure the extent of change to underlying structures, processes and institutions in society. Developments that seek to respond to these gaps are discussed again in section 2.6 and Chapter 9.

Most commentators judge the effectiveness of redistribution in monetary terms — annual Budget analysis tells us how much was spent on any redistribution measure. However this is a very limited assessment of what has actually been achieved with the expenditure. Budget day illustrations of redistribution outcomes often refer to the "typical" income effect of the policy change (Le Grand's final income). This "personal impact" picture does not tell us very much about the outcomes of the redistribution on society in general, for example across classes or across gender. What matters most is the final impact of any intervention: what discernible difference is any one intervention going to make in a person's or a community's life. The most important measurement is how public spending impacts on people outcomes (Le Grand's equality of outcome). Measurement difficulties mean a focus on outcomes is difficult to translate into policy but this focus is an important shift in ideological thinking and is reflected in the NESC Strategy 1999 and in the language of the Programme for Prosperity and Fairness (PPF). However as acknowledged by NESC, serious data deficiencies remain in trying to benchmark improvements in outcomes (NESC, 1999).

When trying to judge the effectiveness of any redistribution policy or measure we cannot measure the opportunity cost of that investment: what was the money not spent on, what might have produced better redistribution results? Most measurement of redistribution outcomes compares them to a "no policy change scenario". In this way, the outcomes tend to be justified because they improve or reform what already exists rather than because the policy outcomes were the best possible use of available resources. Comparison to an alternative redistribution mechanism is a harder test as it seeks to answer to what extent a policy measure has progressed towards more genuine redistribution outcomes. The ESRI has recently begun to measure the impact of government's budget changes against a base of earnings indexation rather than no policy change (see Chapter 5 and ESRI, 1998).

Social spending, the social wage or expenditure on public services like health, education and housing are generally accepted as redistribution mechanisms. ICTU (Irish Congress of

Trade Unions), for example, in its call for a review of PPF (July 2000) called for a combination of tax credits and increased public expenditure on transport, housing and childcare as compensation for higher inflation. It is far harder to measure the redistribution impact of spending on areas like health, education and housing. International work (LeGrand, 1982; Miliband, 1994) suggests that overall public service spending produces negative redistribution outcomes. In an Irish context, the latter chapters of this book on health, housing and education discuss this more fully. More generally the more one can participate in the economy and society the more benefit is accrued from public services like culture, sports, arts, transport, tourism, heritage and so on.

Social spending on health, education, housing etc is motivated by policy objectives beyond redistribution. Universality of healthcare in the UK (while distributing more to the rich) may, in fact have been the most efficient way to guarantee the poor a much better *quality* health service as well as delivering less unequal outcomes compared to market provision. An unequal income distribution outcome may be a worthwhile price to pay for achieving other social objectives. While there may well be regressive distribution outcomes from some public spending this is not to question the validity of social spending. It is a necessary component of solidarity, the very basis of our taxation and social welfare systems.

There are ways to ensure that social services are designed and delivered in an accessible way that provide for equality of participation. Debates about better quality in policy design and implementation focus on the need to include the end user of the public services in the design and delivery of the services. Policymaking also needs to examine better targeting of services, not necessarily from the perspective of means testing services but designing services to enable specific communities of interest; for example, removing barriers re accessibility, literacy etc. Appropriate data collection and disaggregation mechanisms are required to monitor access, usage and outcomes across groups or regions experiencing inequality. This is reflected in a number of data commitments in the current partnership agreement, A Programme for Prosperity and Fairness.

2.5 TOOLS OF REDISTRIBUTION

The redistribution of income and wealth by government typically employs two main tools: transfers and regulation (Le Grand et al., 1992: 206). In a mixed economy such as Ireland's redistribution operates in the public, private, voluntary and informal sectors of society. The state, the market, community-based, voluntary and/or charitable organisations and the family have varying roles in relation to the development and implementation of policies, legislation, regulations, services and programmes relating to, for instance, income maintenance, education, employment, housing and health care. The primary focus of this chapter is restricted to government approaches.

Transfers involve collecting income *from* people through the tax system and giving income *to* people through direct payments or subsidies. Unemployment assistance is a direct payment; mortgage interest relief is a subsidy. Regulation refers to interventions that legislate or regulate the payment that individuals get for the market sale of their resources or services. The minimum wage or rent controls are good examples. Regulation also relates to the structure of public expenditure and primary and secondary legislation that underpins policies and practices. These determine who receives services. The local delivery of services increasingly plays a crucial role in securing intended outcomes from economic and social policy. This is increasingly recognised in the Strategic Management Initiative and the Integrated Services Process. Direct provision of resources by the state is a third key mechanism. This is usually instead of provision by the market. Public transport and council housing are examples. Government can also distribute social services to specific citizens (e.g. medical cards to social welfare claimants or those on low incomes) or to all citizens (e.g. "free" education). Education, housing and health are themes in Chapters 6, 7 and 8. The tax and social welfare systems are covered in detail in Chapter 5 and are discussed briefly in the next section.

2.5.1 Taxation System

Taxation provides the material resources to facilitate redistribution of income, to finance public services and to correct market failures. In general four main categories of taxation prevail: personal income tax on wages, salaries and capital investment returns; corporate profits; expenditure on goods and services; taxes on wealth holdings, transfer of wealth, savings tax or inheritance of property, land, capital assets and investments.

A progressive taxation system is considered an effective redistribution mechanism as it takes a higher proportion of income from the rich than from others in society. The degree of progressivity determines the extent to which there is a fair structure of taxation. Tax rates rise in tandem with income or expenditure rises. Average and marginal tax rates are key to determining the redistribution capability and progressivity of the income tax (Le Grand et al., 1992). High marginal tax rates on low incomes are counter productive and a redistribution failure. Marginal tax refers to the amount of tax paid on an additional unit of income. Progressivity also incorporates the notion of the capacity of the taxpayer to pay and is also relevant to tax base issues. The taxation base refers to what is taxed, e.g. income, wealth, property, expenditure or consumption. If a taxation base is narrow, as in Ireland (Lane, 1991: 121), resources for redistribution are taken from the employed sections of a population while capital contributes relatively less for redistribution. Discretionary tax reliefs also dilute the tax base. The tax burden refers to the effects of taxes on certain sectors or types of taxpayer. Indirect taxes such as expenditure taxes (VAT) are known to have a disproportionately negative effect on low income groups. The taxation system is an important influence on income and wealth distribution outcomes as a fair taxation system can generate a more equal income distribution after-tax. It is also important because it provides the financial resources to fund direct income transfers and subsidies and pay for direct services provision.

A move to a system of tax credits gives policymakers the option of distributing a tax reduction equitably, e.g. at the same tax value to all taxpayers. Having such a tool also has the advantage of making the distribution outcomes from tax decisions more transparent and visible. However having an equitable distribution tool does not mean that there will be equitable distribution. The tax debate in Ireland leading up the 2000 Budget repeatedly illustrated the efficiency/equity trade-off described earlier. Equity advocates argued that all money available for tax reductions should be channelled through tax credits. They also argued this would be efficient as it would reward work at the lower end of the market and encourage the long-term unemployed back to work. Others, on pure efficiency grounds, argued to cut the top tax rates in order to promote labour supply and attract married women and former Irish migrants back into the Irish labour market. The end result was highly inequitable with over 75 per cent of the IR£942 million tax reduction going to people in the higher tax band. The overall income distribution outcome saw the richest 10 per cent of families increase their already high income six times more than the poorest 10 per cent managed to increase their already too low income (Combat Poverty Agency, 2000). Within the debate on tax reductions there are those who argue, from a strong equity perspective, that because 40 per cent of Irish households are outside the tax net, the tax credits mechanism will need to be refundable. This is discussed further in section 5.3

2.5.2 Social Welfare System

In Ireland there are three strands to the social welfare system: universal payments such as child benefit; means-tested payments such as family income supplement or unemployment assistance and contributory benefits such as unemployment benefit. The social welfare system is an important direct income redistribution mechanism. Policies target different types of individuals, groups or areas to achieve certain redistribution outcomes. Income transfers from EU Structural Funds target on the basis of disadvantage in particular geographical areas. Transfers of income through social welfare payments target people living in poverty. Other social welfare payments such as old age pension or child benefit, target benefits at different stages of one's life. Social welfare transfers are more effective at reducing income inequality than tax but, in Ireland, these transfers do not greatly mitigate the growth in widening income inequality. Transfers are more efficient than taxes at narrowing disposable income inequalities (with 40 per cent of citizens outside the tax net this is not surprising). However indexation of social welfare to net earnings is crucial if relative income poverty is to be contained.

Concern about the impact of social welfare provision on the incentive to work is primarily a concern about efficiency. Welfare reforms that have an emphasis on "welfare to work" derive from this as do concerns with keeping social welfare payment levels below potential earnings. Most recently in an Irish context, the Minister for Social, Community and Family Affairs, Dermot Ahern TD, put forward the government view on income inequality and the role of social welfare in relation to redistribution: "We have had to have a widening of income distribution to ensure it pays people to work, to reward people for their skills and to ensure there is incentive to take chances". In this scenario distribution happens through better access to education and employment. Redistribution through social welfare is only appropriate for those who cannot work such as the aged. He continued: "fair distribution of wealth is achievable by ensuring equality of opportunity — we do not believe that a fair distribution of resources can be achieved by mechanistic distribution through the social welfare system" (*The Irish Times*, 20 July 2000). The European Employment Strategy favours reform of the welfare and tax systems to increase incentive to work. These reforms will have obvious impact on the potential of the tax and social welfare system as direct income redistribution tools.

2.5.3 Integration of Tax and Social Welfare Systems

An alternative redistribution tool is to restructure the tax and social welfare systems. Negative income tax and basic income are often argued as approaches with more equal redistribution potential. This debate recognises that the tax system is the primary agent of redistribution and that those outside the tax system only benefit from welfare increases. Integrating the tax and welfare systems will not only make the distribution outcomes more transparent but will also result in more equitable outcomes. Both negative income tax and basic income seek to integrate the tax and social welfare systems. Negative income tax establishes a minimum income level, taxing those above it and giving tax credits to those below it. This idea is already discussed in section 2.5.1 above. Basic income means that each adult receives an unconditional payment from the state. This would, in general, replace all other transfers or subsidies and any income in addition to the basic income is taxable. This has been put forward as an approach to improve substantially the distribution of income with particular reference to the lowest income deciles of the population and it is intended to remove poverty and unemployment traps. Its proponents argue that it can contribute to the common good by providing citizens with greater liberty to achieve self-fulfilment and contribute to the development of society. This approach has been developed and analysed in several papers by CORI (Conference of Religious of Ireland), ESRI and most comprehensively in the Report of the P2000 Working Group on Basic Income which analysed basic income from an income distribution and economic efficiency perspective.

The option of these fundamental structural reforms like refundable tax credits or basic income crystallises the equity and efficiency trade-off. Structural reform may well bring greater equity to lower income groups but opponents are not satisfied that this very equity and the cost to the economy will not jeopardise economic growth through lost work incentives. However, within the more complex relationship between equity and efficiency many believe there are ways to restructure the tax and social welfare systems to achieve both equity and efficiency. Chapter 5 discusses in further detail social welfare and taxation as redistribution tools and charts the progress from the Commissions on Taxation (1982) and Social Welfare (1986) to the most recent PPF which commits to a review of social welfare adequacy and refundable tax credits.

2.5.4 Regulation

Redistribution can also be achieved through governments regulating to control market outcomes (e.g. the minimum wage). Governments intervene in personal financial income decisions between households; for example, the British Child Support Act and the Irish Liable Relatives Act. Governments seek to redistribute opportunities or life chances at individual level or across groups (e.g. access to education and training). Governments can also intervene to try to break down Weber's concept of "social closure" where classes or specific status groups retain power and income. This is often done through intervening in the market by, for example, increasing the number of taxi-driver and publicans' licences or by breaking down barriers that prevent access to specific professions (restructuring grades for hospital consultants, reforming the appointment process to the judiciary).

2.6 AIMING FOR MORE EQUAL DISTRIBUTION OUTCOMES?

The chapter now moves on to map and critique a number of new developments in political and social thought which offer new approaches to the debate about the politics of redistribution. Three important developments are discussed: new approaches to policy planning and governance, economic, social and cultural rights and new approaches to measuring distribution outcomes.

2.6.1 Current National Planning

Forward economic and social planning is characterised in recent years by a number of mechanisms at national level. These include a seven year National Development Plan. This broadly sets out the parameters of spending under EU Structural Funds and the government's capital investment programme. The National Anti-Poverty Strategy, National Spatial Strategy, National Children's Strategy, White Papers on Rural Development and Supporting Voluntary Activity, a sustainable development plan and many other initiatives characterise policy development concerned with future priorities. National planning also involves negotiation of a social partnership consensus every three years or so by the state, employers, trade unions, community and voluntary sector and the farming sector. The most recent programme is the PPF. While primarily concerned with tax and wage bargaining it also features commitments on equality and social inclusion and the ten-year National Anti-Poverty Strategy (NAPS). This section reviews and assesses aspects of the NAPS for achieving a more equal distribution outcome in Irish society. The following section reviews social partnership as a potential catalyst for redistribution.

National Anti-Poverty Strategy (NAPS)

"Sharing in Progress" (Government of Ireland, 1998) is the first ten-year strategy statement of an Irish government to tackle poverty. Derived from the UN Social Summit in Copenhagen in 1995, NAPS is a potential way for the policymaking process to be more accountable and transparent on redistribution objectives. NAPS has mechanisms such as consultation, target setting and poverty proofing. It includes important education and information mechanisms where all stakeholders are encouraged to better understand the structural causes of poverty: unemployment, inadequate income and educational disadvantage. The focus on education and unemployment reflects a strategy that is characterised by a coalescing of labour market integration with social integration. Echoing EU priorities, this has implications for particular groups for whom the labour market may be particularly inaccessible, e.g. older people, people who are ill, refugees and asylum seekers, Travellers, ex-prisoners, people with disabilities and so on. The NAPS commitments in relation to income adequacy aim "to provide sufficient income for all those concerned to move out of poverty and to live in a manner compatible with human dignity". The policy action in relation to this priority, reflecting the labour market integration emphasis above, suggests that increases in social welfare rates need to be complemented by actions to help the unemployed back to work (Government of Ireland, 1998).

This strongly reflects liberal ideology discussed previously where the relations of exchange between labour and capital are crucial to determining relationships within society and to accessing resources within the market. In contrast, a social rights approach facilitates citizens to both consume such resources and socially participate without the prerequisite of making a productive contribution (Levine, 1995: 99). This is discussed further below and also in Chapter 9. In the NAPS there is less concern with relative income poverty and wealth distribution and inequality. There is no discussion on wealth or capital taxation.

The NAPS contains principles, targets and actions and its principles are reviewed here. A review of these suggests that they are concerned with the liberal idea of equality. For example, there is no explicit commitment in the principles to social solidarity or social change though self-reliance through respecting individual dignity and promoting empowerment is encouraged. There is a commitment to guaranteeing the rights of minorities through anti-discrimination measures reflecting a concern with formal equality. From a radical perspective this could be strengthened by commitments to affirmative action to redress existing inequalities. The equal access principle is provided for but the equal participation principle is encouraged rather than say, guaranteed. The other principles relating to participation in decision-making are vague in the extent of their commitment. For example, the commitment to actively involve the community and voluntary sector and to engage in appropriate consultative processes suggests very little about the extent to which these processes will provide for an actual involvement in decision-making and transfer of power by the parties involved. The NAPS principles commit to reduce inequalities but other than the gender dimensions of poverty no other types of inequality are specified. The NAPS principles limit its capacity to achieve more radical equal distribution outcomes though NAPS clearly aims to reduce poverty. In this way they echo Le Grand's minimum standards objective of redistribution policy discussed earlier in section 2.2 and the liberal idea of equality referred to in section 2.3 above. The relationship between wider inequality and poverty is also elaborated on in Chapter 1.

In 1999 the government revised the overall NAPS target, aiming to reduce consistent poverty to 5 per cent by 2004 (Government of Ireland, 1999). At present there is no relative income target. A relative income target would have more practical application in influencing redistribution outcomes as would a target for income adequacy based on the 50 per cent average disposable income. The government in the course of negotiations on the current social partnership agreement, PPF, strongly resisted both a NAPS relative income target and a 50 per cent average disposable income adequacy target (CORI, 2000). Targets are potentially important as they can link to monitoring and evaluation mechanisms and can be used to focus debates on accountable policymaking. However, they are only useful if relatively ambitious targets are set, they can be measured and understood by all and have some relevance to and support within the political system. A relative income target would be important. Setting a target Gini coefficient would extend NAPS to go beyond an income poverty concern to also being concerned about income inequality and distribution. . The Gini coefficient is the most commonly used measure of income inequality. It is a numerical value of income inequality where a score of zero means perfect equality in income distribution. The higher the level of income inequality, the higher the Gini coefficient. Based on the 1996 wave of the European Community Household Panel, Ireland, Britain and Portugal have a pre-transfers (original incomes) Gini coefficient of 39. The EU average is 35. After transfers are taken into account the EU average drops to 31 while Ireland's Gini coefficient is 33 along with Britain and Spain. Portugal is the most unequal (37, Eurostat, 2000). While the Gini coefficient is not a perfect measurement tool, NAPS might nonetheless be strengthened by setting a target Gini coefficient.

Poverty proofing is seen by many to be potentially the NAPS' most powerful tool. Poverty proofing is the process by which government departments, local authorities and state agencies assess policies and programmes, at design and review stage, in relation to the likely impact they will have or have had on poverty and on inequalities which are likely to lead to poverty, with a view to poverty reductions. Poverty proofing is centred on three questions: does the public policy help to prevent people falling into poverty, does it contribute to the achievement of NAPS targets and what options might be considered for the proposal to have a more positive effect on poverty? (Combat Poverty Agency, 2000).

As yet, there is no evidence that administrative proofing mechanisms can or will change the outcomes of policymaking, with Budget 2001 being a case in point. Few applications of proofing have been published or are in the public domain though some key policy documents, such as the National Development Plan (Government of Ireland, 2000), have acknowledged undertaking the process. A review of the poverty proofing process is underway by the National Economic and Social Council. A second study by the Equality Authority and the Combat Poverty Agency is examining the inter-relatedness of equality and poverty proofing and this will have important implications for the future operation and priority of proofing within the public sector.

The PPF also commits to poverty proof the tax components of future budgets and this will be a genuine test of the strength of the proofing process as a tool for policy change in favour of those at the lower end of the distribution profile. This will be important as otherwise poverty proofing may be at risk as cynically being seen as a paper exercise rather than having influence on policy, in particular redistribution. The publication of the application of the poverty proofing guidelines to Budget 2001 tax measures suggests that to significantly impact on redistributional policy in favour of those on low incomes, the guidelines and their implementation need to be reconsidered to be more effective. As the poverty proofing process is relatively new within the public sector it is likely that the review will address the need for staff training, information systems and promotion of proofing within the sector itself. It may also be necessary to reinforce the political commitment to proofing by establishing it on a statutory basis and/or by obligatory publication of proofing exercises. These would then provide for the opportunity to monitor proofing and then to consider meaningful sanctions for failure to proof. Both as a concept and a tool, poverty proofing offers the capacity to change the culture of public policy decision-making. It is about mainstreaming equality and social inclusion issues into the heart of policy formulation, planning, implementation and review systems at national and local levels. We now move on to consider aspects of the social partnership process and its relevance to redistribution policy.

Social Partnership

Since 1987 the process of governance in Ireland includes an Irish model of social partnership based on three yearly economic and social agreements between government and three pillars, employers, trade unions and farmers. From 1996 it involved a fourth pillar in social partnership, the community and voluntary pillar. The widening of the social partnership process also brought about a widening of the agenda so that equality, poverty and redistribution were more explicit objectives of the later rounds of social partnership. As Chapter 5 shows there is evidence of an explicit redistribution agenda in the latter two partnership programmes.

The coexistence of representative democracy and social partnership have, on the surface, since 1987, delivered remarkable results for Ireland. These include increased GNP, decreased national debt, increased employment, reduced unemployment and emigration and a substantial reduction in the numbers of people experiencing consistent poverty (Callan et al., 1999). The impact on income inequality has been mainly achieved through increased numbers in employment. The four national agreements have included the introduction of tax credits, the minimum wage and an achievement of minimum adequate rates of social welfare payments.

The social partnership model has been critiqued as a form of elite interest group dominance of the policymaking arena. Walsh and Leddin (1998) argue that partnership represents a rigid system that protects insiders at the expense of outsiders. However there is some evidence to show that the influence of the social partners has brought about more equal distribution outcomes than would otherwise have been the case. The tax debate in the run up to the 1999 Budget focused on cutting tax rates versus increasing personal allowances. Pressure from trade unions and the community and voluntary sector certainly influenced a government decision to increase personal allowances, a U-turn on its tax policy. However the 2000 Budget reversed this approach where tax rates were cut by two percentage points at both the higher and standard rates, effectively ensuring that the better-off gain more from the biggest ever package of tax measures of almost IR£1bn. Budget 2001 continued this trend with two further percentage points cut from both personal income tax rates. Social partners may be limited in their capacity to influence.

In 1999, alongside the social partnership and representative democracy approaches, a direct action and conflict approach re-surfaced to influence the redistribution agenda. Arguably, strike action for increased pay by public sector workers such as the nurses and the Gardaí suggests that direct action can sometimes deliver greater income outcomes for certain groups than the consensus-building or social partnership approach. However, given the very limited capacity to organise the poor into conflict style action, partnership may be a more powerful tool than the alternative conflict approach, at least from the perspective of those dependant on social welfare who have little bargaining power in any conflict approach (Allen, 1998).

The social partnership process may act as a diversion away from debate about redistribution in that the process and model appear to be to deny any ideological discussion. Social partnership has moved from a crisis solving model (Programme for National Recovery) to a consensus building model (Programme for Economic and Social Progress) to a model that prides itself on its problem solving capacity (Government of Ireland, 2000, PPF). Both consensus models and problem solving models work by setting aside ideological differences to allow shared understanding to develop (NESF, 1997; O'Donnell, 1999). This backdrop reinforces the dominant liberal ideology. The net effect is that ideologies that underpin inequality and the dominant economic model in use today are rarely if ever challenged in the policymaking system. When they are challenged it is often in the guise of arguments about sustainability rather than concern to transform the inherent inequality they produce.

During the years of social partnership, redistribution has primarily happened through job creation and employment. At present, the primary beneficiaries of growth are those who profit and those who earn. Within these two categories, investors and very high earners have profited much more than middle and low income workers, (CORI, 1999). Many wealth holders and higher earners have benefited from tax incentives designed to bring about economic growth and employment growth. People who previously contributed their labour to creating growth also benefit in return for their effort — in particular this is the case for pensioners who are often classified as the "deserving poor". What we get in the name of equality is often focused on the needs of the economy or the labour market. For example, individualisation of the tax system, introduced in Budget 2000, was not motivated by redistribution but by the need to get married women back to work. The inequitable outcomes from Budget 2001's tax measures were motivated by "the objective to reward work and enterprise by tax reform" (McCreevy, 2000).

These outcomes reflect Le Grand's (1982) ideology of inequality, characterising key liberal ideas. Its main features are: a supposition that a certain level of inequality is fair; that there are deserving and undeserving poor; that a certain level of inequality even if unfair is necessary; greater income equality would, for example, produce inefficiencies in the market in the form of work disincentives. Certainly growing income disparity in Ireland appears justifiable within this ideology of inequality.

2.6.2 A Rights Approach

Rights, at their strongest, are judicial and provide a claim or legal entitlement to a particular resource or opportunity. Rights point to the development of social goals such as an adequate living standard or secure and decent accommodation. Economic and social rights usually include legislative, administrative, judicial, policy, economic, social and educational measures that underpin and effectively deliver the right to, e.g. welfare, health, education, income, social security. A right is also "a conceptual device used in political discussion to allocate resources and prioritise aspects of human nature and social relations" (Freedon in Yeates, 1995: 6). The reference to "allocate resources" clearly makes a rights approach relevant to shaping both the development and implementation of redistribution policy.

Plant's (Coote, 1992) understanding of rights captures the contrast between a rights approach concerned with social justice and a classic liberal approach. The social justice view means that:

> . . . market outcomes should not be just accepted with all the resulting inequalities: rather, citizenship confers a right to a central set of resources which can provide economic security, health and education — and this right exists irrespective of a person's standing in the market.

In other words, a rights approach is an active approach to correcting unjust market outcomes in a collective way in which we all share the cost. The welfare state and a progressive tax system are embodiments of the incorporation of social rights into citizenship. Advocates of the social rights approach see them as a way of providing an intermediate way between the market and democracy through the public sector and as being an essential prerequisite to support the individual capacity to act on one's own initiative. Sjoberg's (1999: 276) analysis connects the relationship between political ideologies, economic structures and the realisation of social rights and specifically, the importance of the dominant social view of taxation. He says:

> Social rights . . . demand active efforts on behalf of the state to a substantial degree. These rights must be provided in the form of concrete measures directed to individuals, and they require an extensive administrative apparatus and some kind of distribution mechanism. This costs money, and the development and existence of social rights are thus

highly dependent upon the capacity of the state to extract revenue.

Novak (1988: 186) draws attention to some of the tensions between a rights-based approach and capitalism. Some fear that the rights approach has uncertain implications for capitalism by turning a need for work or income into a right. When there is a right to a job it could reduce the power of employers and dilute the insecurity of a wage labour market by provision of an income guarantee. However, if those who seek full employment and the right to work accept the reciprocal obligation to accept an offer of decent employment, the debate then focuses on what is reasonable. When there is a right to receive social welfare benefit, it erodes the discretionary power of the state to provide for or refuse to satisfy the needs of particular individuals or groups. This is important as theoretically, at least, it denotes that a rights approach potentially offers a route to transfer power from the powerful to the less powerful and a subsequent narrowing of power differentials. As McCormack states: "Sharing power does not come easy but its imbalance in relationships needs to be underpinned by rights of access and accountability " (McCormack, 2000).

There is mixed evidence on the performance of rights in creating more equal distribution outcomes. For example, Harvey (1999: 16) points out that countries with constitutional or legislative protection of social rights such as a right to housing have more systematic and effective responses to homelessness. In countries with the least protection the homeless are poorly housed and most neglected. Four European countries (Portugal, Spain, Netherlands, Belgium) have a right to housing in their Constitution; in Italy the right to housing was upheld in the Supreme Court and in Britain, France and Belgium a right to housing is enshrined in housing law. Notably, Ireland is missing from these lists and Harvey highlights that the Dáil and a High Court judgement firmly rejected a right to housing. Yeates (1995: 14) also points to extensive poverty in Europe residing alongside already existing formal rights to a minimum income.

A number of contexts provide a backdrop to recent commentary and an emerging Irish public policy debate on rights.

These include Ireland's examination at the United Nations about its performance under the UN Economic and Social Rights Covenant (1999); the work of the Review Group on the Constitution (1996) and EU policy developments. In its Concluding Observations on Ireland's first report under the Covenant, the UN Committee observed that:

> . . . while the State Party's National Anti-Poverty Strategy addresses issues relating to, inter alia, educational disadvantage and rural poverty, the Strategy does not adopt a human rights framework consistent with the provisions of the Covenant (UN Economic and Social Council, 1999).

The Committee also noted its regret that the Covenant "has not been fully incorporated or reflected in domestic legislation and is rarely, if ever, invoked before the courts".

The Report of the Review Group on the Constitution (1996) considered if socioeconomic rights should be included in the Constitution "as a counterweight to economic inequality". The Report sets out six arguments for not including in the Constitution a personal right to freedom from poverty or specific economic rights. One of the reasons was the Review Group's view of the primacy of political decision making to determine issues of social and economic policy. This assertion brings into sharp relief again the interplay between the prevailing dominant political ideologies and their related economic systems. Resistance to the realisation of practical judicial economic and social rights is also based on fears of insatiable public expenditure and related fears about loss of economic efficiency due to high taxation. NESC (1999) recently acknowledged that:

> . . . citizenship rights encompass not only the core civil and political rights and obligations but also social, economic and cultural rights and obligations which are embedded in our political culture and which underpin equality of opportunity.

A reply by the Irish Commission for Justice and Peace (1998) to the Constitution Review Group puts the case for new social and economic rights on housing, health, nutrition and an adequate standard of living. In addition the embryonic Equality Authorities and Human Rights Commissions in both N. Ireland and the Republic of Ireland, set up following the Good Friday Agreement, provide a new institutional framework for a debate about rights and for the legal protection and guarantee of such rights.

Within the EU, the 1997 Treaty of Amsterdam reaffirms the commitment to social rights spelt out in other EU texts such as the 1961 European Social Charter and the revised 1996 European Social Charter. The Treaty also includes a new article 117 that sets out as an objective for each EU member state "proper social protection, the development of human resources with a view to lasting high employment and the combating of exclusion" (op. cit, 1998, 88). However, the Charter "will set the stage for any future negotiations on the future of an EU constitution" (Quinn, 2000). Quinn also considers that the Bill of Rights for Northern Ireland will also contain distributional rights:

> This is important because the new Human Rights Commission in the Republic . . . will have to work with the Northern Ireland Commission . . . on an all-Ireland Charter of Human Rights (ibid.).

On its own, a rights approach is insufficient. A commitment to economic, social and political equality of condition needs to inform its development. This is a more expansive view of rights. It avoids the liberal propensity to see rights as the rights of the poorest. It seeks to address the processes and structures underpinning inequality that results in particular groups continuing to enjoy privilege while it excludes others from equal enjoyment of resources and opportunities. The Taoiseach's 1999 comment that "democracy is about the fullest possible participation and it is not just narrowly confined to parliamentary institutions, it is also about the development of economic and social rights and fuller participation" illustrates a political direction for Ireland on rights.

2.6.3 Alternative Approaches to Measuring Distribution Outcomes

The Programme for Prosperity and Fairness requires the National Economic and Social Council (NESC) to benchmark progress in respect of the five operational frameworks of the Programme. NESC's earlier work in benchmarking progress under Partnership 2000 included the identification of policy areas to be monitored, appropriate indicators and relevant data to benchmark progress across time and internationally. NESC has commented that present data is often insufficient as the available range does not capture the range of variables that effect quality of life, most are not disaggregated across age, gender, class, family type or location.

There are considerable time lags in availability and there is methodological difficulty in comparing data, across time or across countries. This has led NESC to embark on an *Information for Policy* exercise, sub-sets of which are the development of indicators for sustainable development and benchmarking. NESC has also noted the importance of data presentation, accessibility and transparency. Access to appropriate data is a prerequisite for widespread participation in the policy debate and the widening of the social partnership approach. It is critical that these weaknesses in the policymaking process are addressed to enable a stronger analysis and argument for more equal distribution outcomes. At the same time it is important to acknowledge that research methodologies themselves derive from and operate within specific philosophical frameworks. Even when a research consensus emerges the ensuing policy action does not always necessarily reflect this, with taxation policy in recent times being a case in point (Cantillon, 1998).

We discussed earlier the shortcomings in using GNP as indicator for the state of society. Much work has been undertaken to generate alternative development indices by the UN, social indicators by the OECD, "green" accounting in the US and the Social Progress Index in Ireland. No alternative measurement has yet gained wide international acceptance. The *Human Development Reports* from the UN focus on the link between income and welfare and extend themselves to the provision of social infrastructure and services for all citizens, emphasise gender equality and equal opportunities for participation on economic and political decision making. While attributed with "contributing for theory formation concerning the preconditions for, and obstacles to, particular patterns of development" the same commentator also considers the limitation of the UN reports which are "purely descriptive and normative, rather than explanatory" (Martinussen, 1996: 304). Other UN-related work seeks to use UN human rights conventions such as the Convention on the Rights of the Child and the Convention on the Elimination of all Forms of Violence against Women as benchmarks for policy assessment (Fajth, 2000). This approach may offer potential for the use of the UN Convention on Economic, Social and Cultural Rights, ratified by Ireland in the 1990s, as a benchmark for policy assessment on redistribution outcomes but also on non-economic outcomes related to wider human well-being within society.

Feminist theorists such as Beechy, Delphi and others have undertaken work on other approaches that highlight the gaps in measuring unearned work. In Ireland under the last national agreement this has also been considered and a time use survey is under development by the Central Statistics Office. CORI and the National Women's Council of Ireland have both developed proposals for alternative social indicators to encapsulate broader concepts of economic and social progress. CORI proposes four key areas for progress indicators. These are economic, political, cultural and social and that measures of poverty, income and wealth distribution should be incorporated as well as the need to identify the participation levels of people in public decision-making and in social development (Healy, 1998). There is a need for indicators on equality working across the spectrum from equality of opportunity to equality of condition. Importantly, Healy stresses the need for widespread social involvement in both choosing these indicators and in deciding their application.

There has also been progress in developing an understanding of social investment and social protection as a factor of productivity (OECD, Bentley, forthcoming). ICTU's submission to Budget 2000 encouraged government to see spending on social inclusion as social investment.

While there are practical measurement difficulties, understanding social protection as an element of productivity is likely to be a key factor in successfully arguing for increased investment in social protection in the future. One of the obstacles to agreeing new indicators is the absence of agreement of what else needs to be measured, e.g. a new vision that is wider than simple economic growth; this has to be resolved through political rather than technological debate.

Advancing Redistribution Priorities

It is becoming clearer, by practical illustration, that the dynamic of economic growth feeds on itself, that the inherent dynamic of our economy is to continually delay redistribution for greater equality. Two complementary approaches have the potential to move forward the debate about growth and redistribution and their relationship to wider social development. It is beyond the scope of the chapter to do little more than sketch these here. Action here would include incorporation of judicial economic and social rights. Mayo and Craig (1995: 10) propose that strategies for change have to be formulated within a framework of alternative critical economic, social and political perspectives. Democratic approaches to planning that draw on the experiences of community participation and notions of empowerment are key to developing such alternatives. To equalise political power, the fundamental inequalities of condition that cause structural inequalities must be tackled. This thinking is a challenge to the controlling structures of power and wealth that have a vested interest in the status quo.

The first approach adopts an explicit social justice viewpoint that embraces a commitment to implementing expansive rather than minimal social rights and to facilitating participation and empowerment strategies for decision making in policy formulation, design and implementation. This approach can contribute to redistributing economic and political power more equally and help to transform social, political and economic structures. This would need to be anchored with an infrastructure of information, promotion and advocacy supports. Empowerment involves mobilisation of people and resources in new ways such that marginalised groups can expand their participation in mainstream decision making. It suggests a participatory model of policymaking based on citizens' rights. Baker (2000) points to the role of the political system and the education system in making this happen. As Kirby (1998, Chapter 8) says, "the process of empowerment has the potential to radically redesign the current paradigm that continues to produce social exclusion even with all our safety nets". The second complementary approach below is important as it can address the resistance to social rights based on fears about loss of economic efficiency due to high taxation.

This approach implies conceptualising a reciprocal relationship between social inclusion, equality and competitiveness. It accepts Kenworthy's view outlined in section 2.4 that there is no empirical evidence that more equality has a negative impact on investment or work effect. Investment in equality will lead to increased and more sustainable levels of competitiveness and this will allow greater long-term social inclusion through full employment affording increased public expenditure. The NESC Strategy document (1999) sets this out: "Competitiveness helps to generate the resources to enhance social inclusion, increased social inclusion facilitates competitiveness". Despite the rhetoric of the shared understanding of social partnership, understanding the dynamic of this reciprocal relationship remains underdeveloped. Social inclusion remains a residual. However the challenge is still there to make social inclusion a central objective of economic growth.

In effect applying the combination of these approaches means more balance between the efficiency and equity trade-off with equity reasons moving from a secondary rationale to a primary rationale, in this way bringing the economic, social and political into a more dynamic interdependency. A rights based approach means redistribution would not be seen as a residual but as an integral part of its design and of inherent value. In a period of high economic growth, a rights based approach is an opportunity to ensure that redistribution objectives survive into a recession or down turn. At the same time greater equality will equip the economy to better outride the impact of any recession. This means using the economic boom to embed the policies into legal rights or outcomes. Ultimately, these approaches can evolve to a new model based on a new ethic, where economics is simply a means that serves the interests of a just and equitable society.

2.7 CONCLUSION

This chapter has sought to demonstrate that redistribution is a political response to the unequal income and wealth distribution outcomes inherent in a capitalist market economy. Redistribution policies are limited to a minimum standards approach. This ensures that the core value of efficiency is protected as being the primary value and equity as secondary or residual. Efficiency is promoted as essential to maintaining the incentive to work and invest, considered key to competitiveness in an increasingly global capital market. Its dominance over equity considerations also ensures that substantial numbers of people experience income inequality and poverty. In effect, this is an ideology of inequality.

The fact that the capitalist market economy is designed on a base of inequality points to the urgent need to develop an alternative model of economic, social and political development. Strategies for change have to be formulated within a framework of alternative critical economic, social and political perspectives. An approach that adopts an expansive view of social rights and a commitment to empowerment strategies, allied with deeper understandings of the interdependent relationship between competitiveness and social inclusion, offers the potential to transform the unequal economic, social and political structures and power relations that are at the heart of unequal income and wealth distribution.

References

Ahern, Bertie (1999), Taoiseach's speech at ICTU Biennial Conference July, Dublin, Government Press Office

Ahern, Dermot (2001), "Labour's Conspiracy Theory has no Basis in Fianna Fáil's Reality", *The Irish Times*, 12 January

Allen, Kieran (1998), "Dimensions of Inequality", paper at Irish Social Policy Association, Annual Conference, 4 September

Baker, John (1996). "Studying Equality: An Interdisciplinary Project", paper delivered at the 1996 Annual Meeting of the American Political Science Association, San Francisco, 29 August – 1 September 1996

Baker John (2000), "The Challenge of Irish Inequality" in *Questioning Ireland: Debates in Political Philosophy*, eds Joseph Dunne, Attracta Ingram, Frank Litton, Dublin, Institute of Public Administration

Barr, Nicholas (1994). *The Economics of the Welfare State*, Oxford, Oxford University Press

Blair Tony and Gerard Schroeder (1999), *The Third Way*, London

Breen, Richard, D.F. Hannan, D.B. Rottman, C.T. Whelan (1990), *Understanding Contemporary Ireland: State, Class and Development in the Republic of Ireland*, Dublin, Gill and Macmillan

Callan, Tim and Brian Nolan, Brendan J. Whelan, Christopher.T. Whelan, James Williams (1996), *Poverty in the 1990s: Evidence from the 1994 Living in Ireland Survey,* Dublin, Oak Tree Press in association with the Combat Poverty Agency and the Economic and Social Research Institute

Callan, Tim, David Duffy, Tony Fahey, Bernard Feeney, Brian Nolan, Philip O'Connell, Sue Scott, John Walsh, (1998), *Budget Perspectives: Proceedings of a Conference*, 29 October, Dublin, ESRI

Callan, Tim and Richard Layte, Brian Nolan, Dorothy Watson, Christopher T. Whelan, James Williams and Bernard Maître (1999), *Monitoring Poverty Trends*, Dublin, Stationery Office and the Combat Poverty Agency

Cantillon, Sara (1998), "Research and Policy Making", in *Social Policy in Ireland*, ed. Sean Healy and Brigid Reynolds, Dublin, Oak Tree Press

Combat Poverty Agency (2000), *Planning for an Inclusive Society An Initial Assessment of the National Anti-Poverty Strategy,* Dublin, Combat Poverty Agency

Combat Poverty Agency (2000), *Pre-Budget Submission for Budget 2001*, Dublin, Combat Poverty Agency

Conroy, Pauline (1999), "From the Fifties to the Nineties: Social Policy Comes Out of the Shadows", in *Irish Social Policy in Context*, ed. Gabriel Kiely et al., Dublin, UCD Press

CORI Justice Commission (1999), *Social Partnership in a New Century*, Brigid Reynolds and Sean Healy

CORI Justice Commission (2000), "Resources and Choices: Towards a Fairer Future", *Socio-Economic Review 2000*, Dublin

Crompton, Rosemary (1993), *Class and Stratification: An Introduction to Current Debates*, Cambridge, Polity Press

Dahrendorf, Ralf and Frank Field, Carolyn Hayman, Ian Hutcheson, Will Hutton, David Marquand, Andrew Sentance, Ian Wrigglesworth (1995), *Report on Wealth Creation and Social Cohesion in a Free Society*, London, Commission on Wealth Creation and Social Cohesion

Dahrendorf, Ralf (1999), "Whatever Happened to Liberty?", *New Statesman*, 6 September

Dáil Éireann (2000), Debates, 27 June

Eurostat (2000), *Statistics in Focus, Theme 3-9/2000 Population and Living Conditions, Social Benefits and their Redistributive Effects in the EU — Latest Data*, Brussels

Fajth, Gaspar (2000), *Regional Monitoring of Child and Family Well-being: UNICEF's MONEE Project in CEE and the CIS in a Comparative Perspective*, Innocenti Working Paper No. 72. Florence, UNICEF Innocenti Research Centre

Giddens, Anthony (1999), "Why the Old Left is Wrong on Equality", *New Statesman*, 25 October

Giddens, Anthony (2000a), *The Third Way: The Renewal of Social Democracy*, Cambridge, Polity Press

Giddens, Anthony (2000b), *The Third Way and its Critics,* Cambridge, Polity Press

Government of Ireland (1990), *Bunreacht na Éireann*, Dublin, Stationery Office

Government Publications (1996), *Report of the Constitution Review Group*, Dublin, Stationery Office

Government of Ireland (1997), *Sharing in Progress: The National Anti-Poverty Strategy*, Dublin, Stationery Office

Government Publications (1997), *Partnership 2000 for Inclusion, Employment and Competitiveness*, Dublin, Stationery Office

Government of Ireland (1999), *Annual Report of the Inter-Departmental Policy Committee: National Anti-Poverty Strategy*, Dublin, Stationery Office

Government of Ireland (1999), *National Development Plan*, Dublin, Stationery Office

Government Publications (2000), *A Programme for Prosperity and Fairness*, Dublin, Stationery Office

Haralambos, Michael and Martin Holborn (1991), *Sociology, Themes and Perspectives*, London, Collins Educational

Harvey, Brian (1999), "A Right to Housing — The European Perspective", *Poverty Today*, No. 44: 16

Healy, Sean (1998), "Progress, Paradigms and Policy" in *Social Policy in Ireland*, ed. Sean Healy and Brigid Reynolds, Dublin, Oak Tree Press

Held, David (1987), *Models of Democracy*, London, Polity Press.

Irish Commisson for Justice and Peace (1998), *Re-Righting the Constitution: The Case for New Social and Economic Rights-Housing, Health, Nutrition, Adequate Standard of Living*, Dublin

The Irish Times, 16 August 1999; 20 July 2000

Kenworthy, Lane (1995), "Equality and Efficiency: The Illusory Tradeoff", *European Journal of Political Research*. 27: 225-254

Kirby, Peadar (1998), "Issues Raised and Agenda for Action", in *In the Shadow of the Celtic Tiger: New Approaches to Combatting Social Exclusion*, Dublin, Dublin City University Press

Lane, Philip (1991), "Government Intervention", in *The Economy of Ireland: Policy and Performance*, John O'Hagan (ed.), Dublin, Irish Management Institute

Le Grand, Julian (1982), *The Strategy of Equality, Redistribution and the Social Services*, London, George Allen and Unwin

Le Grand, Julian, Carol Propper and Ray Robinson (1992), *The Economics of Social Problems*, London, Macmillan Press

Levine, David P. (1995), *Wealth and Freedom, An Introduction to Political Economy*, Cambridge, Cambridge University Press.

Lynch, Kathleen (1998), "Workshop Presentation on Equality" in *Conference Report: Civil and Social Rights in the European Union*, Dublin, National Social Services Board

Martinussen, John (1996), *Society, State and Market: A Guide to Competing Theories of Development*, London, Zed Books

Mayo, Marjorie and Gary Craig eds (1995), "Community Participation and Empowerment: The Human Face of Structural Adjustment or Tools for Democratic Transformation?", in *Community Empowerment: A Reader in Participation and Development*, London, Zed Books

McCormack, Iñez (2000), "Meeting and Owning Change", in CORI (2000), *Participation and Democracy: Opportunities and Challenges*, Dublin, CORI Justice Commission

McCreevy, Charlie (2000), Department of Finance, *Budget 2001*, Dublin, Stationery Office

Miliband, Ralph (1994), *Paying for Inequality*, London, Rivers Oram Press

Morrisson, Ken (1995), *Marx, Durkheim, Weber: Formations of Modern Social Thought*, London, Sage Publications

National Economic and Social Council (1999), *Opportunites, Challenges and Choice*, Dublin

National Economic and Social Forum (1997), Report No 16, *A Framework for Partnership: Enriching Strategic Consensus through Participation*, Government Publications

Novak, Tony (1988), *Poverty and the State*, Milton Keynes, Open University Press

O'Donnell, Rory (2000), "Public Policy and Social Partnership", in *Questioning Ireland: Debates in Political Philosphy*, eds Joseph Dunne, Attracta Ingram, Frank Litton. Dublin, Institute of Public Administration

O'Donnell, Rory (1999), "Reinventing Ireland from Sovereignty to Partnership", Jean Monet Inaugural Lecture, (unpublished) 22 April

Parkin, Frank (1993), *Max Weber*, London, Routledge Press

Plant, Raymond (1992) "Citizenship, Rights and Welfare" in Anna Coote ed., *The Welfare of Citizens: Developing New Social Rights*, London, IPPR/Rivers Oram Press

Plant, Raymond (1995) *Modern Political Thought*, Oxford, Blackwell

Platform of European Social NGOs (2000), "Response of Social Platform and ETUC to Complete Draft of EU Charter produced by Convention", 1 September

Quinn, Gerard (2000), "Making Economic, Social and Cultural Rights an Irish Reality", *Poverty Today*, No. 49:8

Rawls, John (1972), *A Theory of Justice*, Oxford, Oxford University Press

Sjoberg, Ola (1999). "Paying for Social Rights", *Journal of Social Policy*, 28: 275-297

United Nations Development Programme (1999), *Human Development Report*, Oxford, Oxford University Press

United Nations Development Programme (2000), *Human Development Report*, Oxford, Oxford University Press

United Nations Economic and Social Council (1999), *Concluding Observations of the Committee on Economic, Social and Cultural Rights,* Ireland, 14/05/00 E/C. 12/1/Add.35

Walker, Alan and Carol Walker (1997), *Britain Divided: The Growth of Social Exclusion in the 1980s and 1990s,* London, Child Poverty Action Group

Walsh, B. and A. Leddin (1992), *The Macroeconomy of Ireland,* Dublin, 1992

Yeates, Nicola (1995), *Social Exlusion, Social Rights and Citizenship: The Contribution of a Social Rights Perspective to Combatting Poverty and Social Exclusion,* Combat Poverty Agency (unpublished)

Chapter 3

Social Expenditure, Redistribution and Participation

Sara Cantillon and Eamon O'Shea

3.1 INTRODUCTION

This chapter examines the issues of social expenditure, redistribution and participation. Specifically it addresses three themes: social expenditure; the evidence of the effect of social expenditure on income redistribution; and a critical approach to these through an alternative emphasis on the more recent concept of "social quality". The objective of the chapter is to tease out the relationship between these themes and their potential relevance and application to the Irish context. The aim is to open the debate on new ways of thinking about social objectives and the measurement of social progress that go beyond the current remit of social expenditure.

Section 3.2 looks at the differences in understanding the term social expenditure and at the variety of definitions. It is not a question of commitment to the validity of one definition over another — clearly there are trade-offs between the broader ones and more specific ones. Rather the aim is to view the relative merits of the different approaches. Section 3.3 addresses measurement issues in social expenditure, drawing out the distinctions between gross and net expenditure and providing some cross-country comparisons. Section 3.4 looks at social expenditure in Ireland and reviews the literature on its distributional impact and Section 3.5 provides a comparison with the EU. Section 3.6 deals with outcomes within the framework of social quality indicators and seeks to broaden the discussion of the effectiveness of social expenditure beyond simple redistribution measures and effects.

The first part of the chapter focuses on the narrow, contingency definition of social expenditure. The second part focuses on the qualitative effects of a lack of broader support services that "enable" independent living and participation and that is where the wider definition of social expenditure comes back into play.

3.2 ISSUES OF DEFINITION

The Organisation for Economic Co-operation and Development (OECD) defines social expenditures as benefits provided by public and private institutions to households and individuals "in order to provide support during circumstances which adversely affect their welfare" and that such expenditure can be in the form of cash transfers, or direct (in-kind) provision of goods and services (OECD, 1999). Similarly, Ferrera (1997) defines social expenditure, within a welfare state framework, as "public mechanisms of support (in cash, in kind, or through public services) against a catalogue of standard social risks: old age, death of a supporting spouse, invalidity, sickness, maternity, and unemployment". The common themes running through both of these definitions of social expenditure are the social risk and adversity origins of public intervention and social support.

Underlying the OECD definition of social expenditure which focuses on its contingency elements is the assumption that social expenditure has particular qualities that make it different to other forms of public expenditure. The first of these is that it is aimed primarily at individuals and households that face situations which adversely affect their material and personal well-being such as unemployment or illness. Second, social provision usually contains some aspect of redistribution, usually involving redistributing resources vertically, i.e. from the better off to the less well off and as such the spending is related to an objective, albeit implicit, of equality or social justice. The third aspect is that social expenditure does not usually involve a direct payment for a good or service.

However, other economists and researchers question whether all public expenditure (education, transport, environmental services, policing etc.) could not be regarded as social on the grounds that it benefits the whole community (Harding, 1982; Le Grand, 1982). Yet others adopt a mixture of definitions with some items from total government expenditure such as community amenities and roads added to the areas of education, health, social security and welfare services (Saunders, 1994).

One of the broadest definitions of social spending is that offered by the term *social wage* which was popular in the UK in the 1970s and is increasingly coming back into use (Larragy, 1999; Rankin, 1997). The social wage refers to the total income received by the state (either through taxation or earnings) or to total state expenditure including an income support system that pays pensions, benefits, subsidies and tax concessions. The breadth of this definition is particularly relevant to distribution insofar as it takes account of "hidden" expenditure or subsidies in the form of discretionary tax reliefs. For example, where government commitments to the old age contributory pension can be compared with the value of subsidies in tax relief to contributory occupational pension and state schemes. It is this recognition of tax reliefs as a form of fiscal or enterprise welfare that makes the broader definition appealing as it demonstrates the limits of examining the issues of distribution or redistribution in isolation from all aspects of the taxation system.

Underlying the lack of definitional boundaries is a lack of clarity as to the objective of social expenditure. Implicit in the employment of the narrower contingency-based definition of social spending is the view of a very specific type of spending based on the belief that "there is a direct and intimate relationship between social expenditure and social equality" (Crossland, 1956: 519). The common perception is that social expenditure is a necessary diversion of resources from the unequal individualised market process so that they can be put to use to achieve greater equality than would otherwise be the case.

What exactly constitutes equality could be anywhere from a minimum standards approach of providing a floor below which no one falls (along the lines of Beveridge's Freedom from Want) to attempting the equalisation of welfare and life chances through income redistribution and provision of the same standard of social services for all citizens. But, of course, the attainment of equality, however perceived, is not the sole aim of social, or public, spending. The promotion of a more efficient functioning of the economy also underlies state involvement in the economy. So judging involvement wholly in terms of redistributional impact is not sufficient, in the same way as judging the intervention only on the basis of efficiency is incomplete. The absence of a consensus about the definition of social spending or the extent to which it is meant to be an instrument for achieving greater equality are fundamental issues which are returned to throughout the chapter.

Finally, social provision can be divided into public or private social provision. Public social provision means provision of government benefits. Unemployment benefits, disability benefits and social housing are examples of gross public social provision. Private social provision of benefits is taken to mean those provided by individuals or employers and has two dimensions: mandatory or voluntary. For example, if sickness benefit is required by law to be provided by employers, then this is mandatory employer-provided private social benefit. If this is not a legal obligation but still provided by an employer, then it is voluntary private social provision. Not all private social benefits are provided by employers; some are also provided voluntarily by non-governmental organisations such as charities.

3.3 SOCIAL EXPENDITURE — GROSS AND NET DISTINCTIONS

Social expenditure can be divided into gross and net expenditure. The most basic approach to determining the level of social provision is to measure the monetary cost of cash transfers and social services. This does not give the complete picture because it overlooks the social support provided through the tax system in the form of tax breaks for social purposes. This can be considered expenditure because it reflects the opportunity cost of the revenue that could have been raised if the tax break was not granted. So a more complete picture of social provision takes into account both the money value of benefits and social services and tax breaks for social purposes. Some of the benefits to recipients of social provision may be offset because they may have to pay taxes. The benefits themselves may be taxed, or the recipient may pay tax indirectly when they buy goods and services. Thus, their effective value in net terms is usually less than the gross expenditure. To determine the real level of total social provision one must define social expenditure in net rather than gross terms.

Recent work by the OECD (Adema, 1999) is part of an overall effort to generate consistent data so that accurate cross-country comparisons can be made on the basis of the gross net distinctions discussed in the previous section (Table 3.1). Gross public social expenditure in Ireland amounts to 21.8 per cent of GDP at factor cost. Direct taxes on public benefits in Ireland amount to 0.4 per cent of GDP, while indirect taxes are 4.4 per cent of GDP. Public benefits are taxed only to a very limited extent, similar to Australia, the United States and the United Kingdom. Indirect taxes in Ireland are in line with other European countries, but are much higher than in the United States or Australia. Tax breaks for social purposes are relatively unimportant in Ireland. When private social benefits are added in, overall net social expenditure in Ireland is 18.8 per cent of GDP, three percentage points below the gross level. It is likely, however that if data on the value of tax concessions to private pensions were available for Ireland then the net figure would be higher.

Table 3.1: Net Social Expenditure Indicators, 1995, as a Percentage of GDP Factor Costs

Item	Aus	Bel	Can	Den	Fin	Ger	Irl	Ital	NL	Nor	Swe	UK	US
1. Gross public social expenditure	20.3	31.9	20.8	37.6	35.7	30.4	21.8	26.5	30.1	31.5	36.4	25.9	17.1
2. Direct taxes and social contributions paid over public cash benefits	0.3	1.9	1.5	6.1	5.1	1.2	0.4	2.3	5.1	2.7	5.2	0.4	0.3
3. Indirect taxes	1.6	4.4	2.0	8.0	5.5	4.2	4.4	3.3	3.9	6.9	5.8	3.7	0.9
4. Net direct public social expenditure	18.4	25.6	17.3	23.5	25.1	25.0	17.0	20.9	21.1	21.9	25.4	21.7	15.9
5. Net tax breaks for social purposes	0.3	0.9	0.4	0.1	0.0	0.9	0.3	n/a	0.1	0.0	0.0	0.4	0.3
6. Net current public social expenditure	18.7	26.5	17.7	23.6	25.1	25.9	17.3	20.9	21.2	21.9	25.4	22.1	16.2
7. Net direct mandatory private social expenditure	0.3	..	..	0.3	0.0	1.0	..	..	0.4	0.6	0.2	0.3	0.5
8. Net publicly mandated social expenditure (4+5)	19.0	26.5	17.7	23.9	25.1	26.9	17.3	20.9	21.6	22.5	25.6	22.4	16.7
9. Net direct voluntary private social expenditure	2.7	..	3.5	0.5	0.7	0.8	1.5	1.4	3.4	..	1.4	3.6	7.8
10. Net total social expenditure (6+7)	21.6	..	21.2	24.4	25.8	27.7	18.8	22.3	25.0	..	27.0	26.0	24.5

Source: Adapted from Adema (1999)

On the basis of gross levels of benefit provision Denmark and Sweden have the highest level of social expenditure in the OECD countries. However, the ranking changes when net expenditure data is used. Germany replaces Denmark as the highest public social spender in net terms. For all OECD countries considered, except Australia and the United States, public social effort is below what is suggested by an examination of gross budget data. In addition, accounting for private social benefits and the impact of the tax system on social expenditure increases the convergence of social expenditure across the OECD. However, Ireland remains a relatively low spender in both gross and net terms in the OECD, having the lowest net total social expenditure for the countries for which full data is available.

3.4 SOCIAL EXPENDITURE AND REDISTRIBUTION IN IRELAND

Looking at the trend of gross social expenditure in Ireland in relation to gross national expenditure, spending as a percentage of GNP has varied in recent decades from around one quarter in the late 1970s and the latter half of the 1990s to one third in the first half of the 1980s. The 1970s and the first half of the 1980s show a steady upward trend in social expenditure as a percentage of GNP. After the fiscal adjustment of the late 1980s social expenditure fell from 33 per cent of GNP in 1986 to 24 per cent of GNP in 1990. The ratio of social expenditure to GNP rose again in the first half of the 1990s to 26 per cent in 1995. With the improvement of the economy in recent years, the ratio has fallen again and is now close to the 1990 share of 24 per cent of GNP. However, these ratios can only take us so far in identifying the optimal scale of social expenditure on inequalities. The critical question is whether spending is broadly in line with levels of prosperity as measured by GNP per head. There are differences across countries with similar levels of prosperity in the priority given to social expenditure. In the early 1990s social spending in Ireland was higher than might have been expected on the basis of income per head (Callan and Nolan, 1992b). Given the economic growth in the second half of the 1990s and the slower growth in social spending this

finding is unlikely to be still valid. A recent welfare state classification by Bonoli (1997) places Ireland in the low-spending social expenditure category.

The effectiveness of social expenditure matters as much as
its size and scale. To determine whether social expenditure has
been successful, it is necessary to have a clear idea of the aims
of the programme itself. In Ireland, social objectives have
tended to remain implicit and, therefore, quite ambiguous. In
1981, NESC recommended a clear analysis of the distributive
aspect of current and proposed social policies. The issue of redistribution was also raised by the Commission on Taxation
(1982) and Commission on Social Welfare (1986). The former
viewed equity in a fairly narrow sense as meaning tax in line
with ability to pay rather than playing any major role in redistribution or redressing income inequality. The latter was more directly concerned with redistribution and argued that the higher
social welfare payments the more progressive the overall welfare system. It also underlined the importance of progressivity in
the financing of the system. However, as Hills (1995) observed:

> The issues involved in funding the welfare state are much
> more complex than simply aggregate questions of who pays,
> who benefits or what is going to happen to costs in the future.

Rottman and Reidy (1988) also argued that the objectives of
many social expenditure programmes were very general and
the extent to which redistributive objectives underlay these programmes was rarely explicit. To date there is little emphasis on
setting redistribution objectives for social expenditure, beyond
statements of general aspirations for a more equitable society
and a fairer distribution of resources. There has been some
analysis of the redistributional impact of various programmes of
social expenditure from the 1970s onward and below is a very
brief review of some of those studies from 1984 to 1998.

Rottman and Reidy (1988) looked at the trend of tax and
benefit redistribution in Ireland for 1973 and 1980 using unad-
justed income. They found there was a significant increase in
overall redistributive impact, mainly due to increased taxation
and transfers. Inequality in final income was lower in 1980 than

in 1973 because of greater redistributive effort despite the fact that inequality in market income increased. The same pattern emerges, adjusting for differences in household size and composition (Murphy, 1984). They concluded that the tax and benefit system had a major influence on income distribution in Ireland and cash benefits have had the largest influence in reducing inequality.

The Central Statistics Office (CSO) analysis of the redistributive effects of state taxes and benefits for 1973, 1980, and 1987 showed that while income tax itself was progressive, expenditure taxes were generally regressive. Thus, returning to tax reliefs, we can see that the progressivity of income tax is significantly reduced by expenditure taxes which can be deducted (often at the top rate of tax) on a wide range of items including business investment, private insurance, and pension contributions. Figures from the Revenue Commissioners Survey (1997) suggest that in 1994-95 over one quarter of individuals with incomes above IR£250,000 faced an average tax rate of less than 25 per cent and another quarter with incomes above IR£250,000 were liable for an average tax rate of 40 per cent or more despite the fact that their nominal tax rate was 48 per cent.

Income tax and expenditure tax work in opposition to each other in relation to overall redistributon or tax equity. Indeed the CSO analysis for 1987 suggests that the two produce a tax system which is proportional to income. This conclusion that progressive taxes like income tax tend to be offset by regressive indirect taxes in Ireland, while non-cash transfers are only mildly progressive is reiterated by Callan and Nolan (1992a: 198).

Using data from various Household Budget Surveys, Collins and Kavanagh (1998) calculate different measures of inequality for direct and disposable income for 1973, 1980, 1987 and 1994. Collins and Kavanagh argue that over these four time periods rising inequality in market incomes was counteracted by a redistributive effect from social expenditure, but that disposable income remains highly concentrated in the upper deciles of income distribution.

Another area of interest is the inequality in employees' earnings. Using the 1987 and 1994 ERSI surveys, Callan and

Nolan (1998a) show that there has been a consistent widening in dispersion at the top for weekly and hourly earnings. Using the ratio of the top to the bottom decile inequality rose from 4.2 to 4.8 for hourly earnings, and from 3.7 to 4.1 for weekly earnings, in the period 1987 to 1994. While earnings among employees became more unequal, the distribution of disposable income among households was little changed during the same period, having become more equal between 1980 and 1987. Direct taxation contributed to income inequality not increasing, even though earnings inequality did increase. This effect was more pronounced in 1980-87 than between 1987 and 1994. Survey data for 1997 indicates that there was a marked increase in inequality in the distribution of household income between 1994 and 1997 with a shift away from the bottom half of the distribution. An increase in the dispersion of earnings, a declining share of social welfare transfers in total income and greater inequality in the distribution of income of the self-employed are suggested as the main factors (Nolan and Maître, 2000).

Callan et al. (1996) argue that increases in current social welfare in line with prices are not adequate to prevent poverty because of a growing disparity with average take home pay. They recommend that social welfare rates should be indexed to average income growth rather than to inflation. The redistributive effects of tax and social welfare policies should be analysed against a more realistic benchmark, such as average earnings, than a "no change" in policy (in nominal terms). Budgetary policy has generally allowed the incomes of welfare recipients to fall further behind average incomes because the baseline chosen has not reflected the income growth in the economy. This is reflected in the increase in the numbers below the 50 per cent poverty line between 1994 and 1997 (Callan et al., 1999), a period of strong economic growth. In an analysis of budget changes between 1994 and 1998 Callan and Nolan (1998b) have shown that the poorest 30 per cent of the population have gained 2 per cent less from budget changes than they might have through an indexation of social welfare and taxes to average income growth.

Madden (1996) uses data from the 1987 Household Budget Survey to analyse income inequality by source of income. He uses disposable income which excludes imputed rents from home ownership, indirect taxes and social expenditure on health, housing and education. The largest marginal contributor to increasing inequality is wages and salaries, while the largest marginal contributor to decreasing inequality is income tax. For policy purposes, if wages and salaries are outside the direct control of policymakers (which they usually are for some important categories of workers, particularly in high paid jobs), then changes in income tax are the most important instrument for reducing inequality. Some caution is necessary in interpreting this result, since income tax may also have other welfare effects and the policy implications are ambiguous. Changes in income tax should be geared to the lower paid and, where possible tax adjustments focused more on increasing personal allowances than cutting taxes, given the more favourable effect of the former policy on the income of the lower paid (Callan and Nolan, 1998b). This has not happened in recent budgets as rate cuts and band widening have tended to dominate increases in personal allowances. This has led to higher gains for richer than for poorer households. In their analysis of Budget 2000, Duffy et al (1999) calculate that the richest 20 per cent of families gained about 4 per cent compared to less than 1 per cent for the poorest 20 per cent.

The source with the next greatest marginal impact on reducing inequalities is the old age pension. The results suggest that 1 per cent increase in pensions could reduce inequality in equivalised incomes by almost 0.2 of a percent (Madden, 1996: 8). In contrast, private pension provision contributes to inequality only to a limited degree. This may have something to do with the dynamics of income inequality. Richer households can afford to make private pension provision during their working years and are likely to remain in the upper part of the income distribution; less well-off households have to rely more on state transfers in their retirement to maintain their relative position. Unemployment payments comprise the third strongest effect on inequality with an effect of just over 0.1 per cent. Children's allowance has a very weak effect on inequality, the likely explanation being that it is a universal payment which is not subject to taxation.

Discussion of transfer payments must include some reference to the adequacy of social welfare payments which have now reached the uprated minimum levels recommended by the Commission on Social Welfare (1986). Current priorities include an increase in the old age pension to IR£100 per week over five years, with considerable progress towards achieving this target already made. Current rates of social welfare payment are clearly not enough, having failed to prevent increases in the numbers in relative poverty between 1994 and 1997, suggesting they are too low and need to be adjusted upwards. Social welfare payments must rise in line with the growth of other incomes. The fairest way is to link social welfare increases to changes in gross earnings. This would be an important demonstration of solidarity within society, that at a minimum, social welfare income recipients would not be allowed to fall in relative terms. The evidence is that countries with more generous levels of social provision tend to have both lower absolute and relative poverty rates (Kenworthy, 1998).

3.5 SOCIAL EXPENDITURE AND REDISTRIBUTION: IRELAND COMPARED WITH THE EU

The following discussion is based on a recent study carried out by Eurostat and DREES[1] and the 1995 wave of the European Community Household Panel which analysed the redistributive effect of social benefits for 13 member states including Ireland. The results are compatible with our review of the literature above. It is clear that a large percentage of the population receive some form of social transfer, that these transfers are concentrated on people with a low standard of living and that the redistributive effect, measured in terms of the impact of social transfers on the distribution of income, is significant. However, it is equally clear that considerable inequalities remain even after the transfers.

---

[1] Directorate of the French Ministry of Employment and Solidarity.

Table 3.2 below indicates the percentage of households receiving some form of social transfer in selected countries. Social transfers are divided into pensions and other social transfers including unemployment, invalidity, child benefit, housing benefits etc. Indirect social transfers and income in kind are not included. The average across the EU is 70 per cent and for Ireland the figure is 88 per cent with the total less than the combined pension and other social transfers figure because some households receive more than one social transfer. The figure is lower in Italy and Greece than in other countries mainly because of the lower proportions (less than 20 per cent) drawing social benefits other than pensions.

Table 3.2: Percentage of Social Benefit Recipients in Selected EU Countries

Countries	Pensions (%)	Other Social Benefits (%)	All Social Transfers (%)
Belgium	29	70	90
Denmark	19	75	85
Greece	42	18	53
Ireland	22	81	88
Italy	39	17	50
Netherlands	19	68	80
Portugal	37	63	85
United Kingdom	26	73	86

Source: Eurostat, 1999

Throughout the EU social welfare payments, excluding pensions, are concentrated on those with a low standard of living. The figures from this study indicate that while income from social transfers makes up 9 per cent of the total equivalised income of EU citizens, 51 per cent of that goes to people on low original income. This varies across different countries: the share of income from social transfers is highest in Denmark at 16 per cent and lowest in Greece at 2 per cent. The figure for Ireland is 12 per cent. The distribution of social transfers, other than pensions, by quintiles of the population in terms of original

incomes shows the extent to which social benefits are targeted
on those with lowest original incomes. In Ireland and the Netherlands, the bottom quintile receive 56 per cent of social transfers. In the UK the comparable figure is 58 per cent, in Denmark
52 per cent while in Portugal it is 34 per cent.

The redistributive impact of the social transfers is very significant in a number of EU countries, most notably Denmark and
the Netherlands but also in Ireland and the UK where the effect
is measured by looking at the reduction in the percentage of
those on low incomes before and after transfers. In Denmark
and the Netherlands the reduction is around 60 per cent; in
Greece, Italy and Portugal the reduction is smallest at between
7 and 15 per cent whereas in Ireland and the UK the reduction
is 38 per cent and 41 per cent respectively.

**Table 3.3: Impact of Social Transfers on the Distribution of
Household Income in the EU12, 1993**

Country	Transfers as % of Net House- hold Income	Gini Coefficient before Transfers	Gini Coefficient after Transfers
Belgium	36.5	0.544	0.281
Denmark	30.5	0.485	0.246
Germany	27.9	0.490	0.286
Greece	24.8	0.511	0.368
Spain	29.7	0.540	0.340
France	37.4	0.554	0.312
Ireland	27.8	0.553	0.333
Italy	32.7	0.546	0.330
Luxembourg	27.0	0.511	0.318
Netherlands	30.2	0.512	0.315
Portugal	22.1	0.543	0.405
UK	27.3	0.558	0.357
EU12	30.4	0.532	0.319

Source: European Commission, 1998

The impact of social transfers on income distribution across Europe has also been examined for twelve EU member states (European Commission, 1998). The income distribution between households before social transfers did not vary a great deal among the twelve member states in 1993 (Table 3.3). The value of the Gini coefficient before transfers ranged between 0.49 for Denmark and 0.56 for the UK, with the higher value representing a more uneven income distribution between households. Ireland had a pre-transfer Gini coefficient of 0.55 in 1993, third highest behind the UK and France. Social transfers helped to reduce the dispersion of income in every EU country. After transfers, the Gini coefficient for Ireland fell to 0.33. Across the EU (12) income remained more evenly distributed in Denmark after transfers, but Portugal had replaced the UK as the most unequal country of the twelve. The distribution of income between households after social transfers also varied more among countries than the pre-transfer distribution of income. Transfers had clearly a more pronounced effect in some countries than others. Ireland was at the top range of effect, particularly when the scale of transfers is taken into account.

Looking at the redistributive effect of social transfers in comparative terms leads to a straightforward conclusion. While the impact of social transfers, excluding pensions, is significant and while Ireland does quite well in comparison with other EU countries, inequalities in Ireland are still considerable even after social transfers. It is not that the welfare state is any less effective than elsewhere but largely because of the considerable and increasing inequality in market incomes. This leads us back to the issue raised in the Introduction — the need to revisit the more fundamental questions around resource allocation, welfare provision and setting equality objectives. Social expenditure, as currently defined, can only achieve so much. More fundamental reform will be necessary to make progress in dealing with prevailing and persistent social inequities in this country.

3.6 SOCIAL EXPENDITURE AND SOCIAL QUALITY

The data discussed above confirms the importance of social expenditure in mitigating the harsh economic realities of the market system. Social expenditure is, therefore, an essential and necessary component of the redistributive process. Whether it is both a necessary and sufficient condition for social progress is another matter. There are strong arguments to support the view that, notwithstanding its successes, social expenditure as currently formulated and constituted, does not go far enough in addressing the underlying needs of people. At a fundamental level, the Irish welfare system remains "pay related," in the sense that higher income individuals can supplement public provision from their own resources (O'Connell and Rottman, 1992). This dimension of the welfare state is evident in pensions, health care and education, where people on higher incomes enjoy better standards of provision, with significant levels of state subsidy. This leads to a widening of market inequalities rather than a reduction and promotes what O'Connell and Rottman refer to as the concept of dual citizenship with respect to social provision.

The lack of a common social citizenship is partly due to the absence of an integrating framework for reconciling the dual objectives of economic and social progress. Economic progress is, of course, much easier to measure than social progress, which is a much more disparate and elusive concept. Looking at changes in GNP or GDP tells you something about economic progress. But many more indicators are required to explore changes in social well-being because of the many different dimensions to need, fairness and equality. It is difficult to know where to begin measurement. Traditionally, social expenditure has focused on ensuring continued, if reduced, economic participation for certain categories of workers excluded from the labour market. People who cannot participate for reasons of unemployment, age, sickness and disability receive social protection in the form of social insurance and social assistance payments. While this is very important, it does not go far enough towards maximising the well-being and individual potential of recipients.

Intervention of a more radical kind is required which would focus on ways to bridge the gap between the actuality of people's lives and maximising their participation in economic and social life. At the core of this approach are policies that preserve and enhance the dignity and self-respect of people. So much in the market society serves to humiliate people who are not successful, who are outside the various circles of growth and prosperity, that social policies should be focused more on addressing individual and social need in a way that gives people maximum control over their own lives. This type of intervention requires a much more comprehensive, pervasive and integrated approach to policymaking than up to now. Even if the "pay related" aspects of the Irish welfare state are dealt with, it will not be enough. The emphasis must expand to include policies that enhance the capabilities of people to engage in both economic and social life.

A potential framework for exploring the effectiveness of social expenditure is the concept of social quality which seeks to integrate the economic and social consequences of public policymaking in a range of different fields. It recognises that both social and economic objectives are important, and that progress in the economic sphere does not necessarily imply progress in the social sphere. Social quality also rejects the view that economic growth and development are likely to be undermined by progress in the social sphere. Instead, the emphasis is on making progress in both spheres. Social quality can, therefore, be defined as the extent to which citizens are able to participate in economic and social life under conditions which enhance their well-being and individual potential (Beck, 1997). The essence of social quality is an emphasis on participation within a citizenship framework, where the objective is the maximisation of individual capabilities and potential.

The key focus is on the way we lead our lives within an increasingly individualised and fragmented market economy. Income transfers remain important within this framework, but additional objectives and benchmarks also need to be set for social expenditure beyond simple income distribution effects. Social expenditure could become an instrument for social change based on the enhancement of people's capabilities, the nurturing of self-respect within vulnerable groups and individuals and the development of social relations among citizens. This approach will involve innovative and radical equal opportunity measures to deal with current inequalities (Baker, 1998; Lynch, 1999) and is likely to be costly given the need to focus on the elimination of all barriers to participation and not just income transfers based on a contingency rationale. Nevertheless, a radical approach is needed if real progress is to made with respect to participation and full citizenship.

Social quality is, therefore, about more than equalising resources or ending discrimination, although action in both these areas is important. To participate in economic and social life people must have adequate economic resources. This is a necessary condition for a fairer and more ethical society. But it is not a sufficient condition and this is where social quality becomes important, requiring an inclusive and cohesive society where people have control over their own lives within a genuine representative democracy. While progress has been made towards meeting poverty targets within the framework of the National Anti-Poverty Strategy, there remains a culture of inequality and exclusion. The key target, therefore, is to expand the horizons of equality beyond income transfers and social provision. A conventional analysis of social expenditure cannot, for example, tell us why so many students leave the education system unfulfilled and unprepared for their role as citizens, why rich and poor people live in different areas and why people with various types of disability are largely absent from economic and social discourse.

These issues are inextricably bound up with the form and extent of structural inequality within Irish society, the remedies for which cannot be redressed through social expenditure alone. However the way we formulate, implement and evaluate social expenditure policies plays a role in reducing some of these inequalities. The first step is to evaluate economic and social programmes in terms of their contribution to social quality, i.e. to examine the impact of the way we organise production and exchange on people's capabilities, their self-respect and the nature of their social relations. This is not the language of the market, nor is it the language currently used to explore the meaning and measurement of inequality in this country. It is a language that will have to be learned, not from intellectuals or experts, nor the powerful, but primarily from the people who are disadvantaged and marginalised in this society (Phillips, 1995). Taking ritual humiliation out of economic and social relationships, building up what Margalit (1996) calls "the decent society", will require innovative and far-reaching changes in public policy that go beyond dealing with the normal contingencies and uncertainties. We now explore the application of the social quality concept in two areas of social policy: disability and ageing.

3.6.1 Disability

One of the key elements in being disabled is the absence of choice (O'Shea and Kennelly, 1998). The absence of choice is not only because of an absence of income. The problem is that the preferences and needs of people with disabilities are generally mediated through others. Inevitably this relationship leads to difficulties, since it is highly unlikely that third party preferences will equate with the expressed needs of disabled people. Yet, all the conditions for consumer sovereignty are present for people with disabilities. They are as likely to be rational as the next and their preferences are as likely to be transitive and in line with the assumptions of consumer theory. What tends to happen, however, is that people with disabilities are systematically denied a meaningful role in economic and social life, and learn not to want what they have not got. Their well-being is consequently low since their preferences have been adapted and distorted in order to fit the needs and wants of others. Within this environment conventional social expenditure programmes and, in particular, income transfers can only achieve so much.

Ultimately, the full participation of people with disabilities in economic life will depend on how much society is willing to pay to educate, employ and support disabled people on the same basis as able bodied people. The Rawlsian concept of primary goods, particularly the primary good of self-respect, is very important in considering the relevance of moral philosophy and justice for disabled people. It is only with a strong sense of self-worth allied to self-confidence, both of which come from self-respect, that individuals with disabilities can acquire a sense that what they do in everyday life is worthwhile and appreci-ated by others. Without self-respect, a person can have no sense of self-worth and consequently will have a lower feeling of well-being than those who do. People with disabilities, given their position in society, may place an even higher premium on policies and programmes that promote self-respect. Education and work are the two critical areas where self-respect is nur-tured and developed. There is a strong relationship between them and self-respect in modern capitalist economies. Recog-nising this relationship implies that people with disabilities should have a special claim on education and employment op-portunities as a means of equalising access to primary goods.

It is inequitable if disabled people are denied access to em-ployment or education as a result of factors beyond their con-trol (Sen, 1982; Le Grand, 1991). Le Grand (1991) explains this in terms of "equalising choice sets", which means that people should broadly have the same opportunities to develop their capabilities and enhance their self-respect as everyone else. Putting this right will require a policy response of positive dis-crimination in favour of the disadvantaged through the judi-cious manipulation of economic and other barriers to the ad-vantage of the less well-endowed. Accepting this view implies a holistic, eclectic approach to supporting disabled people; an approach that requires broad-based public intervention at an early stage in life. Families must be supported while, at the same time, nurturing the individuality of the person with dis-abilities. It may also require innovation in the form of public funding for personal assistants in both the education and work environments. Positive discrimination would not only apply to education and work, but would also encompass other areas like housing, transport and social care, since choice sets are deter-mined by opportunities for all types of commodities and serv-ices. The overall objective is to allow autonomy and sovereignty to prevail thereby maximising capabilities, self-respect and social relations.

One of the problems of this egalitarian approach is to explain whether such theories would be widely accepted by society. Although caution must be exercised about deducing moral values from empirical observations, the weight of evidence from party voting experiments and social indicators suggests that the views on fairness expressed above may not be universally shared. The implications for other important values like freedom may be simply too severe. The resource, or efficiency, implications of equalising choice sets are also likely to act as a constraint on policymakers. Equality of choice sets requires inequality of opportunity in the sense of positive discrimination. This costs money, much more money than governments have historically been willing to pay. Nevertheless, as Le Grand (1991) points out "a society with less inequality in choice sets will be one with less inequity". At the very least, considering the problem in terms of social quality is a much more satisfactory way of dealing with values than the current implicit approach of always relegating equity to a secondary position behind technical, individualistic and market functional based concerns about efficiency and freedom. Certainly, this would expand the domain of intervention in disability way beyond the current focus on income transfers. The focus would be on the potential of people with disabilities, the enhancement of their self-respect and self-worth and the development of their economic and social relations with other groups in society.

3.6.2 Ageing

Social policy has an important role in influencing the participation of older people in society. That role has been too narrowly defined in the past and cannot be captured by current levels of social expenditure on older people. The emphasis has mainly been on pensions and provision for long stay care requirements of vulnerable older people. Healthy ageing is, however, only possible and meaningful if older people are able to participate fully, on their own terms, in all aspects of economic and social life. What sometimes stops them from participating fully

are ageist attitudes on the part of others which sets limits on
what they can and cannot do and be (Walker, 1993; Bytheway,
1995). Older people are sometimes characterised as helpless
or defenceless, as not able to make decisions for themselves.
More perniciously, older people may be stigmatized as redundant, dependent, and, in more extreme language, as a drain on
society's resources (Walker, 1990). Social policy for older people has a key role to play in challenging stereotypical negative
images of ageing and older people by promoting the individual
and positive dimensions of ageing. Paying older people more
money is a necessary but not sufficient condition for greater
inter-generational solidarity.

The labour market for older people is a key area in need of
social reform (Taylor and Walker, 1995). Flexibility in retirement decision making is a very important part of healthy ageing. There is no provision for flexible retirement in Irish law
and early retirement is a matter for negotiation between employers and employees, or their representatives (National
Council on Ageing and Older People, 1998). The number of
people aged 65 years and over in the paid labour force has declined significantly throughout the last century, mainly due to
the reduction in the numbers employed in agriculture and improvements in the social welfare system. However, participation rates have also declined significantly for males in the 60-64
age category and also in the 55-59 category. The reason is the
shedding of older workers during periods of high unemployment. Some of the early exit has been voluntary with workers
opting to leave the paid labour force to pursue other interests
and activities. Unfortunately, for many early exit has not been
voluntary. In periods of high unemployment, for example during the 1980s, older workers were often selected for redun-
dancy. Older workers who are made redundant find it very difficult to re-enter the labour force and are de facto retired before they reach 65 years of age. While discrimination on the basis of age up to 65 is now outlawed by recent anti-
discrimination legislation, there is little doubt that discrimination has been an insidious part of the labour market experience

of older workers, and this remains the case for some workers above the age limit, notwithstanding the equality legislation.

Demographic changes occurring with varying speeds across Europe are causing governments to rethink the role of older workers in the labour force. In Ireland a significant increase in the numbers of older people and a decline in younger people is predicted in the next two decades. Labour shortages and the cost of pensions will mean that the emphasis will be on exploring ways to keep older workers in the labour force. This can be very positive if handled properly. How we value older people is the important question. They cannot be used simply as a reserve labour force to be used when and where the economy needs them. Active ageing implies a high degree of flexibility in how individuals choose to allocate their time over their later years in work, learning, training, in leisure and caregiving. The more active older people are and the more flexibility they have to pursue their interests, the better the quality of their lives. Through a combination of education, training and flexible retirement the labour market experience of older people can be transformed for the good of the economy and society. This points to the need for a public policy for ageing that emphasises individual capabilities, autonomy and real choice for older people, all within a social quality framework.

Social policy also needs to be transformed for dependent older people. Even if some become dependent they should be facilitated in reaching decisions about the type of services they want and value. Most older people want to live at home but community care services are not always developed enough to allow this. In addition, older people are not always directly involved in decision making about their future. Asking older people where they want to live and which services they want is better than telling them what they should want and is one of the central tenets of citizenship. A basic principle of social policy for older people should be to facilitate the genuine choices of people in need. This is a long-neglected area in social care provision and is seldom raised in discussions of equity. When it is, this usually relates to income but there can be equally pernicious inequities associated with the exclusion of older people from making decisions about their lives. The public subvention scheme for private nursing home care is encouraging people to choose in-patient long-stay care rather than care in their own homes. Allowing older people genuine choice in social care would not cost that much in terms of additional expenditure, but demands a significant change in the organisation and delivery of health and social care services. The involvement of older people in decisions about resource allocation in care of the elderly would transform current placement decision making leading to higher social quality for patients, families and providers.

Once more, the most useful approach to thinking about ageing issues is to focus on ways to bridge the gap between the actual and the potential in the lives of older people: between what they currently achieve and what they might achieve given more opportunities. That gap is larger for some older people than for others, but is there for the vast majority. This is very relevant in the case of people with dementia who are often ignored in the search for optimal care strategies and efficiency in resource allocation. But, even if capabilities have to be qualified for them, it is a good starting point, because it focuses on the person as the key to the whole process of care and not as an object of care (O'Shea and O'Reilly, 1999). The individuality, complexity and diversity of dementia can only be addressed within a person-centred approach to care (Sixsmith et al., 1993). When we establish solidarity with the people we want to help and their lives become part of some shared sense of humanity or community, we can think about genuine equality. This is where the focus on social quality becomes important. Equality is too vague a concept when formulating policy for people with dementia and social expenditure is too functionally defined to address all the important issues raised above. Social quality provides the basis for a more comprehensive treatment of all of the issues in protecting and developing the autonomy and personhood of the individual with dementia.

Public policy has a role in increasing the participation levels of older people in society. Equality legislation, flexible retirement, life-long learning, adequate income, social housing, health promotion and investment in community based health and social care services all contribute to healthy ageing. In that regard, continued economic growth, allied to the change in the population structure, may free up more resources for spending on older people in the future. The important point is to see beyond income distribution as the only strategy for achieving greater equity and solidarity between the generations. While current and ongoing increases in the basic pension are welcome the focus on income is a distraction from the more pervasive structural inequalities between the generations. What is needed more than ever is to identify new resources and new organisational structures within which to develop the social quality of the lives of older people across a wide-ranging set of circumstances and capabilities. In that regard, the more emphasis there is on the basic humanity of people's lives the greater the return in terms of increased solidarity between the generations. Attitudes will only be transformed by recognition and representation of older people in the decision making process.

3.7 CONCLUSION

Social spending has had a positive impact on measured income inequality in this country. This effect is strongest for people at the bottom of the income scale who have no other source of income. The narrowing of income disparities achieved by social transfers is higher in Ireland than in the majority of EU countries. The importance of scale and adequacy with respect to contingency based social expenditure should not be underestimated. Given the high level of inequalities associated with market incomes in Ireland, social expenditure can significantly reduce the gap between rich and poor. So also does direct taxation which has helped to prevent income inequality increasing, even though earnings inequality has increased in recent years. On the other hand, other aspects of the taxation system, especially expenditure taxes, have acted as a counterbalance to the progressivity of the income tax system.

The question is whether social expenditure can do more than reduce income inequalities especially in light of the structural inequalities in Irish society. We believe it can provide a means and impetus for more meaningful involvement in the economy and in society when its explicit goal is one of capability enhancement, linked to the attainment of higher levels of social quality and social citizenship for every person. This is a demanding task, both in terms of required resources and institutional change. We have provided two examples in the fields of disability and ageing of what might be achieved with a more comprehensive, social quality oriented, approach to goal setting in the area of social provision.

References

Adema, Willem (1999), "Labour Market and Social Policy-Net Social Expenditure", *Occasional Papers* No.39, Paris, OECD

Baker, John (1998), "Equality", in Healy, Sean and Brigid Reynolds (eds.), *Social Policy in Ireland*, Dublin, Oak Tree Press

Beck, Wolfgang (1997), "Social Quality: From Issue to Concept" in W. Beck et al. (eds), *The Social Quality of Europe*, The Hague, Kluwer Law International

Bonoli, Giuliano (1997), "Classifying Welfare States: A Two Dimensional Approach", *Journal of Social Policy*, 26, 3, pp. 351-72

Bytheway, Bill (1995), *Ageism*, Buckingham, Open University Press

Callan, Tim and Brian Nolan (1998a), "Income Inequality in Ireland in the 1980s and 1990s" in Barry F. (ed.), *Understanding Ireland's Economic Growth*, Dublin, Gill & Macmillan

Callan, Tim and Brian Nolan (1998b), "Income Tax and Social Welfare Policies" in *Budget Perspectives*, Dublin, ESRI

Callan, Tim and Brian Nolan (1994), "The Role of the Tax and Social Welfare Systems" in Nolan and Callan (eds.), *Poverty and Policy in Ireland*, Dublin, Gill and Macmillan

Callan, Tim and Brian Nolan (1992a), "Distributional Aspects of Ireland's Fiscal Adjustment", *Economic and Social Review*, 23(3), pp. 319-42

Callan, Tim and Brian Nolan (1992b), "Income Distribution and Redistribution: Ireland in Comparative Perspective" in Goldthorpe and Whelan (eds.), *The Development of Industrial Society in Ireland*, London, Oxford University Press

Callan, Tim and Brian Nolan and C. Whelan (1996), "A Review of the Commission on Social Welfare Minimum Adequate Income", *Policy Research Series*, no. 29, Dublin, ESRI

Callan, Tim et al. (1999), *Monitoring Poverty Trends: Data from the 1997 Living in Ireland Survey*, Dublin, Stationery Office and Combat Poverty Agency

Collins Michael and Catherine Kavanagh (1998), "For Richer, for Poorer: The Changing Distribution of Household Income in Ireland 1973-1994" in Healy, Sean and Reynolds, Brigid B. (eds.), *Social Policy in Ireland*, Dublin, Oak Tree Press

Commission on Social Welfare (1986), *Report of the Commission on Social Welfare*, Dublin, Stationery Office

Commission on Taxation (1982), *First Report: Direct Taxation*, Dublin, Stationery Office

Crossland, Anthony (1956), *The Future of Socialism,* London, Cape

Duffy, David, John Fitzgerald, Kieran Kennedy, and Diarmuid Smyth (1999), "The Domestic Economy", *Quarterly Economic Commentary*, Dublin, ESRI, December

European Commission, (1998), *Social Protection in Europe, 1997*, Luxembourg

Eurostat, (1999), "Social Benefits and Their Redistributive Effect in the EU", *Statistics in Focus Population and Social Conditions,* Theme 3 13/1999

Ferrera, Maurizio (1997), "New Problems, Old Solutions? Recasting Social Protection for the Future of Europe" in *European Social Policy Forum: A Summary*, Luxembourg, European Commission

Harding, Ann (1982), "An Introduction to the Social Wage", *Social Security Journal*, December

Hills, John (1995) "Funding the Welfare State", *Oxford Review of Economic Policy,* 11(3), pp. 27-43

Honohan, Patrick (1992), "Fiscal Adjustment in Ireland in the 1980s", *Economic and Social Review,* 23(3), pp. 285-314

Kennedy, Finola (1989), "Family, Economy and Government in Ireland", *General Research Series*, no. 143, Dublin, ESRI

Kennelly, Brendan and Eamon O'Shea (1998), "The Welfare State in Ireland", in Healy, Sean and Brigid Reynolds (eds.) *Social Policy in Ireland*, Dublin, Oak Tree Press

Kenworthy, Lane (1998), "Do Social Welfare Policies Reduce Poverty? A Cross-national Assessment", *Luxembourg Income Study,* Working Paper No. 188

Korpi, Walter (1992), "Welfare State Development in Europe since 1930: Ireland in a Comparative Perspective", Twenty-third Annual Geary Lecture, Dublin, ESRI

Larragy, Joe (1999), "Social Welfare and Public Health Services: Towards a Social Wage as Part of the National Product", paper presented to Retired Members Consultative Conference of SIPTU, 9 November

Le Grand, Julian (1991), *Equity and Choice: An Essay in Economics and Applied Philosophy* London, Harper Collins

Le Grand, Julian (1982), *The Strategy for Equality,* London, Allen & Unwin

Lynch, Kathleen (1999), "Redistribution, Recognition and Representation: The Importance of Economic Equality", paper read to ICCL Conference on Equality, 22-3 October 1999

McGuire, Maria (1986), "Ireland" in Flora (ed.), *Growth Without Limits,* vol. II, Florence, EUI

McGuire, Maria (1984), "Components of Growth in Income Maintenance Expenditure in Ireland" 1951-79, *Economic and Social Review*, 15(2), pp. 75-85

Madden, David (1996), "Sources of Income Inequality in Ireland", working paper, Centre for Economic Research, University College, Dublin

Margalit, Avishai (1996), *The Decent Society*, Boston, Harvard University Press

Murphy, Donal (1984), "The Impact of State Taxes and Benefits on Irish Household Incomes", *Journal of the Statistical and Social Inquiry Society of Ireland*, 25, pp. 55-110

National Council on Ageing and Older People (1998), *The Law and Older People*, Dublin

National Economic and Social Council, (1996), *A Strategy into the 21st Century*, Report no. 98/99, Dublin

National Economic and Social Council, (1993), *A Strategy for Competitiveness, Growth and Employment*, Report no. 96, Dublin

National Economic and Social Council, (1986), *A Strategy for the Nineties*, Report no. 89, Dublin

National Economic and Social Council, (1981), *Irish Social Policies: Priorities for Future Development,* Report no. 61, Dublin

Nolan, Brian (1993), "Charging for Public Health Services in Ireland: Why and How?", *Policy Research Series*, No. 19, Dublin, ESRI

Nolan, Brian and Bertrand Maître (2000), "A Comparative Perspective on Trends in Income Inequality in Ireland", paper presented to the Irish Economic Association, April

O'Connell, Philip J. and David B. Rottman. (1992), "The Irish Welfare State in Comparative Perspective", in Goldthorpe, J. H. and C.T. Whelan (eds.), *The Development of Industrial Society in Ireland*, London, Oxford University Press

OECD, (1999), *OECD Social Expenditure Database*, 1980-96, Paris

O'Hagan, John and M. Kelly (1984), "Components of Growth in Current Public Expenditure on Education and Health", *Economic and Social Review*, 15(2), pp. 87-93

O'Shea, Eamon and Brendan Kennelly (1998), "The Economics of Independent Living: Efficiency, Equity and Ethics", *International Journal of Rehabilitation Research*, 19, pp. 13-26

O'Shea, Eamon and Siobhan O'Reilly (1999), *An Action Plan for Dementia*, Dublin, National Council on Ageing and Older People

Phillips, Ann (1995) *The Politics of Presence*, Oxford, Oxford University Press

Rankin, Keith (1997) "Social Wage as Definitive Component of Political Parties' Philosophies", paper given to conference of New Zealand Political Studies Association

Revenue Commissioners (1997), "Effective Tax Rates for High Earning Individuals", Dublin

Rottman, D. (1994), *Income Distribution within Irish Households*, Dublin, Combat Poverty Agency

Rottman, D. and M. Reidy (1988), "Redistribution through State Social Expenditure in the Republic of Ireland", Report no. 85, Dublin, NESC

Saunders Peter (1994), *Welfare and Inequality: National and International Perspectives on the Welfare State*, Cambridge, Cambridge University Press.

Sen, Amartya (1982), *Choice, Welfare and Measurement*, Oxford, Blackwell

Sexton, Jerry, Brian Nolan and B. McCormick (1999) "A Review of Earnings Trends in the Irish Economy since 1987", *Quarterly Economic Commentary*, December, Dublin, ESRI

Sixsmith, A, J. Stilwell and J. Copeland (1993) "Dementia: Challenging the Limits of Dementia Care", *International Journal of Geriatric Psychiatry*, 8, pp. 407-12

Taylor, P and Alan Walker (1995), "Utilising Older Workers" *Employment Gazette*, April, pp. 141-5

Walker, A (1993), *Age and Attitudes-Main Results from a Eurobarometer Survey*, Brussels, CEC

Walker, Alan (1990), "The Economic Burden of Ageing and the Prospect of Inter-generational Conflict: *Ageing and Society*, 10, 4, pp. 377-96

Chapter 4

Inequality in the New Irish Economy

Colm O'Reardon[1]

4.1 INTRODUCTION

Much hyped and hackneyed as a certain *feles hibernaie*[2] may be, the pace of change in the Irish economy in the late 1990s has been extraordinary. Among the advanced European economies, the rate of economic growth experienced in Ireland in recent years is astonishing. Growth in national income, however, is but one element of the story. Irish economic life has changed enormously in a variety of ways, having a significant impact on the daily lives of millions of citizens. These changes range from the number of jobs available and the types of work people do, to the myriad of congestion effects which economic growth has caused. Economic change has been both rapid and profound. Moreover, in the absence of any major shock to the world or European economies, this period of change and growth is likely to continue in the medium term (Duffy et al., 1999).

Amid this process of change, one can become mesmerised by astonishing growth rates, accelerating house prices and ever more frustrating traffic problems, particularly when economic change

[1] This chapter was prepared while the author was an economic consultant with Indecon Economic Consultants. The views expressed are his alone and do not necessarily reflect those of Indecon or the NESC. I am grateful to the editors, reviewer and colleagues for their assistance. The usual disclaimer applies.

[2] That the term Celtic Tiger is now in common usage reflects the extent and pace of economic change in Ireland since 1994. At the same time, and for that reason, it now almost defies definition.

alters (sometimes literally) the signposts by which people live their lives. While much interest has been focused on the production of wealth, however, its distribution has also attracted considerable attention, with no little comment on how the fruits of growth have been shared. In fact, these distributive issues go to the heart of the relationship between economic activity and economic well-being, as well as shaping the society in which we live in a variety of ways.

This chapter is concerned with the relationship between the productive and distributive functions of the new Irish economy. It attempts to trace the implications of economic change in Ireland, at a macroeconomic level, for the distribution of economic well-being. In doing so, it is important to place these relationships within the context of the system of political economy that has underpinned this period of economic change. The discussion begins by describing the major watershed in economic governance, which occurred in 1987, and the pattern of accumulation and growth which has emerged since that time. This involves reviewing a number of the major macroeconomic indicators. The impact which this pattern of growth and accumulation has had on the distribution of well-being is then considered. For practical purposes, the focus of attention is predominately on the distribution of incomes, and in particular the Economic and Social Research Institute's (ESRI) research results from household surveys. The chapter then attempts to look behind the income distribution data, by examining changes in the components of household incomes over time. This allows a picture to be built up of how the pattern of change, at a macroeconomic level, has influenced the distribution of incomes. As will be seen, however, there are a number of gaps in our knowledge of how income is distributed in Ireland, and a primary concern of the chapter is to point to areas where information deficiencies exist, or where further research is merited.

4.2 ECONOMIC GOVERNANCE AND GROWTH, 1987–99

In order to understand the distribution of income in Ireland in the 1990s, one must examine the mode of economic governance which has underpinned recent growth and shaped the pattern of economic development. The backbone of that mode of governance is social partnership. While one cannot ascribe recent Irish prosperity to a single cause, social partnership has been a fundamental driver in economic change and has come to constitute a system of political economy which has had a profound effect on how the economy has developed, how wealth is produced and how it is distributed.

Social partnership, in the form of the Programme for National Recovery (PNR), emerged at a time of deep economic crisis. While centralised wage bargaining had existed in the 1970s, that process collapsed in 1981, and was followed by a period of decentralised bargaining. This coincided with an excruciating period in Irish economic history, with negative employment growth, unemployment reaching some 17 per cent, high outward migration and seemingly insoluble problems in the public finances. Within this context, the social partners worked out an agreed socioeconomic strategy within the National Economic and Social Council (NESC), which subsequently formed the basis for the PNR. That agreement and its successors have shared a number of central features, which include, but go well beyond, centralised pay determination. Certainly, pay moderation has been a key feature of the system. So too, however, have been other aspects of macroeconomic management. A non-accommodating exchange-rate policy within the European Exchange Rate Mechanism (ERM), for example, was an important element of the PNR, which has since developed into full European Monetary Union (EMU) membership. The stabilisation of the debt/GNP ratio, adherence to the Maastricht guidelines and movement towards current surpluses have been features of a consistently prudent fiscal policy established through social partnership, and marking a radical departure from the approach taken in the 1970s and early 1980s. Within the process of social partnership, pay bargaining has also been accompanied by a considerable input from the social partners to other important areas of economic and social policy. This included the maintenance of the structures of the welfare state, the preservation of the real value of welfare payments and significant increases in certain payments during the period of rapid fiscal stabilisation. Moreover, the process of social partnership has provided the social partners with an ongoing input to policy formation, which has had a significant impact on the way in which economic and social policies are developed and implemented (O'Donnell and O'Reardon, 1997, 2000; O'Reardon, 1999).

This mode of economic governance has been extraordinarily successful, in part, because of a virtuous circle which social partnership has established. The social partnership arrangement reached in 1987 effectively constituted a form of "solidarity pact" between those who were employed, and those who were unemployed (O'Reardon, 1999). Pay moderation, which was central to the deal, was to be a key factor in improving competitiveness and hence increasing employment. At the same time, it was expected that a hard currency policy, accompanied by consistent policy stances in fiscal policy and wage determination, would help to drive down interest rates, and hence improve growth and employment. Meanwhile, the basic fabric of the welfare state was protected during fiscal stabilisation. In more recent years, as productivity has increased and employment has grown, revenue buoyancy has allowed the state to reduce income taxes for those in employment, which has increased real incomes and allowed for further wage moderation. Hence, real net incomes have increased, employment has increased and (until 2000 at least) inflation has been low.

When social partnership developed in the late 1980s it was initially heavily criticised in political and academic debate, particularly by neo-classical economists, but also by some industrial sociologists (O'Donnell and O'Reardon, 1997). Among policy makers, however, the process was quickly seen as yielding important successes, as can be seen in Table 4.1 which shows a number of the main macroeconomic indicators between 1987 and 1999. After 1987, economic growth increased rapidly, but was stalled by the international recession of the early 1990s. From 1994 onwards rapid growth resumed and a remarkable transformation in economic life began. While employment growth had been sluggish, rapid increases in employment were achieved from 1994 onwards and inflation remained low throughout. Meanwhile, the public finances were stabilised and a government surplus has been recorded in recent years.

Table 4.1: Selected Macroeconomic Variables for Ireland, 1987-99

	Economic Growth %	Inflation %	Employment Growth %	Government Surplus/ (Deficit) % of GDP	Labour Costs, % Change
	(1)	(2)	(3)	(4)	(5)
1987	4.7	2.2	1.3	(8.6)	0.5
1988	5.2	3.2	0.1	(4.5)	-0.9
1989	5.8	5.5	0.0	(1.8)	0.9
1990	8.5	-0.7	4.4	(2.3)	-0.3
1991	2.0	1.7	-0.3	(2.4)	4.4
1992	4.2	2.5	0.6	(2.5)	3.0
1993	3.1	4.4	1.4	(2.4)	4.9
1994	7.3	1.2	3.0	(1.6)	-0.9
1995	11.1	0.4	4.8	(2.1)	-3.1
1996	7.4	1.7	3.4	(0.3)	1.1
1997	9.8	2.3	4.8	1.0	0.3
1998	10.4	4.0	8.4	2.4	3.7
1999*	7.5	4.0	5.2	2.3	5.3

Source: OECD Economic Outlook, December, 1999

*Data for 1999 are OECD projections.

Notes: (1) Percentage change in GDP; (2) percentage change in the GDP deflator; (3) percentage change in employment; (4) General government financial balance as per cent of GDP; (5) percentage change in unit labour costs.

The extraordinary success of the economy can be judged from the data in Table 4.2 which compares Ireland in the period 1994-99 with the Euro-zone and with the Organisation for Economic Cooperation and Development (OECD) as a whole for the same period. Average annual GDP growth of 8.5 per cent can be contrasted with figures of less than 3 per cent in the Euro-zone and the OECD, while employment growth averaged 4.5 per cent compared to 1.5 per cent in the rest of the Euro-zone. Meanwhile, over the period as a whole inflation in Ireland remained below the OECD average, although it was above the Euro-zone average.

Thus Irish national income increased by 63 per cent in six years, compared to the Euro-zone average of 13 per cent.

Table 4.2: Ireland's Comparative Economic Performance, 1994-99

	Ireland	Euro-zone	OECD
	Annual Averages		
Economic growth	8.5	2.1	2.9
Inflation	3.2	2.0	3.9
Employment growth, %	4.5	1.5	1.1

Source: *OECD Economic Outlook*, December 1999. Data for 1999 used in calculations are OECD estimates. Variables used are as for Table 4.1 above.

4.3 INCOME DISTRIBUTION

4.3.1 Irish Data

What impact has this pattern of economic change had on the distribution of incomes? As a result of a major ongoing suite of research projects undertaken by the ESRI, we now know quite a lot about the distribution of incomes in Ireland. This research has been based on analysis of a number of large scale household surveys which have gathered information on a variety of related issues, including incomes from different sources and access to necessities. The first of these surveys was conducted in 1987, with a limited follow-up in 1989. A further major survey was conducted in 1994, which was the first of an ongoing household panel study due to continue to at least 2001.[3] Collating the results of these studies, we can trace important features of the distribution of incomes from 1987 onwards.

There are a number of ways to examine the distribution of incomes. A standard approach is to calculate net equivalent households incomes, using an equivalence scale which adjusts the incomes of the household for the number of adults and children it contains, and hence measures household income in relation to household needs. Using this data, the Gini coefficient is the most

---

[3] Background information on these studies, including the methodological problems involved can be found in Callan et al. (1996).

commonly used method of describing the overall level of income inequality. The Gini measures inequality on a scale between zero and one, with higher values indicating greater inequality. Table 4.3 below shows Gini coefficients for Ireland in 1987, 1994 and 1997, as well as the share of total income which accrues to each decile[4] of the population distributed by equivalent household income.[5]

Table 4.3: Decile Shares in Equivalised Disposable Income for Irish Households, 1987, 1994 and 1997, ESRI Surveys

Decile	1987	1994	1997
Bottom	3.2	3.8	2.9
2	4.8	4.8	4.6
3	5.8	5.3	5.2
4	6.5	6.0	5.8
5	7.4	7.0	7.3
6	8.7	8.6	8.8
7	10.2	10.5	10.5
8	12.3	12.7	13.1
9	15.2	15.7	16.1
Top	25.9	25.5	25.7
all	100.0	100.0	100.0
Gini	0.330	0.331	0.348

Source: Nolan et al. (2000), Tables 3.3 and 4.3. Note: The (1/0.66/0.33) equivalence scale is used.

Looking at the period between 1987 and 1994, there is a remarkable stability in the Gini coefficient, particularly when we consider that a major fiscal stabilisation occurred during this period. Between 1994 and 1997, however, the Gini coefficient increased significantly. The income shares of the bottom four deciles fell between 1994 and

---

[4] In other words, the population is ranked according to the equivalent income of each household and then divided into ten groups or deciles, with the bottom decile being the poorest 10 per cent, the second decile being the next poorest, and so on.

[5] In making these calculations, the equivalent income of each household is weighted by the number of persons in each, so as to calculate the distribution of income across the population of persons, and not just of households.

1997, while the shares of the top six deciles increased (with the exception of the 7th, which was constant).

A sense of what lies behind these Gini coefficients can be had from examination of poverty measures calculated using the same data. The ESRI has made considerable use of relative poverty measures to describe the lower portion of the distribution of incomes. In Table 4.4 we show measures of the proportion of persons living in households where equivalised household incomes fall below a number of relative poverty lines, defined in terms of percentages of mean equivalent income.

Table 4.4: Percentages Below Relative Poverty Lines, Ireland, 1987, 1994, 1997

	1987	1994	1997
40% Line			
% of households	8.9	7.0	9.1
% of persons	11.8	10.7	12.5
50% Line			
% of households	17.6	16.9	20.3
% of persons	21.8	22.7	23.3
60% Line			
% of households	27.7	33.3	36.2
% of persons	32.2	35.2	36.6

Source: Callan et al. (1996); Callan et al. (1999).

Note: The OECD equivalence scale (1/0.7/0.5) is used. Poverty lines are defined in terms of mean equivalent income.

Comparing the situation in 1994 with that in 1987, we see that the percentage of persons below the 40 per cent poverty line fell, while the percentages below the 50 per cent and 60 per cent lines increased. Between 1994 and 1997, however, there were increases in the percentages falling below all of these poverty lines.

These measures are intended to describe the distribution of incomes in relative terms. In general, household incomes increased significantly during the decade after 1987, so the income in absolute terms of those at the lower end of the income distribution did increase significantly. This is an important factor, and has contributed to falls in poverty measures which combine relative income criteria with qualitative deprivation indicators. These qualitative indicators are measures of poverty based on household responses to survey questions concerning their inability to access certain basic needs because of financial constraints. Callan et al. (1999) show that the proportion of those falling below the 60 per cent relative poverty line and experiencing basic deprivation fell from 16 per cent to 15 per cent between 1987 and 1994, and then to 10 per cent in 1997. Thus while the incomes of those at the bottom of the distribution did not increase at the same pace as those on higher incomes in recent years, this is a markedly different situation than one where the incomes of the poor actually decline in real terms.

Further detail on changes at the lower end of the income distribution are available by looking at poverty measures which examine the poverty gap, i.e. the average amount by which households fall below some particular poverty line. Data on two such measures — the average poverty gap, labelled P_2, and the distribution-sensitive poverty gap measure, labelled P_3, are shown in Table 4.5. Each measure can be calculated for each of the three poverty lines discussed above. P_2 measures the mean of the differences between each poor person's income and the relevant poverty line, while the P_3 measure weights those gaps according to their size, thereby taking greatest account of the situation of the poorest. The data in Table 4.5 show improvement for both measures with all three poverty lines between 1987 and 1994. This data shows that, in the context of increasing aggregate real incomes, although some headcount measures increased, the position improved for many of those at the bottom of the income distribution. Between 1994 and 1997, however, we see a significantly different story. During this period there were substantial increases in both measures at all poverty lines. Again, this pattern of change is consistent with rapidly rising average incomes, with those in positions at the lower end of the distribution of incomes receiving smaller increases than those at the top and falling behind in relative terms.

Table 4.5: Additional Poverty Measures

	40% Poverty Line			50% Poverty Line			60% Poverty Line		
	1987	*1994*	*1997*	*1987*	*1994*	*1997*	*1987*	*1994*	*1997*
P_2	0.027	0.015	0.038	0.056	0.046	0.065	0.091	0.087	0.105
P_3	0.014	0.004	0.021	0.024	0.014	0.032	0.039	0.030	0.048

Source: Callan et al. (1996); Callan et al.(1999).

Note that the OECD equivalence scale (1/0.7/0.5) is used.

4.3.2 International Comparisons

It is interesting to compare the Irish pattern of income distribution with the experience of other countries. International comparisons of income distribution statistics, however, are fraught with difficulties, since data comparability problems arise in a number of areas. Table 4.6 below compares the level of income inequality as measured by the Gini coefficient for Ireland with a number of other countries, using the results from two studies. The first, by Gottschalk and Smeeding (1998) uses national datasources brought together in the Luxembourg Income Study databank, in a manner which attempts to minimise comparability problems. The second study, by Nolan, Maître and Callan (2000), uses data from the European Community Household Panel study, which was designed to harmonise household questionnaires across countries, and hence address comparability problems, as far as possible, at source. The Gottschalk and Smeeding study also provides us with data on the percentage change in the Gini coefficient for a number of countries between 1987 and 1994, the years for which we have Irish data. While the Nolan, Maître and Callan study provides data for fewer countries, their dataset involves fewer comparability problems. Nonetheless, it is important to treat both sets of results with some caution, not least because no attempt is made to adjust for the economic cycle. Moreover, because different measurement techniques may be used, one cannot compare the Gini's for particular countries across datasets.

Table 4.6 Cross-national Comparisons of Levels and Changes in Gini Coefficient

	Gottschalk and Smeeding LIS Data		Nolan, Matre and Callan ECHP Data
	Gini (year)*	Average Annual % Change in Gini, 1987–94**	Gini 1993–94***
Finland	0.223 (1991)	4.5	N/A
Sweden	0.229 (1992)	3.7	N/A
Belgium	0.230 (1992)	N/A	0.29
Luxembourg	0.235 (1994)	N/A	0.32
Denmark	0.239 (1992)	3.0	0.23
Norway	0.242 (1995)	1.7	N/A
Netherlands	0.249 (1991)	1.5	0.28
Italy	0.255 (1991)	0.3	0.33
Canada	0.287 (1994)	-0.1	N/A
Germany	0.300 (1994)	1.4	0.30
Spain	0.306 (1989)	N/A	0.34
Australia	0.308 (1989)	N/A	N/A
Japan	0.315 (1992)	1.3	N/A
France	0.324 (1989)	0.8	0.32
Ireland	0.328 (1987)	0.0	0.35
UK	0.346 (1995)	1.7	0.35
US	0.368 (1994)	1.0	N/A
Greece	N/A	N/A	0.36
Portugal	N/A	N/A	0.39

Source: Gottschalk and Smeeding (1998), Nolan, Maître and Callan (2000).

Notes: Gottschalk and Smeeding data is taken from the Luxembourg Income Study data bank with the exception of Japan, which is from a country study. Nolan, Maitre and Callan data is taken from the European Community Household Panel.

* Gini coefficients are based on incomes which are bottom coded at 1 per cent of disposable income and top coded at 10 times the median disposable income.

** Reference period is approximate. Exact period depends on data availability, hence annual average percentage change is used. Note that Danish data refers to 1987-90 only.

*** The Gini coefficient from Nolan, Maître and Callan here uses the OECD equivalence scale with annual income data.

Despite these measurement problems, the results are striking in a number of respects. Both sets of data show significant differences between the most and least unequal countries. To put this difference in context, in the Gottschalk and Smeeding data, a person at the 90th percentile[6] of the income distribution in Finland had 2.75 times the income of a person at the 10th percentile, whereas the equivalent figure for the US was 6.44, and for the UK 4.56. The Irish Gini shown in the Gottschalk and Smeeding dataset is somewhat dated, since it refers to 1987, but as we have seen above the Gini coefficient on incomes was virtually static between 1987 and 1994, so it is reasonable to take this 1987 data as a proxy for the Irish situation in the early-1990s. By doing so, we see that, with the exception of the UK, Ireland was the most unequal of the European countries in the Gottschalk and Smeeding dataset. There is a striking contrast between Ireland and other EU countries, such as Sweden and Finland, or even the Netherlands and Belgium.

There are significant inconsistencies in the ranking of countries between the two datasets. While we cannot sort out these inconsistencies here, the key point to note is that Ireland ranks as a highly unequal country in both datasets. In the Nolan, Maître and Callan data, only Greece and Portugal are more unequal. This fits in with a pattern observed by Atkinson (1995), whereby the Southern European economies (including Ireland) are the most unequal in Europe, while the Scandinavian countries such as Denmark, Finland and Sweden are the least unequal.

On the other hand, the table also shows Gottschalk and Smeeding data on changes in inequality for the period 1987-94 (approximately) for a number of countries. This data shows that Canada was the only country where inequality declined during this period, and Ireland was the only country where inequality remained constant. In the other countries for which there is relevant information, inequality tended to increase, in some cases quite significantly. (The UK and the US had also experienced significant increases in inequality in the early and mid 1980s.) While

---

[6] Just as deciles divide the population into groups of 10 per cent, ranked by income, percentiles are divisions of 1 per cent ranked in the same way. Hence, a person at the 90th percentile is at the bottom of the top decile, while a person in the 10th percentile is at the top of the bottom decile.

it is important to stress that this data does not take account of factors such as the business cycle in each country, nonetheless it is striking that while Irish income inequality did not decline during this period, neither did it increase. As was seen above, however, inequality did increase between 1994 and 1997.

Nolan and Maître (1999) also present comparative data on poverty for a variety of poverty lines. In Table 4.7 below we show their results for each of three poverty lines defined in terms of different percentages of mean equivalent income. Of the twelve EU countries for which data is shown, Ireland places in the middle of international ranking using a 40 per cent relative income poverty line. The Irish ranking deteriorates, however, as the relative poverty line is shifted upwards. With the 50 per cent line, Ireland is on a par with the UK and Greece, and only Portugal has a significantly higher percentage of persons in poverty.

TABLE 4.7: INTERNATIONAL COMPARISONS OF POVERTY HEADCOUNT MEASURES, 1994-95

	40% Line	**50% Line**	**60% Line**
	% of Population below Relative Line		
Germany	9.9	15.2	21.4
Denmark	2.9	6.0	12.2
Netherlands	4.7	8.8	19.1
Belgium	7.3	13.3	21.5
Luxembourg	6.5	15.4	25.9
France	7.7	14.9	24.5
UK	12.3	21.3	30.8
Ireland	7.7	21.6	32.9
Italy	11.2	17.7	26.2
Greece	14.8	21.8	29.3
Spain	11.0	19.8	29.1
Portugal	17.1	25.2	32.9

Source: Nolan and Maître (1999)

The contrast with Denmark and the Netherlands here is stark. With a 60 per cent line, Ireland has the highest poverty rate in the EU, with one-third of the population in poverty, compared to approximately one person in eight in Denmark. Thus while there are limited numbers of Irish people with very low relative incomes by EU standards, the proportion of the population which falls between the 40 per cent and 60 per cent lines in Ireland is the highest in the EU — fully 25 per cent, whereas the next highest is Luxembourg at 19.4 per cent, while the lowest is Denmark at 9.3 per cent. This aspect of Ireland's income distribution is also reflected in the poverty gap measures. While Ireland rates quite well in terms of both P2 and P3 at the 40 per cent line, its ranking deteriorates markedly for the P2 measure as the poverty line is shifted upwards.

4.3.3 Information Gaps

An interesting feature of this literature is that, while major advances have been made in the availability of information on poverty and the lower end of the income distribution, we know considerably less about the top of the income distribution. Of course, research resources are limited and the concentration on poverty and low incomes reflects a pressing policy need. Moreover, the incomes of the rich are complex and may be subject to particular problems of under-reporting in household surveys. Nonetheless, since a quarter of all incomes accrue to the top 10 per cent of households in the distribution, it would be interesting to know more about the type of households involved, the sources of their income and the impact of the tax system at the highest levels. Without such data, we are confined to anecdotal and indirect evidence. We know, for example, that sales of cars such as Mercedes Benz, Porsche and Jaguar have increased significantly in recent years, suggesting that a greater number of households have access to such luxury brands. It would be interesting to know, however, whether this is part of a general increase in prosperity, or one which is skewed towards a few. More data on high incomes would provide a further insight into the relationship between the productive and distributive functions of the new Irish economy, i.e. how income generated in different sectors of the economy is shared, what are the main sources of income for the richest 10 per cent of households etc. It would also provide a basis for debate about how the costs and benefits of economic progress are shared.

4.4. GETTING BEHIND THE GINI

The pattern of inequality described above and the manner in which inequality changes over time, are determined by a variety of economic and political factors. A number of the main driving forces behind income inequality in Ireland are discussed below. In order to develop our understanding and to organise our discussion, it is useful to make a distinction between what we shall call first moment and second moment explanations of changes in the distribution of income. With first moment explanations, one is concerned with the share of a particular type of income such as wages or profits in total income. Making assumptions about how these various types of income are distributed among households, one can consider the implications of changes in these shares. Second moment explanations, on the other hand, are concerned with the dispersion of income from these sources, i.e. with the variance of the distribution of the different components of household incomes. The most important example which we shall refer to below is the distribution of earnings. Whereas early economists once focused on first moment explanations, as the advanced economies have developed, the number of persons who can live without recourse to some form of labour has fallen and the number of households for whom labour earnings are an important source of income has increased. Thus the second moment of the distribution of earnings has become an increasingly important determinant of the overall distribution of incomes.

4.4.1 First Moment Explanations

For the purposes of discussion, we can think of household disposable income as being made up as follows:

Disposable income   = Primary market incomes
                     + Secondary market incomes
                     + Social welfare benefits
                     − Direct taxes

The term primary market incomes refers to payments for labour i.e. wages and salaries. Secondary market incomes means those from other market activities which are not direct payments for labour, such as rents, dividends and interest. Since both taxes and benefits are largely influenced directly by the state, they are considered together under a separate heading below. We focus here on primary and secondary market incomes.

The division of national income between wages and profits has been the subject of some comment in recent times (e.g. Lane, 1998). In terms of inequality, given that profits, dividends and interest are more unevenly distributed across households than wages, the finding that profits have increased as a share of national income can be taken as a force for greater inequality. Data on the capital income share in the business sector for Ireland from the *OECD Economic Outlook* is shown in Table 4.8 below, together with similar data for the EU. Calculating capital income shares is difficult, however, and data problems in this area make cross country comparisons of capital income shares particularly difficult.[7] Nonetheless, the data in Table 4.8 suggests a convergence of the Irish capital income share with the (increasing) EU average.

Table 4.8: Evolution of the Profit Share, Ireland and the EU, 1987-98

	Ireland	EU Average
1987	25.2	35.9
1988	27.6	36.5
1989	29.4	36.6
1990	30.4	36.1
1991	30.2	35.1
1992	28.6	35.2
1993	29.7	35.9
1994	30.3	37.5
1995	33.6	38.2
1996	34.7	38.3
1997	35.9	38.4
1998	37.8	38.6

Source: OECD Economic Outlook[8]

---

[7] In particular, it is necessary to apportion the income of the self-employed between wages and profits. This is usually achieved by imputing a wage to the self-employed with the balance designated as profits.

[8] While the datasource used here has its problems, other sources for Ireland confirm the general picture of an increasing profit share. This is true of analysis

An increasing capital income share is likely to give rise to greater inequality. A higher share of such secondary incomes in total households incomes can be shown to be associated with a higher Gini coefficient across households (O'Reardon, 1999).[9] So, how can this increasing share of profits be reconciled with stable income inequality between 1987 and 1994? There are a number of reasons why the major increase in profit share would not show up in the Gini coefficient on household incomes. Firstly, secondary markets incomes are generally significantly under-reported in household surveys. As Atkinson et al. note (1995: p. 36): "Incomplete reporting of property income plagues virtually all types of income surveys" often resulting in the under-recording of such incomes by as much as 50 per cent or more. Moreover, a large proportion of profits is retained in companies and not paid out to shareholders. While these profits represent an increase in the net worth of the firm, and hence of the shareholder's assets, they will not be recorded as income in a household survey. Nor would imputed rents from home ownership, which have recently been included in the Irish national accounts. As shown in Table 4.9 below, undistributed profits of companies increased by an average of 16.3 per cent per annum between 1990 and 1997, compared to 7.7 per cent for wages. Perhaps more importantly, however, a large proportion of the profit earned in Ireland is not distributed among Irish households, but rather is repatriated by foreign-owned firms. Such profit outflows increased by 15.3 per cent per annum in the 1990-97 period. Data in Table 4.9 from the Irish national accounts on the personal income of households and private non-profit institutions shows only profits that have actually been distributed and we can see that while there have been individual years when profit incomes have increased more rapidly than wages, the employees' remuneration component actually increased at a faster pace than the interest dividends and rent component between 1990 and 1997. Hence, apart from the measurement problems with household sur-

---

of the 1998 National Accounts, Table 1, when looking across the economy as a whole and adjusting for changes in the proportion of self-employed persons in the total number at work; and of the profit share in industry, transport and communications in OECD historical statistics.

[9] Unfortunately, internationally comparable data on the share of rent, dividends and interest in household incomes, is not available for Ireland.

veys, the flow of profits out of the country and the retention of profits in companies suggests that the increase in capital income shares
may not have had a strong impact on household income inequality.

Table 4.9: Annual Percentage Changes in the Main
Constituents of Personal Income

	1990-97	1990-91	1991-92	1992-93	1993-94	1994-95	1995-96	1996-97
Remuneration of employees	**7.7**	6.2	7.3	7.7	6.4	7.7	8.2	10.4
Income of independent traders	**6.1**	-0.7	10.2	6.4	6.7	7.7	6.8	6.3
Interest, dividends and rent paid to households and private non-profit institutions	**6.4**	7.2	-13.3	14.1	-19.5	4.3	15.5	49.9
Current transfers to households (including net transfers from the rest of the world)	**7.6**	11.5	5.6	7.3	5.1	8.0	6.1	9.4
Personal income of households and private non-profit institutions	**7.3**	6.2	4.9	8.1	3.4	7.5	8.2	13.0
Memo:								
Undistributed profits of companies	**16.3**	-2.9	20.9	17.4	42.1	33.7	1.9	7.7

Source: CSO, National Income and Expenditure Accounts, 1999

4.4.2 Second Moment Explanations

As discussed above, first moment explanations of income inequality look at the division of the national cake on the basis of assumptions about how different types of income are distributed.
Second moment explanations, on the other hand, are concerned
with the distribution of the different components of household incomes. Here, we are interested in the distributions of profits and
wages themselves, and how changes in the distribution of these
components of household income affect income inequality.

Capital Incomes

Unfortunately, we have little or no published information on the distribution of secondary market incomes across households in Ireland.[10] This is a significant lacuna in our knowledge concerning a potentially important determinant of income inequality. The lack of emphasis on this area might be explained in terms of the international experience of under-reporting of this type of income in household surveys. This makes it difficult for any study to produce reliable results. Moreover, as discussed above, the literature on income distribution in Ireland has tended to focus on the lower end of the income distribution, where secondary market incomes are not a major issue. The poor tend to hold few shares or bonds. This area, however, is likely to attract greater attention in the future. The prospect of an ageing population and longer average retirement periods, for example, will make pensions and other forms of investment income a more significant element in determining the distribution of economic well-being. With more flexible working arrangements such as greater contract working, pension provision and other forms of saving for retirement could become a major political issue.[11] Alternatively, if the state were to actively pursue a policy of privatisation through the sale of state-owned companies to individual investors, such as in the case of the Telecom Eireann floatation, personal investment in company stocks could become more widespread. Apart from the question of the distributional implications of these sales, the more widespread holding of such shares could affect the relationship between aggregate secondary market incomes and the distribution of income across households.

The Distribution of Earnings

Primary market incomes compose the bulk of household incomes in advanced economies, and Ireland is no exception. In addition to this empirical significance, the role which paid work plays in the daily lives of individuals gives the distribution of earnings an added importance. Working for low pay may involve an experi-

---

[10] While Nolan and Holohan (1993) analysed the holding of financial assets by households, the holding of wealth is not the same as the income flows which wealth generates.

[11] See, for example, Hughes and Nolan (1999). See also Pensions Board (1998).

ence of alienation which is additional to purely financial considerations. Here we consider the distribution of earnings from employment in two stages. Firstly, we examine the question of access to any earnings, i.e. employment and unemployment. Secondly we look at the distribution of wages among those in work. It is important to note that the discussion here is couched in terms of individuals rather than households, since data on wages tends to be collected and collated for the former.

Access to Earnings. An important feature of the distribution of earnings from work across all individuals in the population is that many individuals have no such income at all. Of course, in many cases, this is to be expected, as the person may be retired, may choose to be in full-time education, may be sick or disabled, may be engaged in full-time home duties, or may otherwise not be seeking work. Persons not working or seeking work are deemed to be outside the labour force and are not included in calculations of unemployment rates. Yet the decision to stay out of the labour force is often not independent of conditions in the labour market. The availability of full-time employment and the rates of pay on offer in such jobs can be a major determinant of labour force participation decisions, particularly among young people deciding whether to remain in full-time education, among female workers considering full-time home duties, or among older persons considering retirement.

For all of these reasons, the actual rate of unemployment may not fully reflect the numbers of persons who would choose to work if they could.[12] In considering access to earnings from employment therefore, we should consider both the unemployment rate and the employment rate, i.e. the proportion of those over 15 who have access to earnings from work (while bearing in mind that not everyone will choose or have the option to be economically active). Table 4.10 sets out data for these variables from 1987 to the present.

---

[12] In Ireland, this is further complicated by the tradition of economic migration in response to poor employment prospects. If large numbers of people are leaving the country because they cannot obtain work, this also affects the distribution of well-being among the potential population.

Table 4.10: Employment and Unemployment Rates for Ireland, 1988-98

	Unemployment Rate, %	Long-term Unemployment Rate*, %	Employment Rate**, %
1988	16.3	10.4	43.0
1989	15.0	9.8	43.2
1990	12.9	8.3	44.8
1991	14.7	8.8	44.0
1992	15.1	8.5	43.7
1993	15.7	8.9	43.6
1994	14.7	9.0	44.5
1995	12.2	7.1	46.1
1996	11.9	6.9	47.2
1997	10.3	5.6	48.2
1998	7.8	3.9	51.7
1999	5.7	2.5	54.4

Source: CSO Labour Force Surveys 1988-97, Quarterly National Household Surveys, 1998-99.

* Persons unemployed for more than one year. **Excludes part-time workers recording themselves as under-employed.

Table 4.10 shows that the fall in the unemployment rate has been accompanied by an increase in the employment rate. Thus a greater proportion of the population now has access to paid employment. Another key factor to bear in mind here is the rate of long-term unemployment. Lack of access to earned income over a prolonged period can have a more significant impact on economic and social well-being than short-term unemployment. In the early 1990s, it was feared that long-term unemployment would be subject to a ratchet effect, whereby once the numbers of long-term unemployed had increased, they would not fall, since they are thought to face particular difficulties in finding employment. The data on long-term unemployment in Table 4.10 suggest that this has not been the case, as long-term unemployment has fallen significantly since 1994. There are some concerns, however, that these figures may reflect the impact of increases in the numbers of long-term unemployed taking up places on employment schemes such as Community Employment. Such schemes take people off the live register, but can have low success rates in terms of subsequent employment of participants, and may therefore simply recycle people into the short-term register.

Wage Dispersion. For a given proportion of the population in work, the distribution of earnings among the population will depend on the dispersion or distribution of wages among those in work. Throughout the advanced economies, wage dispersion has been the subject of considerable research in recent years, largely prompted by the observation that wage inequality has increased rapidly in a number of countries. The initial focus of attention was on the US, where a major increase in wage dispersion took place, but significant increases have also been observed in a number of other advanced economies.[13]

Table 4.11 below presents data from Nolan (2000) on the dispersion of earnings in Ireland in 1987, 1994 and 1997, while Table 4.12 situates this data within the context of earnings dispersion in other OECD countries. What we observe for Ireland in the period 1987 to 1994 is a considerable widening in earnings differentials. This is most noticeable at the top end of the earnings distribution, where the hourly earnings of those at the 90th percentile increased from 196 per cent of median earnings to 224 per cent, between 1997 and 1994, and increased further to 232 per cent by 1997. Movement at the bottom end of the distribution is less striking, but not insignificant. Those at the bottom quartile,[14] for example, saw their hourly wages fall from 73 per cent of the median to 68 per cent between 1987 and 1994, before increasing slightly to 69 per cent in 1997.

---

[13] See, for example, Gottschalk and Smeeding (1997).

[14] Quartiles divide the population, in this case ranked by earnings, into groups of 25 per cent.

Table 4.11: Earnings Dispersion in Ireland, 1987, 1994 and 1997

	1987	1994	1997
	As a Proportion of the Median		
All Employees, Hourly Earnings			
Bottom decile	0.47	0.47	0.48
Bottom quartile	0.73	0.68	0.69
Top quartile	1.37	1.50	1.53
Top decile	1.96	2.24	2.32
Full-time Employees, Weekly Earnings			
Bottom decile	0.50	0.48	0.51
Bottom quartile	0.75	0.72	0.71
Top quartile	1.35	1.43	1.42
Top decile	1.82	1.97	2.02

Source: Nolan (2000)

In fact, the level of wage dispersion in Ireland in 1987 was already high by OECD standards, as shown in Table 4.12. Despite having the second highest level of wage dispersion among the countries shown in 1987, however, Ireland experienced the greatest increase in wage dispersion over that period. Another striking feature of the data is the extent to which this increase in dispersion took place at the top of the distribution of earnings. Apart from Portugal, no other country experienced such an increase in the 90/50 ratio.[15] Looking at other countries where total dispersion increased, such as Austria, France, Italy, The Netherlands and Sweden, the increase was somewhat concentrated in the 50/10 part of the distribution, while in Portugal, Australia, New Zealand and the UK increases in dispersion were concentrated in the 90/50 ratio.

---

[15] The 90/50 ratio is the ratio of the earnings of a person at the 90th percentile to the earnings of someone at the 50th percentile (the median). Similarly, the 50/10 ratio expresses the median wage as a proportion of the wages of someone at the 10th percentile, while the 90/10 ratio relates earnings at the 90th percentile to earnings at the 10th percentile.

Table 4.12.: Earnings dispersion in selected OECD countries c.1987 and 1994

	90/50		50/10		90/10		Change, 1987–94		
Country*	*1987*	*1994*	*1987*	*1994*	*1987*	*1994*	*90/50*	*50/10*	*90/10*
Ireland	1.82	1.97	2.00	2.08	3.64	4.10	0.15	0.08	0.46
Australia	1.68	1.75	1.67	1.64	2.81	2.87	0.07	-0.03	0.06
Austria	1.80	1.82	1.93	2.01	3.47	3.66	0.02	0.08	0.19
Canada	1.86	1.84	2.39	2.28	4.45	4.20	-0.02	-0.11	-0.25
Finland	1.70	1.70	1.48	1.40	2.52	2.38	0.00	-0.08	-0.14
France	1.97	1.99	1.62	1.65	3.19	3.28	0.02	0.03	0.09
Germany	1.64	1.61	1.55	1.44	2.54	2.32	-0.03	-0.11	-0.22
Italy	1.60	1.60	1.51	1.75	2.42	2.80	0.00	0.24	0.38
Japan	1.84	1.85	1.71	1.63	3.15	3.02	0.01	-0.08	-0.13
Netherlands	1.64	1.66	1.54	1.56	2.53	2.59	0.02	0.02	0.06
New Zealand	1.67	1.76	1.70	1.73	2.84	3.04	0.09	0.03	0.20
Portugal	2.14	2.47	1.69	1.64	3.62	4.05	0.33	-0.05	0.43
Sweden	1.57	1.59	1.32	1.34	2.07	2.13	0.02	0.02	0.06
UK	1.81	1.86	1.77	1.78	3.20	3.31	0.05	0.01	0.11

Source: OECD *Employment Outlook,* 1996, Table 3.1.

*Data for Austria, Germany, Italy and Sweden refers to the period 1987-93. Data for Canada and New Zealand refers to 1986-94. Data for Portugal refers to 1985-93. Data for Ireland from Tables 4.6 and 4.7 above.

How are we to explain this trend in wage dispersion? In particular, how can we reconcile this increasing wage inequality with the practice of centralised wage bargaining after 1987? Various cross-country studies have shown that centralised wage bargaining tends to be associated with lower levels of wage dispersion.[16] Moreover, the post-1987 social partnership agreements have included wage agreements which were intended to be biased in favour of the low paid. How then can it be that wage dispersion has increased so significantly?

O'Donnell (1998) examines the change in earnings dispersion between 1987 and 1994 from the supply-demand-institutional (SDI) perspective. This approach has been widely used in the in-

---

[16] See, for example, Rowthorn (1992).

ternational literature to explain trends in earnings distribution and focuses on the supply of and demand for various sub-groups within the labour force, as well as institutional change.[17] Hence, for example, attention has been focused on the numbers of workers with various levels of skill, and attempts made to relate changes in relative wages to shifts in supply and demand for such groups. O'Donnell argues that supply and institutional factors (i.e. the centralisation of wage bargaining) would lead one to expect a decrease rather than an increase in earnings inequality between 1987 and 1994. This period saw considerable structural change among the Irish labour force, particularly with respect to its skill profile, with the effects of changes in education policy from the 1960s onwards becoming increasingly evident. The level of qualifications among workers coming into the labour market was considerably higher than that of older workers retiring. Between 1987 and 1994, for example, the proportion of employees with post-secondary qualifications increased from 18 per cent to 28 per cent (Barrett et al., 1999). Hence, there was a strong increase in the supply of skilled workers. Despite this trend, returns to education (i.e. the additional wages received by workers with various educational qualifications relative to similar workers without lesser qualifications) increased between 1987 and 1994, reflecting changing patterns of labour demand. Barrett et al. find that, in addition to changes in wage dispersion caused by changes in the distribution of positions (as defined in terms of qualifications and experience) there was also a significant price effect which accounted for between 40 per cent and 60 per cent of the increase at the top end of the distribution (90/50). Thus, higher wage dispersion was driven both by increasing skill intensity and higher prices being paid for those skills. O'Donnell shows that much of the change which took place was within-industry.[18] She argues that increasing within-industry dispersion suggests that technological change was the primary underlying force, rather than, for example, shifting patterns of trade. Technological change, demanding greater numbers of skilled work-

---

[17] See, for example, Levy and Murnane, (1992).

[18] Indeed, inter-industry wage dispersion actually declined after 1987 (O'Reardon, 1999).

ers, therefore, would have driven up returns to education and skill and hence wage inequality. Employment in the foreign-owned sector was an important element in driving this technological change.

If this was the case, why was centralised wage bargaining unable to restrain the increase in wage dispersion? After all, these agreements were intended to favour the low-paid, and should, therefore, have limited the rise in inequality. A number of possible explanations present themselves. The first relates to the coverage of centralised bargaining. The available evidence suggests that the PNR and its successor the Programme for Economic and Social Progress (PESP) were widely implemented. One survey of 173 firms conducted in 1988, for example, showed that 94 per cent had concluded pay arrangements which complied with the terms of the PNR, and the remaining 6 per cent had concluded agreements which were not greatly in excess of the provisions of the PNR. A subsequent and considerably larger survey showed that the coverage of the PESP was also similarly broad.[19] Hardiman (1992) also notes evidence of widespread adherence to the terms of the centralised agreements. Barrett et al. (1999) note, however, that adherence to the centralised bargains may have diminished over time, citing evidence from a survey of industrial relations practices conducted in 1996. In this latter survey, some 44 per cent of firms stated that pay increases had exceeded the terms of the national agreements, and this proportion was considerably higher in non-unionised firms. This data suggests that as the Irish labour market has tightened and labour shortages have emerged, the rate of pay for highly skilled staff has tended to exceed the terms of national agreements. Whether this would have had a major impact before 1994, however, is open to question.

Another possible explanation is that the high-tech sectors are dominated by foreign-owned firms who have increasingly shown a tendency to adopt non-union wage policies which are independent of the national wage bargaining system. Hardiman (1992), for example, notes that firms in sectors such as pharmaceuticals, chemicals and electronics, which are dominated by foreign-owned companies, agreed to pay increases in excess of the

---

[19] Cited in Sexton and O'Connell (1996).

PNR terms. If this were true, however, one might also expect wages in the high-tech sector to have increased more rapidly than in other areas and we have noted that inter-industry wage dispersion fell after 1987. Given that wage dispersion has increased within all industries, wage setting in foreign-owned firms is likely to be only part of the story.

On the other hand, it is striking that the change in dispersion was so heavily concentrated at the top end of the distribution; unusually so by OECD standards. It may be that those at higher wage levels were more likely to fall outside of the collective bargaining context and could secure higher pay increases than were provided for in the PNR. In 1992, for example, some 40 per cent of managerial staff and 32 per cent of professional staff had their wages determined individually, rather than through collective bargains, compared to only 17 per cent of clerical staff and 8 per cent of manual employees. By contrast, 71 per cent of manual workers had their pay set by national arrangements.[20] Thus, if higher paid staff can have their wages determined on an individual basis, they may obtain wage increases in excess of the norms established by centralised wage bargains.

Even more striking, however, is the pace of change in the Irish economy and labour market. During the period 1987 to 1994, the numbers employed increased by 7.7 per cent, while from 1994 to 1997 employment grew by a further 11.6 per cent, and the types of employment available changed significantly. In contrast the pay terms of the centralised bargains were defined in terms of a static labour force, i.e. they set out how the wages of persons holding specific positions in the labour market should increase over a specified period. Many of the jobs which people held in 1997, however, and indeed many of the firms in which they worked, did not exist in 1987. The creation of new jobs, often in new firms, may have provided the opportunity for the wages of the skilled to be pushed up, while the centralised agreements only referred to how wages should evolve in existing employments.

What are the implications of this trend towards greater wage inequality? To date, there has been a limited connection between low pay and relative poverty in Ireland (Nolan, 1993; Hughes and

---

[20] Taylor (1996).

Nolan, 1997). This could be explained by the fact that many of the low paid were not the only or the main income earners in their household and also because of the large number of households where no one was employed. This is not to suggest, however, that wage dispersion does not translate into greater inequality in general, although this will be mitigated to some degree by a progressive tax system. If the trend towards greater wage inequality continues, and the level of unemployment remains low, however, we may come to see more working poor. This situation could arise as the take home pay of those towards the bottom of the earnings distribution falls below relative income poverty lines pushed up by higher wage increases for others. With fewer unemployed, families which include persons in the workforce could come to make up a greater proportion of households in poverty. Such a trend is already evident in the 1997 ESRI survey data, as discussed below, albeit from a small base. At a more general level, greater wage dispersion may produce or increase a sense of alienation or exploitation among those who work and receive relatively low wages in return. Rising wage dispersion may also diminish the social solidarity which is necessary to maintain social partnership arrangements. The recently introduced national minimum wage has the potential to limit wage inequality at the lower end, although its effectiveness in practice remains to be seen.

4.4.3 Government Redistribution of Incomes

The discussion so far has focused on the distribution of market incomes, both primary and secondary. Clearly, however, the state has a major influence on the final distribution of incomes through both the tax and social welfare systems. Since both tax and social welfare will be considered in some depth in subsequent chapters, the discussion here will be limited, and will concentrate on broad trends. We will focus on two distinct periods: 1987 to 1994 and 1994 to the present, both because of data availability and because of the rapid pace of economic change after 1994.

From 1987-94

The availability of survey data for 1987 and 1994 means that the implications of changes in the tax and social welfare system over this period for income distribution have been examined in some detail (see Callan and Nolan, 1999b). The first part of this period, from 1987 to 1990, saw a rapid fiscal stabilisation, coupled with a strong employment and growth performance (and significant net emigration). From 1990 to 1993, however, the performance of the economy dipped, and the level of unemployment increased as net emigration fell off considerably. Having achieved fiscal stability by 1990, fiscal policy in this sub-period was to maintain a deficit of some 2.5 per cent of GDP.

How did these trends translate in terms of the tax and social welfare systems? During the period of fiscal stabilisation the general rate of increase in social welfare payments was in line with price inflation. In addition, following the recommendations of the Commission on Social Welfare in 1986, there was a policy of increasing the lowest allowances, particularly those paid to the long-term unemployed. In terms of taxation, the PNR included agreement that a process of tax reform and reduction would at least begin. After 1990, a lower rate of growth and higher unemployment put pressure on the public finances, and a number of restrictions were imposed in the social welfare area, as well as a special 1 per cent levy on incomes. These measures had been rescinded, however, by 1994. Looking at the period 1987-94 as a whole, Callan et al. (1999) note that, while the lowest welfare payments were uprated significantly, other payments including pensions, were not treated as generously. Meanwhile, although there were reforms to the tax system such as increases in the exemption limits which favoured the low paid, reductions in tax rates were biased in favour of the better-off. Using a microsimulation model they show that relative to a baseline situation where all parameters of the tax and social welfare system are uprated in line with wage growth, the positions of the bottom two deciles improved as a result of tax and social welfare changes, as did that of the top four deciles. The third, fourth, fifth and sixth deciles lost out. Looking at taxation on its own, Callan and Nolan (1999) show that the Suits Progressivity Index which measures the progressivity of the tax system was broadly stable between 1987 and 1994, with only a slight improvement.[21]

---

[21] Nor were there major changes in the allocation of total tax revenues across different tax bases during this period. Between 1987 and 1994, there was a de-

From 1994-99

After 1994, the rapid pace of growth in the economy and particularly employment growth have produced considerable revenue buoyancy and allowed for significant tax cuts, while at the same time a public sector surplus has emerged. A key distributional issue during this period has been the fact that social welfare payments have kept pace with prices but not with earnings. In terms of taxation, further cuts in rates have been made, the standard rate band has been widened and personal allowances have been increased. Callan et al (1999) show that the combined effect of changes in the tax and social welfare system between 1994 and 1998 was to significantly improve the position of the higher deciles, while worsening that of the lower deciles,[22] relative to a baseline of simply upgrading the system's parameters in line with earnings.[23]

In the 1999/2000 fiscal year, a major change in the structure of the tax system was introduced with the standard rating of personal allowances. This promises a shift towards a system of tax credits, which would make it easier to target tax reductions at those on low incomes. Meanwhile, key issues for the reform of personal taxation continue to include the need for further reduction in the burden of taxation on the low paid and the need to increase the level of income at which the higher marginal rate takes effect.

More broadly, however, there are limits to how much longer the process of tax reductions can viably continue if economic and social objectives are to be met. If we examine taxation in the 15 EU countries, we see that total tax revenue as a percentage of GDP increased from 40.7 per cent in 1987 to 41.5 per cent in 1997. In contrast, over the same period, the ratio of tax revenue to GDP in Ireland fell from 37.4 per cent to 32.8 per cent. Hence, while greater prosperity has allowed for lower taxation, which has in

---

cline in the proportion of taxes made up from personal income tax and an increase in the share of corporation tax in the total. There was also a slight decline in the share of indirect taxes, due to a fall in the share of specific indirect taxes such as excise duties. This is contrary to the UK experience of the 1980s, for example, where indirect taxes, which are generally regressive, were increased.

[22] It is important to note that the 1998 Budget included a special increase in pensions.

[23] Again, there were only minor changes in the balance of taxes.

part helped to underpin wage moderation, there are limits to how far this process can go. It should come as little surprise that the advanced economies with lower levels of income inequality also have above average tax/GDP ratios. The reduction in the Irish tax burden will, in the long run, limit the pool of resources available to the state for expenditures which can reduce inequality.

4.5 GROUPS

The primary focus of the discussion has been on the distribution of incomes across households in general. Hence, little attempt has been made to distinguish between different types of households and the positions which they may hold in the distribution of incomes. Moreover, while the discussion has been couched in terms of equivalent incomes, which adjusts income for needs in terms of the number of people in a household, little attention has been paid to the needs which different types of people have with respect to income.

The ESRI's work on poverty measurement has included analyses of the profile of households falling below various poverty lines.[24] This work has shown significant change in the composition of the poor over time. During the 1980s, as unemployment increased, households headed by an unemployed person, and hence households containing children, came to constitute a greater proportion of the poor. At the same time, as the real value of pensions increased, the proportion of poor households headed by elderly people fell. In more recent times, this change has begun to be reversed. The fall in unemployment after 1994 has meant that, while households headed by unemployed persons still face the highest risk of poverty, they have come to make up a smaller proportion of the poor. So too have households containing children. On the other hand, households without children, particularly those headed by an elderly person, saw their risk of poverty increase as social welfare pensions were under-indexed relative to wages.

In addition, our concentration on incomes tends to assume that households are similar with respect to the relationship between their

---

[24] See, for example, Callan, Nolan and Whelan (1994), Callan et al. (1999).

income and their well-being. Sen (1973), in his seminal work on economic inequality, argues that people differ in their capacity to translate income into well-being. He gives the example of a person with a disability who requires a higher income than most persons in order to achieve a particular standard of living or well-being. Sen's discussion reminds us that some households and individuals in our society require a greater level of resources than others in order to achieve reasonable standards of well-being. The homeless person, the person with a disability, the carer and the addict are all ready examples of those for whom it is easy to see how the relationship between income and well-being is not the same as for the average household. Another way to put this is that the resources required to enjoy certain social rights may vary across individuals and households. Of course, many of these differences are picked up by deprivation indicators, but such indicators may not fully capture the extent to which inadequate income can exclude individuals from full participation in society, or from fully realising their own potential.

Moreover, rapid economic growth in Ireland has given rise to changes in traditionally understood relationships between income and economic well-being. In particular, the rapid rise in house prices has, for the time being at least, provided existing houseowners with windfall gains, while others seeking to enter the housing market have found that their previous expectations concerning the affordability of housing are no longer valid. Similarly, rising accommodation costs would appear to have significantly increased the risk of homelessness for many. Meanwhile, other shifts in prices, such as that of childcare, have imposed significant new economic pressures in an uneven way, while congestion effects such as transport problems have had a negative impact on the quality of life of many.

4.6 IMPLICATIONS

What are the implications of our analysis for policy formulation? In considering this question, let us begin by bringing together the various strands of the discussion to date. It was seen above how the Irish economy has been transformed since 1987, when a new system of political economy emerged, and particularly since 1994, when income and employment growth accelerated rapidly. Unemployment has fallen and the employment rate has increased rapidly, as has the capital income share. Between 1987 and 1994, these factors, as well as changes in the tax and social welfare systems, seem to have cancelled each other out, as the Gini coefficient remained stable, although some headcount measures of poverty increased. During this period, however, the indexation of social welfare payments in line with prices and the special increases afforded to claimants receiving the lowest allowances limited the extent to which low income households fell behind. Since 1994, wage increases have accelerated somewhat as employment growth has continued and we have seen how the incomes of those at the lower end of the distribution of income have not increased at the same rate as the population as a whole. Between 1994 and 1997 the Gini increased considerably.

Our discussion also showed that Ireland has for many years been one of the most unequal countries in Europe. In earlier decades, it might have been argued that this was related to our status as a peripheral economy, with low income per capita by European standards. The success of recent times means that Ireland is rapidly shedding its status as an underdeveloped region of the EU. As the economy develops, Irish society faces choices as to how these new resources will be distributed. As was seen above, there is wide variation among the advanced economies in the level of inequality of income, with some countries having significantly greater levels of inequality than others. This is not merely a matter of chance, but is related to a variety of factors, not the least of which is the model of political economy which prevails in each country. In other words, the way in which countries organise their political and economic affairs has a significant bearing on the distribution of incomes. Social partnership is the dominant theme within the Irish model of political economy which has accompanied recent growth. While this system of political economy was successful in rescuing the economy from crisis without a significant increase in inequality, recent data have shown a tendency for relative income poverty and inequality to increase, presenting a serious challenge to the social partnership model. While we can now reasonably aspire to the same income per capita as other richer member states, we can and should also aspire to a more equal society, with significantly lower levels of poverty. The Irish model needs to find a way to respond to this need.

Moreover, these issues give rise to tensions within the model itself. As was discussed above, for example, the share of taxation in GDP has fallen since 1987 and to some degree tax reductions have been traded for wage moderation. While the public finances are currently in surplus, there are limits to the scope of continued tax cuts in the long run if social objectives are to be met. State redistributive measures must ultimately be financed through taxation. There are fundamental choices to be made by the social partners and by Irish society, therefore, about our willingness to address the problem of social inclusion and to bear the costs of so doing.

In terms of developing policies for addressing these issues, changed circumstances in the labour market may lead to a rethinking of previous approaches. The improvement of labour market conditions in recent times has provided a means for many households to increase their incomes, and for some has provided a route out of poverty. The problem of large scale unemployment is now being replaced by other concerns such as the possibility of a greater number of working poor and a concern for those who remain long-term unemployed, or who may be moved between the short-term register and various schemes.

For those who have the potential to take part in the labour market, policy should be directed at increasing their capacity to find work and to earn. Reducing unemployment of itself is not enough unless those who find jobs have the skills and capacities to command a wage which brings them above the poverty line. This may well require ongoing investment in human capital as skill requirements change. This in turn requires a series of active labour market policies which are focused on the acquisition of marketable skills and which are flexible in the face of changing requirements. Given the current level of labour market shortage in the Irish economy (Williams and Hughes, 1999), this approach serves the needs of both equity and efficiency.

On the other hand, there are several groups for whom changing labour market conditions are almost irrelevant, such as the elderly. For those who cannot support themselves in the labour market, there is no alternative to increasing the level of state support in order to reduce poverty and inequality. This is not to suggest that there is no room for discussion as to how such support is delivered. In some cases it will involve higher direct payments, while in others the direct provisions of state services will be more effective. Other more complex considerations also arise. In the case of pensions, for example, the prospect of an ageing population may turn the minds of policymakers towards mandatory savings measures, or towards pension schemes which include elements of both personal and state contributions. The same point is also true of active labour market policies — there is always room for debate about how the state can best achieve its objectives. Indeed, in an era when resources are finally becoming available to address some longstanding problems in Irish society, it is important to constantly reassess the delivery mechanisms and policy instruments by which public expenditure is intended to achieve its objectives.

Within both groups we can see that some persons will require more assistance than others to fully realise their potential. Those who have been out of the labour force for many years or those who have poor levels of educational attainment may require significant resources to be invested in them if they are to develop their labour market capacities. Among those who cannot work, there will also be varying needs to be met in varying ways. As unemployment recedes, the need for state action to address issues of poverty and income distribution is no less acute.

Finally, we conclude by noting some of the areas where more research may be warranted. Our general level of knowledge on income distribution issues has been advanced beyond measure by the work of the ESRI over the past twelve or more years, but it is interesting to consider likely future directions for research in this area. We have noted above the need for more information on secondary market incomes, and how this is likely to become a more pressing issue over time. We have also noted the need to delve further into the data on those on higher incomes, if only to have a properly informed debate about how income is distributed in Ireland and how the burden of taxation is distributed. The increasing dispersion of earnings and the prospect of a larger group of working poor suggests that on-going analysis of the structure of wages ought to be afforded a high priority. This will include careful study of the impact in practice of the national minimum wage.

References

Atkinson, Anthony B. (1995), "Income Distribution In Europe and The United States", Nuffield College Oxford, Discussion Papers in Economics No. 103. September

Atkinson, Anthony B. (1996a), "Seeking to Explain the Distribution of Income" in Hills, J. ed. *New Inequalities*, Cambridge, Cambridge University Press

Atkinson, Anthony B. (1996b), "Bringing Income Distribution in from the Cold" Nuffield College Oxford, Discussion Papers in Economics No. 117, July 1996

Atkinson, Anthony B. et al. (1997), "Measurement of Trends in Poverty and the Income Distribution" DAE Working Paper No. MU9701, Amalgamated Series No. 9712, Cambridge University

Atkinson, Anthony B., Lee Rainwater and Tim Smeeding (1995*)*, *Income Distribution in OECD Countries*, Social Policy Studies No. 18, Paris, OECD

Barrett, Alan, Tim Callan and Brian Nolan (1999), "Rising Wage Inequality, Returns to Education and Labour Market Institutions: Evidence from Ireland", *British Journal of Industrial Relations*, Vol. 37, No. 1, March, pp. 77-100

Burniaux, J. M., T.T. Dang, D. Fore, M. Forster, M.M. d'Ercole,, and H. Oxley (1998), "Income Distribution and Poverty in Selected OECD Countries", OECD Economics Department Working Papers No. 189, Paris, OECD

Callan, Tim (1991), *Income Tax and Welfare Reform: Microsimulation Modelling and Analysis, General Research Series*, Paper No. 154, Dublin, ESRI

Callan, Tim, Richard Layte, Brian Nolan, Dorothy Watson, Christopher T. Whelan, James Williams, and Bertrand Maître (1999), *Monitoring Poverty Trends*, Dublin, Stationery Office and Combat Poverty Agency

Callan, Tim and Brian Nolan (1992), "Distributional Aspects of Ireland's Fiscal Adjustment", *Economic and Social Review*, pp. 319-342

Callan, Tim and Brian Nolan (1993), "Income Inequality and Poverty in Ireland in the 1970s and 1980s", ESRI Working Paper No. 43, Dublin, ESRI

Callan, Tim and Brian Nolan eds. (1994), *Poverty and Policy in Ireland*, Dublin, Gill and Macmillan

Callan, Tim and Brian Nolan (1999), "Income Inequality in Ireland in the 1980s and 1990s" in Barry Frank ed., *Understanding Ireland's Economic Growth*, Basingstoke, Macmillan

Callan, Tim and Brian Nolan (1998b), *Tax and Welfare Changes, Poverty and Work Incentives In Ireland, 1987-1994*, Policy Research Series No. 34, Dublin, ESRI

Callan, Tim, Brian Nolan, J. Walsh, and Richard Nestor (1999), "Income Tax and Social Welfare Policies" in Kearney, C. ed., *Budget Perspectives*, Dublin, ESRI

Callan, Tim, Brian Nolan, and Christopher T. Whelan, (1994), "Who Are the Poor?" in Callan and Nolan (eds.) *Poverty and Policy In Ireland*, Dublin, Gill and Macmillian

Callan, Tim, Brian Nolan, Brendan J Whelan, and Damian F. Hannan., with S. Creighton (1989*), Poverty, Income and Welfare in Ireland*, ESRI General Research Series, Paper No. 146, Dublin, ESRI

Callan, Tim, Brian Nolan, Brendan J Whelan, Christopher T. Whelan and James Williams (1996), *Poverty in the 1990s: Evidence from the 1994 Living in Ireland Survey*, Dublin, Oak Tree Press

Duffy, David, John FitzGerald, Ide Kearney and Diarmaid Smyth (1999), *Medium Term Review, 1999-2005*, Dublin, ESRI

Fortin, N. and T. Lemieux (1997), "Institutional Change and Rising Wage Inequality: Is There a Linkage?" *Journal of Economic Perspectives*, Vol. 11., No. 2, Spring, pp.75-96

Gottschalk, P. and T.M. Smeeding (1997), "Cross-national Comparisons of Earnings and Income Inequality" *Journal of Economic Literature*, Vol. XXXV, June, pp. 633-87

Gottschalk, P. and T.M. Smeeding (1998), "Empirical Evidence on Income Inequality in Industrialised Countries" Luxembourg, Income Study Working Papers, No. 154

Hardiman, Niamh (1992), "The State and Economic Interests: Ireland in Comparative Perspective" in J. H. Goldthorpe and C. T. Whelan eds., *The Development of Industrial Society in Ireland*, Oxford, Oxford University Press

Hughes, Gerry and Brian Nolan (1999), *Competitive and Segmented Labour Markets and Exclusion from Retirement Income*, ESRI Working Paper, No. 108, Dublin, ESRI

Hughes, Gerry and Brian Nolan (1997), "Low Pay, the Earnings Distribution and Poverty in Ireland, 1987-94", ESRI Working Paper no. 84, Dublin, ESRI

Lane, Philip (1998), "Profits and Wages in Ireland, 1987-1996", Trinity Economic Papers, Technical Paper No. 14, May

Levy, F. and R. Murnane (1992), "US Earnings Levels and Earnings Inequality: A Review of Recent Trends and Proposed Explanations", *Journal of Economic Literature*, vol. XXX, September

Nolan, Brian (1993), *Low Pay in Ireland*, General Research Paper No. 159, Dublin, ESRI

Nolan, Brian (2000), "The Distribution of Earnings" in Nolan et al. (eds), *The Distribution of Income in Ireland*, Dublin: ESRI/Combat Poverty Agency

Nolan, Brian, Tim Callan, Christopher T. Whelan and James Williams (1994), *Poverty and Time: Perspectives on the Dynamics of Poverty*, General Research Series No. 166, Dublin, ESRI

Nolan, Brian, Tim Callan, Bertrand Maître, Donal O'Neill and Olive Sweetman, (2000), *The Distribution of Income in Ireland*, Dublin, ESRI/Combat Poverty Agency

Nolan, Brian and Patrick Honohan (1993), *The Financial Assets of Households in Ireland, General Research Paper* No. 162, Dublin: ESRI

Nolan, Brian and Gerard Hughes (1997), "Low Pay, the Earnings Distribution and Poverty in Ireland, 1987-1994", paper presented to LOWER Conference, Bordeaux

Nolan, B. and Bertrand Maître, (1999), *The Distribution of Income and Relative Income Poverty in the European Community Household Panel*, Working Paper no 107, Dublin, ESRI

Nolan, Brian, Bertrand Maître and Tim Callan (2000), "Ireland's Income Distribution in Comparative Perspective" in Nolan et al., *The Distribution of Income in Ireland*, Dublin, ESRI/Combat Poverty Agency

Nolan, Brian, Christopher T. Whelan and James Williams (1998), *Where are Poor Households?: The Spatial Distribution of Poverty and Deprivation in Ireland*, Dublin, Combat Poverty Agency

OECD (1996), *Employment Outlook,* Paris, OECD

OECD *Economic Outlook*, various issues, Paris, OECD

OECD *Revenue Statistics*, various issues, Paris, OECD

OECD *Historical Statistics*, various issues, Paris, OECD

O'Connell, Philip J. (1997), "The Irish Labour Market", working paper, No. 81, Dublin, ESRI

O'Connell, Philip J and J.J. Sexton, (1994), "Labour Market Developments in Ireland", in Cantillon et al. eds, *Economic Perspectives for the Medium Term*, Dublin, ESRI

O'Donnell, Nuala (1998), "Why Did Earnings Inequality Increase in Ireland: 1987-1994?", EUI Working Paper, ECO 98/17, Florence, European University Institute

O'Donnell, Rory and Colm O'Reardon (1996), "The Irish Experiment", *New Economy*, March

O'Donnell, Rory and Colm O'Reardon (1997), "Ireland's Experiment in Social Partnership, 1987-96", in Fajertag, G. and P. Pochet eds, *Social Pacts in Europe*, Brussels ETUI/OSE

O'Donnell, Rory and Colm O'Reardon (2000), "Social Partnership in Ireland's Economic Transformation" in Fajertag, G. and P. Pochet (eds), *Social Pacts in Europe*, 2nd edition, Brussels, ETUI/OSE

O'Reardon, Colm (1999), *The Political Economy of Inequality: Ireland in a Comparative Perspsective*, D.Phil. Thesis, University of Oxford

Pensions Board (1998), *Securing Retirement Income: National Pensions Policy Initiative*, Dublin

Rowthorn, Robert (1992), "Corporatism and Labour Market Performance" in Pekkeranin et al. eds, *Social Corporatism: A Superior Economic System,* Oxford, Clarendon, pp. 82-131

Sen, Amartya K. (1973), *On Economic Inequality*, Oxford, Clarendon

Sexton, J. J. and Philip J. O'Connell, eds. (1996), *Labour Market Studies: Ireland*, Luxembourg, EU Commission.

Shorrocks, Anthony F. (1983) "The Impact of Income Components on the Distribution of Family Incomes" *Quarterly Journal of Economics*, May, pp. 311-26

Shorrocks, Anthony F. (1987) "Inequality between Persons" in Eatwell et al. eds, *The New Palgrave: A Dictionary of Economics*, London, Macmillan, pp. 821-24

Taylor, George, (1996), "Labour Market Rigidies, Institutional Impediments and Managerial Constraints: Some Reflections on the Recent Experience of Macropolitical Bargaining in Ireland", *Economic and Social Review*, No 27 (3), April, pp. 253-77

Williams, James and Gerard Hughes (1999) *National Survey of Vacancies in the Private Non-Agricultural Sector,* 1998, Dublin, ESRI

Chapter 5

Redistribution through Ireland's Welfare and Tax Systems

Eithne Fitzgerald

5.1 INTRODUCTION

This chapter examines the role of the welfare and tax systems in Ireland in redistributing incomes, looking particularly at the period of modern social partnership. Section 5.1 sets the context of addressing inequalities in market incomes. Section 5.2 on social welfare and Section 5.3 on the tax system outline how the mechanisms in these codes redistribute incomes. Section 5.4 examines the developments in the tax and welfare systems over the period of social partnership. Section 5.5 assesses the distributive impact of tax and welfare changes over this period and Section 5.6 draws some policy conclusions.

5.1.1 The Market Delivers Unequal Incomes

Without state intervention, we would experience a far more unequal command over resources in our society (see Chapter 2). People's incomes from the economy reflect whether or not they have paid work, their earning capacity, and their ownership of property or investments that yield an income. Earning power reflects not just differences in work effort, but also differences in education, skill, contacts, luck, and in asset ownership. Powerful social and economic forces, particularly social class, shape differences in market incomes. Business and property ownership concentrate wealth and income. Wealth and privilege are transmitted from one generation to the next. Education has replaced family property as the most important mechanism for transmitting earning power to the next generation (Breen et al.,1990: 53).

5.1.2 Redistribution

The welfare and tax systems turn unequal incomes from economic activity into a fairer distribution of income in people's pockets. Social welfare transfers and taxes on income convert these market incomes into disposable incomes.

The social welfare system redistributes income from those currently earning an income to those who are unemployed, caring full-time, ill or retired. Over the life cycle, social welfare transfers money from the earning years to the retirement years. The poorest 30 per cent of Irish households have virtually no income from economic activity. Welfare payments bring their share of pre-tax incomes up from under 1 per cent to about 8 per cent (Nolan et al., 2000, Table 3.12, 1998 figures). Compared to most OECD countries our welfare payments are more concentrated on this poorest group of households (Förster and Pellizzari, 2000, Table 3.1).

While in Ireland social welfare is the much more important means of redistributing income (Callan and Nolan, 1992: 189; Nolan et al., 2000: 16), the income tax system also redistributes by taking more from the rich than from those on lower incomes. Such a system is termed *progressive*, where it takes a higher share from those with higher incomes. A tax system is *neutral* if it takes the same percentage from all income groups, and *regressive* if it takes a higher share of income from the poorer. Our modestly progressive income tax system is largely counterbalanced by the regressive nature of taxes on spending (CSO, 1995: Table E).[1] The result is a broadly neutral overall pattern of redistribution over the tax system as a whole. Thus, it is the welfare system rather than the tax system that carries the primary role of redistributing income.

---

[1] This is the latest available detailed study of the distribution of indirect taxes. Similar results were shown in analyses of previous years.

The tax system including pay related social insurance (PRSI) funds redistribution of resources through social welfare and other public services like health, education and housing. The overall impact on redistribution depends on the combined impact of both funding and state transfers. A welfare system that gives proportionately to everyone but is funded by progressive taxes will have an overall progressive impact. A means tested system which concentrates only on the poorest but is funded through regressive tax measures could have a neutral or regressive overall effect (Reddin, 1978). Tightly targeted welfare systems tend to contribute little towards lowering inequality (Shaver, 1998; Korpi and Palme, 1998). In Ireland, where both welfare payments and non-cash benefits are positively skewed to the poor, funded by a broadly neutral tax system,[2] the system is progressive in overall terms.

The scale of intervention in market incomes matters. In international terms, Ireland's welfare payment (National Pensions Board, 1998: Table H1) and tax levels are both relatively low, so the level of redistribution effected through both systems is also low. A result is that Ireland's disposable incomes are among the most unequal in the developed world.[3] In 1999, the social welfare system redistributed almost IR£5 billion, about 8.5 per cent of gross national product (GNP). In 1999, the tax system collected about a third of GNP.[4]

5.1.3 Redistribution versus Wealth Generation

Chapter 2 looked at the policy tension between equity and efficiency, between redistribution and the generation of wealth. The tax and welfare systems do not simply redistribute market incomes, they also can influence how the market itself gener-

---

[2] Redistributive Effects of State Taxes and Benefits on Household Incomes in 1987, Table E..

[3] Atkinson, Rainwater and Smeeding, (1995): Table 4.4 for the 1980s; Förster and Pellizzari, (2000): Table 2.2 for the 1990s. These show our inequality of disposable incomes on a par with the UK; among OECD countries, just Italy, Greece, US, Mexico, and Turkey display more inequality.

[4] DSCFA, Statistical Information on the Social Welfare Services 1999; Department of Finance Accounts, 1999. In the period 90 per cent of tax revenue was spent, with a surplus retained.

ates and distributes income. For example, low taxation of profits may encourage economic growth and jobs, but at the same
time lead to concentration of asset ownership and a widening
inequality gap. Paying through high taxes on labour for a generous welfare system may mean fewer jobs.

The political right tends to favour low taxation and less interference with the income distribution thrown up by the market.[5] This viewpoint usually sees the answer to poverty as about
changing the behaviour of individuals rather than the characteristics of society. This is what Ruth Levitas (1998) has labelled
"marginalised underclass discourse". This views the welfare
system primarily as a financial burden which may undermine
individual effort (Murray, 1984). In much of US public debate,
"welfare" is no longer seen as meaning well-being, but as
something to be avoided or minimised.

The political left puts a greater emphasis on redistribution,
to help correct inequalities in market incomes and takes a positive view of the welfare state as providing basic social protection for citizens. The traditional left saw a main cause of poverty
as low income and redistributing income through generous
welfare benefits as an important answer. "Third Way" social
democracy (see Chapter 2) places an increasing emphasis on
active labour market measures within social protection rather
than on passive income support, perhaps at the expense of a
commitment to redistribution (Levitas, 1998).

That emphasis on welfare to work is embodied for example
in the European Employment Strategy (European Union,
1999b). The EU Communication on a Concerted Strategy for
Modernising of Social Protection (1999: 13) assigned a high priority in the design of social security measures to safeguarding
economic growth:

> Social protection and the welfare of the community depend
> on economic performance and a high participation in the
> labour market. Therefore, social protection *must never ham-*

---

[5] Minister for Finance Charlie McCreevy TD gave a robust defence of this
viewpoint, arguing that people were entitled to keep most of any additional
income they earned, and describing those holding an alternative viewpoint as
"left-wing pinkos" (*The Irish Times*, 7 April 2000).

> *per economic life* by setting up disincentives to work, edu-
> cation, training, mobility, the creation of jobs, or entrepre-
> neurship (author's italics).

Countries like Sweden with a long social democratic tradition
in government have been characterised by high welfare
spending, funded by high taxes. Redistributing large amounts
of income tends to a highly equalising system. The US is at the
other end of the spectrum, with a low tax, low benefit regime.
Ireland is closer to the US model. It is becoming more difficult
with an increasingly global economic system for any one
country to maintain independence in social policy. As countries compete more directly with each other on export markets, higher tax countries may find their goods and services
are less competitive, other things being equal. Increasing
globalisation is thus putting pressure on those countries that
have traditionally chosen the higher benefits, higher taxation
path (Mishra, 1999).

5.1.4 Redistribution as a Goal of the Irish Tax and Welfare Systems

A commitment to tackle poverty has become, with the publication of the National Anti-Poverty Strategy (NAPS, Government of
Ireland, 1997), a very explicit policy objective of government. It
is difficult to locate any corresponding official commitment of
successive governments towards a strategy for redistribution or
to discern any systematic approach to redistribution across the
tax and welfare systems as a whole. The most explicitly redistributive measure of recent decades — the wealth tax introduced in the 1970s — was not intended simply as such, but also
designed to replace lump sum taxation on death by annual
charges on property. Wealth tax was subsequently abolished
following intense vocal opposition.

The two Commissions that sat in the 1980s to review the tax
and social welfare systems set out quite different emphases on
redistribution.

Commission on Taxation

The Commission on Taxation's first report (1982: 83) set out three criteria for the tax system — equity, efficiency and simplicity. The Commission saw equity as meaning taxes levied in accordance with ability to pay, rather than any stronger notion of redistributive or social justice. Indeed, the Commission saw investment in education rather than the tax system as taking on the primary role of redressing income inequality:

> Education policy may be perhaps the most powerful weapon available to democratic government in seeking to introduce equality in the distribution of incomes (ibid.:103).

In other words, market incomes should be made more equal rather than strengthening redistribution via tax. The Commission recommended a single rate of income tax on all income. Progression would be achieved at lower incomes through the welfare system and tax credits and at higher incomes through a direct expenditure tax.

Commission on Social Welfare

Redistribution was one of the five key principles adopted by the Commission on Social Welfare. It saw the welfare system as having the key role in redistributing income, given that overall the tax system proved to be neutral. Therefore it envisaged an enhanced role for social welfare spending (Commission on Social Welfare, 1986: 154-64). The Commission saw its core principle of adequacy of payments as closely linked to redistribution — the higher the welfare payments, the more redistributive the overall system would be. It also emphasised that specific financing for welfare should be progressive.[6]

---

[6] The Commission proposed abolishing the income ceiling for social insurance contributions; op. cit.: 125.

5.2 THE SOCIAL WELFARE SYSTEM

In Irish society, the social welfare system is the most important vehicle for redistribution. This section looks at the nature of our system, at factors influencing payment levels, and how the system is funded.

Ireland's welfare system offers modest flat-rate payments with additions for dependent family members. This contrasts with the earnings-related payments and generous universal child benefits of Continental systems. In terms of Korpi and Palme's (1998) typology, Ireland's is a basic security model, unlike Continental corporatist models or the Scandinavian encompassing social security systems. The Irish system, set up in 1953, closely follows the UK model designed by William Beveridge in 1942 (Beveridge, 1942). Social insurance gives benefits as of right based on a record of social insurance contributions. Social assistance provides a largely parallel system of means tested payments. Universal child benefit is at modest rates. There are also some in work benefits for low earners. Slightly more recipients are on insurance based payments than on means tested payments (Dept of SCFA, 1999, Table A13).

Redistribution via the welfare system is affected by:

- Number of recipients, reflecting coverage, demographic change and unemployment;

- Generosity of payment rates;

- Degree to which payments are concentrated on the poorest families;

- How the system is funded.

Almost a quarter of the population currently receives a weekly welfare payment. Over the 1990s, the proportion on welfare has dropped as unemployment fell, in contrast to the 1980s which saw high redistribution via social welfare as unemployment soared. Thus, the share of welfare transfers in GNP peaked in the late 1980s.[7]

---

[7] Welfare spending peaked in 1986 at 14.8 per cent of GNP, compared to 8.5 per cent in 1999.

Our payments are fairly well targeted on poorer households (Callan et al., 1989, Tables 11.4, 11.5),[8] indeed a high
share of those on non-means tested payments are below the
poverty line (Callan et al., 1996: Table 4.5). Child benefits are
more evenly spread across all incomes. Although proponents
of selectivity argue that means tested payments offer better
targeting of the poor, in fact selective systems achieve less
redistribution because of the small scale of their interventions
in reassigning income (Korpi and Palme, 1998). Thus countries
with basic, targeted, welfare payments achieve less redistribution than countries with more generous and encompassing
welfare systems, although earnings-related systems distribute
their transfers farther up the income ladder. Ireland's welfare
system is among the most targeted (Förster and Pellizzari,
2000), but also among the least generous in the EU at the
spending level (Figure 5.1).

---

[8] In 1987, 58 per cent of contributory payments went to the poorest 30 per
cent of households (by pre-transfer income) compared with 70 per cent of
mean-tested payments. See also Callan et al., 1996: Table 4.4.

Figure 5.1: Social Security (Minus Health) Expenditure as %
of GDP, 1996 (EU states for which data available)

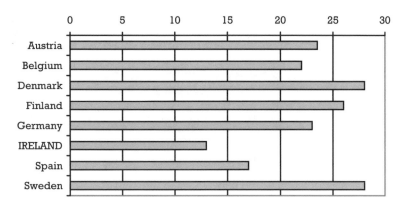

Source: ILO (1999)

5.2.1 Payment Rates

Traditionally, benefit rates reflected ad hoc decisions made from budget to budget. The Commission on Social Welfare recommended that personal weekly welfare rates be brought up to a target of IR£50-60 a week (in 1986 terms), which ultimately became official policy. The Commission was also highly critical of the disparity in social welfare incomes paid to people in apparently similar financial circumstances, and recommended a harmonisation of benefit rates. These recommendations influenced what happened to pension rates (symbolised here by the old age contributory pension) and short-term payments (symbolised here by unemployment assistance). Over the last 20 years of the twentieth century, the real value (measured in terms of consumer prices) of old age pensions grew by almost a half and of unemployment assistance by almost three-quarters (Figure 5.2). From 1982 to 1995, pension rates grew almost imperceptibly, and then began to rise again. Rates for the unemployed, being farther away from the adequacy target, were raised sharply in the immediate years after the Commission reported.

Figure 5.2: Real Value of Old Age (c.) Pensions and Unemployment Assistance Rates, 1980–2000 (at Feb. 2000 prices)

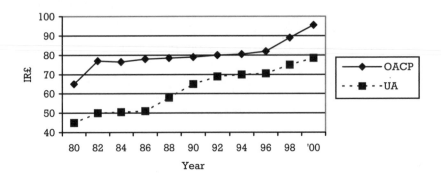

5.2.2 Tracking Incomes in Society

Even if welfare payments are improving in real terms, unless they keep pace with incomes generally in society, the relative position of those who remain on welfare will deteriorate. Figure 5.3 shows that while social welfare rates have risen faster than prices over the 1980s and 1990s, they are failing to keep up with disposable incomes generally. Old age pensions have been falling consistently since 1984 in relation to average incomes, forming a lower proportion at the turn of the century than they did 20 years earlier. Payment rates to the unemployed grew throughout the 1980s and began to drop from the early 1990s relative to average incomes as concerns about work incentives moved more into the foreground.

Since the poorest 30 per cent of the population depend mainly on the welfare system for their income, the level of welfare payments is a critical tool in tackling poverty. Ireland's official definition of poverty is explicitly relative — exclusion from ordinary living patterns and activities of society due to lack of resources (Government of Ireland, 1997).[9] Whenever welfare incomes fall behind income growth in society, poverty rises among the welfare population.

---

[9] This paraphrases the classic definition of relative poverty given by Peter Townsend (1979), also used by the Commission on Social Welfare (1986: 123).

Figure 5.3: Social Welfare Rates and Average Disposable Income per Head, 1980-2000

A. In Real (2000) Terms

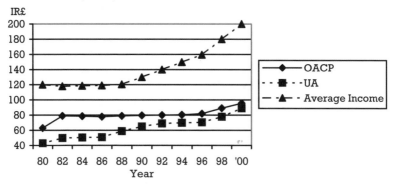

B. % of Average Income

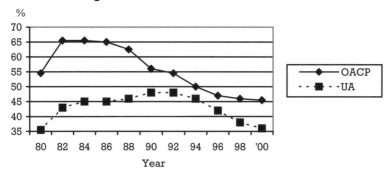

5.2.3 Concerns about Work Incentives

Several national and international studies have charted links between high replacement rates, generous welfare payments for the unemployed and higher unemployment.[10] Government policy looks to strike a balance between ensuring adequate incomes and a share in rising living standards to those who have no jobs, and trapping people in unemployment. This concern became more acute in the 1990s following the narrowing of the

---

[10] Replacement rates are the ratio between welfare income when out of work and take home income in a job. For a discussion of the economic evidence see Government of Ireland, (1996): Chapter 2 and Appendix 5.

gap between average disposable incomes and incomes out of work. The Tax Welfare Integration Group (Government of Ireland,1996: 26, par. 2.50), in acknowledging this challenge for policy, recommended that no further widening of the gap between income in employment and income out of work should take place.

Holding benefit rates down is only one of the possible policy options to maintain replacement rates. Other ways include tax and PRSI reductions targeted on the low paid; improved in-work benefits like family income supplement (FIS); increasing the earning capacity of the unemployed through training; or making child income support independent of the work status of the parents.

5.2.4 Funding the Welfare System — Social Insurance

Social assistance and universal payments (about 55 per cent of overall welfare spending[11]) are funded from general taxation. Social insurance expenditure is met mostly from PRSI contributions from employers and insured workers with employers paying over 70 per cent. Social welfare payments in Ireland have always been funded from current revenue. Up to now this pay-as-you-go financing means that each succeeding working generation funds the previous generation's pensions, through PRSI and tax.

Cross Subsidies within the System

Social solidarity is an underlying principle of social insurance. However, Ireland was slow to develop comprehensive coverage of the social insurance system,[12] and this narrowed the numbers to whom this obligation of solidarity applied. A significant minority of the working community, self-employed people (including farmers), only began paying social insurance

---

[11] The share of total social welfare spending funded by the state was 54.8 per cent in 1999, down slightly in the previous ten years from 57 per cent in 1989.

[12] Social insurance initially covered manual workers, and private sector non-manual workers under an income limit (abolished in 1974). Self-employed were brought into social insurance in 1988, part-time workers in the early 1990s and new public servants recruited after April 1995.

in 1988 with the corollary that a large section of this group have been getting non-contributory benefits funded from general taxation.[13]

Unlike private insurance, contributions and benefits are not actuarially based. Employers and insured workers contribute into a general pool from which benefits are paid. The system involves progressive contributions which rise with income (up to a ceiling — see below) and flat rate benefits, so that those on the lowest incomes can expect greater value for their contributions. The net impact is broadly progressive. The payment of family-based benefits from a wage-based system of contributions can redistribute from those without dependants to those with families.

Effective Incidence of Social Insurance Contributions

Social insurance contributions are formally levied on employers and insured persons, and collected as a deduction from payroll. The effective incidence may be different from the formal shares due, depending on how elastic is the supply of labour or the demand for labour in the job market. In an employers' market, where job opportunities are scarce and employers can pick or choose their workers, they may be able to shift back the PRSI to workers through lower wage offers. When the job market is very tight, the opposite result may happen, with employers effectively carrying the employee share of PRSI through increased wages.

High payroll taxes, which tax labour rather than capital, can mean lower levels of employment at any given level of output, encouraging employers to substitute relatively cheaper capital for relatively more expensive labour. The gap between what it costs an employer to hire a worker, and what that worker takes home is called the *tax wedge*. It includes both employer and worker shares of PRSI, and income tax deductions. The higher the tax wedge, the lower employment is likely to be. Various Irish studies have estimated that a growth in the tax wedge sub-

---

[13] This may partly explain the net transfers from urban to rural Ireland recorded in the CSO's redistribution analysis of the 1987 Household Budget Survey (CSO, 1987).

stantially contributed to the steep growth in unemployment in the 1980s.[14] Therefore, the burden of high payroll taxes can also fall on unemployed people who become priced out of a job.

The Income Ceiling

Pay-related contributions, which replaced the earlier flat rate system, are subject to an income ceiling.[15] There is a floor below which workers pay no PRSI, and tiered rates of PRSI for those on moderate earnings.[16] The result is a system which is highly complex, has anomalies[17] but is quite steeply progressive up to the earnings ceiling. Above that, it is regressive.[18] The Commission on Social Welfare recommended abolition of the earnings ceiling, a move which could fund some general lowering of PRSI rates. Ideal opportunities were missed to do that as part of an integrated package as top rates of tax were being steadily lowered over the 1990s.

Contribution or Tax?

The Commission on Taxation regarded social insurance contributions as principally a tax, and a poorly designed one. It rec-

---

[14] For example, Barry and Bradley (1991) estimated that the growth in the tax wedge accounted for up to 30 per cent of the fall in manufacturing employment in the first half of the 1980s. See Tansey (1998: 216) for a summary of findings on the link between growth in the tax wedge and unemployment.

[15] For the year 2000/1, this ceiling is set at IR£36,600 for employers and IR£26,500 for employees and the self-employed (euro 46,472 and euro 33,648). For 2001/2, the ceiling for employers has been abolished, and for employees raised to IR£28,250 (euro 35,870)

[16] Tiered rates for PRSI were introduced in the mid-1990s, partly to help improve disposable incomes of those below the tax threshold who would not be reached by conventional tax reductions. Reducing PRSI in the Government accounts results in a higher Exchequer share of spending on social welfare and is treated in accounting terms as a spending increase not as a tax reduction.

[17] For example, the 2 per cent health contribution (collected with PRSI) in 2000/1 was nil for someone earning IR£279 a week, and IR£5.62 for someone on IR£281 earning just IR£2 a week more.

[18] In 2000/1, a worker earning exactly the amount of the earnings ceiling would have paid an effective PRSI rate of 5.2 per cent of earnings, but a worker on double that income would pay only 3.8 per cent of income. A worker earning three times the ceiling would pay an effective PRSI rate of 3.2 per cent of income.

ommended their incorporation into the mainstream tax system, in the form of a flat rate social security tax on all forms of income. The Commission on Social Welfare took a different view, placing a high value on the sense of entitlement to benefit which followed from making earmarked contributions.

Ireland now raises a very low share of its total taxation via social insurance contributions in comparison to other EU states (Figure 5.4). This is because of a less generous welfare system and because in many EU states social insurance funds health services, largely funded here from general taxes.[19]

Figure 5.4: Social Security Contributions as % of Total Tax Revenue, 1997, EU

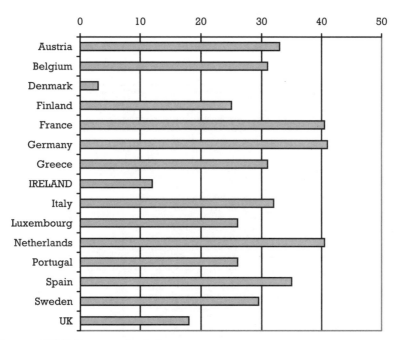

Source: OECD Revenue Statistics

5.3 THE IRISH TAX SYSTEM

This section looks at the structure of the Irish tax system and examines how different elements of that system operate to re-

---

[19] The 2 per cent health levy, collected as part of the PRSI contribution, brought in IR£452 million in 1999.

distribute income and wealth. Discussion is limited to taxes levied by central government, which account for about 98 per cent of the total.

In international terms, Ireland is not a heavily taxed country. In 1997, Ireland had the lowest taxes measured as a share of GDP[20] in the EU, and ranked 22nd out of 29 OECD countries (OECD, 1999: Table 1).[21] Taking taxes in dollars per head, Ireland was still at the low tax end of the spectrum, with just Greece, Spain and Portugal in the EU 15 below Ireland. Tax levels have been falling in Ireland since the late 1980s. However, even with taxes at their peak, Ireland was not particularly heavily taxed, coming in the lower half of the EU countries.

Figure 5.5: Tax Revenue, EU, 1997 (as % of GDP and in US $)

A. Tax as % of GDP

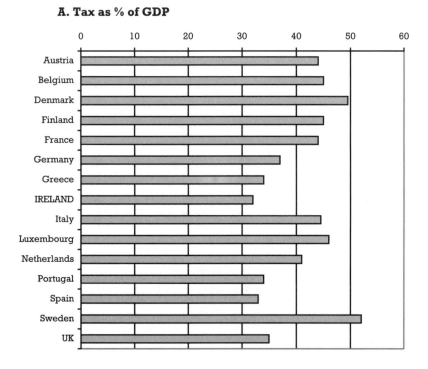

---

[20] Gross national product (GNP) provides a more accurate ranking of Ireland's income level, but comparisons with GDP are the ones readily available.
[21] Total tax here includes social security contributions.

B. Tax in $ per Head ($000s)

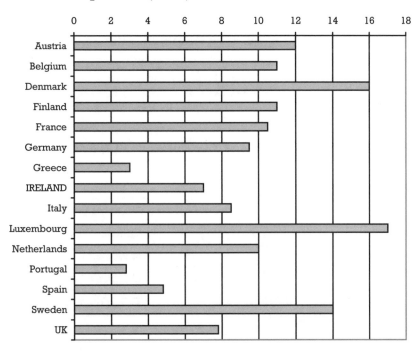

Source: OECD Revenue Statistics

5.3.1 Structure of Tax Revenue

Income tax is the main source of tax revenue in Ireland, followed closely by VAT (Figure 5.6). We have greater reliance on spending taxes, and lower reliance on income taxes, than in our EU partners (Figure 5.7). The long-term trends show significant changes in the structure of taxation over the last 30 years. The share of revenue from corporate income (including employers' PRSI) has increased, and the share from taxes on expenditure and capital taxes has reduced (Figure 5.8). Changes in the corporate tax code that widened the corporate tax base (following recommendations from the Commission on Taxation)[22] and a rapidly growing profit share have boosted revenue from company taxation in spite of falling rates of tax.

---

[22] Among the changes which widened the corporate tax base was the abolition of accelerated capital allowances and the curtailment of group relief.

The core of the Commission on Taxation's blueprint for tax reform — a single rate of tax to be levied on a comprehensive definition of income — has not been implemented. However, the Commission's emphasis on simplifying the income tax code may have influenced the subsequent reduction of the number of income tax rates to two. Apart from the business tax changes, its other proposals implemented were self-assessment and, from 1999, tax credits.

Figure 5.6: *Composition of Tax Revenue, 1999 (excluding PRSI)*

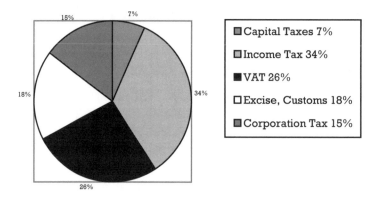

Source: Department of Finance

Figure 5.7: *Taxes on Income and Sales as % of Total Tax Revenue, EU*

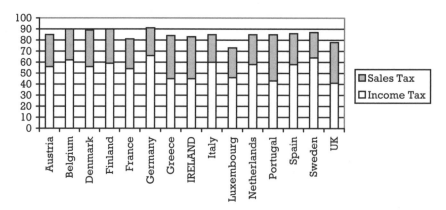

Source: OECD Revenue Statistics

Figure 5.8: Composition of Irish Tax Revenue, 1965–97

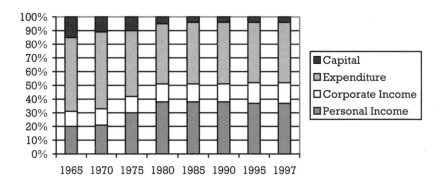

Note: Tax on personal income includes workers' PRSI. Tax on corporate income includes employers' PRSI.
Source: OECD

5.3.2 Progressive Income Tax is Modified by Tax Breaks on Expenditure

Income tax in Ireland, designed with higher rates of tax on higher incomes, is, according to Central Statistics Office (CSO) studies, consistently progressive (CSO, 1973, Table F; 1980: Table E; 1987: 16). People below a minimum income are exempt from tax. Tax credits, which replaced personal tax allowances in 1999/2000, provide a personal deduction which is worth the same to high or low rate taxpayers

People can offset particular expenditures against tax, a form of fiscal welfare (labelled *tax expenditures*) equivalent in value to state cash handouts. These tax breaks blunt the progressive design of the income tax rates and bands structure. Generous tax allowances for investments such as the business expansion scheme (BES), rental housing in seaside resorts or multi-storey car parks offer particularly attractive tax shelters, largely availed of by upper income taxpayers. While tax relief on mortgage interest and health insurance applies at the standard rate of tax,[23] worth no more to the higher rate than the lower

---

[23] Until 1994, mortgage interest relief could be claimed in full at a person's top tax rate. Since then, tax relief on mortgage interest and on health insurance was phased down over a period to apply at the lower rate of tax only.

rate taxpayer, other tax expenditures can be deducted at the top rate of tax. Thus, IR£1,000 spent in such a tax approved way could save IR£440 in income tax in the year 2000 to a top rate taxpayer, but IR£220 to a lower rate taxpayer.

A 1997 Revenue Commissioners' survey of taxpayers earning over IR£250,000 a year found that one in five was paying an effective tax rate of less than 25 per cent; one in nine an effective tax rate of less than 10 per cent (Revenue Commissioners, 1997). This was at a time when people on quite moderate incomes were liable to pay tax at a top rate of 48 per cent.[24] Tax expenditures continue to increase. Budget 2000 increased mortgage interest relief for existing second time buyers at a cost of IR£33 million, a move for which there was no public demand or economic rationale.[25]

Unlike direct expenditure, there is no formal audit of how much these reliefs cost, and who benefits. Their importance can be gauged from the following official estimates of their value in tax foregone.

Table 5.1: Estimated Value of Tax Reliefs, 1998

	IR£ Million	Estimated nos.
Mortgage interest	163.2	415,000
Rent, private tenancies	14.8	84,400
Medical insurance	61.0	442,200
Medical expenses	25.5	76,000
Pension contributions	312.0	n.a.
Pension fund income	59.0	n.a.
Third level fees	0.4	1,600

---

[24] The survey related to the 1994/5 tax year. Business deductions, business losses, BES and film investments, and pension contributions were the main vehicles being used to reduce exposure to tax. At that time, a married couple with an income over IR£16,400 would have been in the top 48 per cent tax bracket.

[25] This measure increased the proportion of mortgage interest on which relief was claimable from 80 per cent to 100 per cent, and reversed the *de minimis* provision introduced in 1993, which had eliminated the relief on the first IR£100 (single) and IR£200 (married) for second time and later buyers. The measure was introduced at a time when interest rates on mortgages had reached historic lows and were negative in real terms.

Business Reliefs		
BES	41.8	n.a.
Urban renewal	48.0	n.a.
"s.23" for landlords	26.2	n.a.
Film investment	19.1	2,500
Seaside resorts	5	n.a.

Source: Department of Finance (1998), Tax Strategy Group 98/03A

5.3.3 Design of Income Tax Changes

Ireland's social partnership deals have been built around a model of trading moderate pay rises for income tax cuts. There has been a significant fall in the effective rates of tax since 1987 (Figure 5.9). As income tax cuts have grown, the distribution of these cuts across different income groups has become more important. Changes to separate elements of the income tax system focus the gains in different directions.

Figure 5.9: Effective Rate of Income Tax, 1974–96

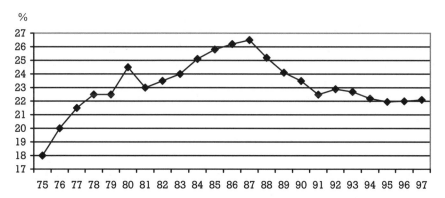

Changes in the tax system announced at budget time are not the only ones which take place — failure to index tax allowances, tax credits or tax bands to inflation constitutes a real increase in tax. The real value of personal allowances fell continuously from 1986 to 1992, for example (Figure 5.10). The dependent relative's allowance, for example, was set at IR£110 in

1982, and not increased again till 2000. By that stage, it had almost halved in value in real terms.

Figure 5.10: Real Value of Personal Tax Allowance, 1985–98

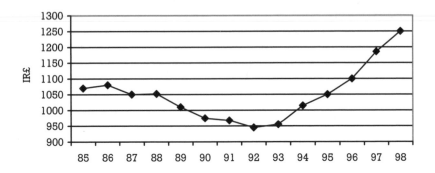

1980 prices

Source: Personal tax allowances adjusted by the consumer price index

People with incomes below the tax threshold do not benefit directly from tax-cutting packages. Changes made to the structure
of PRSI and the health levy during the mid-1990s were designed
to reach lower earners below the tax threshold. Raising income
tax exemption limits offers a cheap and very focused way to direct resources to people below the newly raised limits. However, the Tax Welfare Integration Group (Government of Ireland,
1996: 133) recommended against pursuing this policy as it adds
to marginal tax rates and poverty traps in the system.

An increase in personal tax credits is worth the same in cash
terms to taxpayers at all income levels, and thus proportionately less to those on higher incomes. Reducing taxes through
raising tax credits improves the progressivity of the tax system.

Widening of tax bands confers no benefit on those whose
incomes are already too low to reach the higher tax threshold,
while everyone who pays tax at the higher rate benefits by an
identical cash amount. At a lower tax rate of 22 per cent, a
IR£1,000 increase in the lower tax band saves IR£220[26] for all

---

[26] IR£1,000 extra is levied at 22 per cent rather than 44 per cent, the difference
being worth IR£220 (rates for tax year 2000/2001).

top rate taxpayers. This is worth proportionately more to those in the middle range of income than to those at the very top.

Much of the debate around income tax reduction has centred on headline rates rather than the effective rate of tax paid. A process of tax rate cuts that began in the mid-1980s saw the surtax rate of 60 per cent abolished. By 2001/2, the higher rate of tax had reduced from 48 per cent to 42 per cent, and the standard (lower) rate of tax from 35 per cent to 20 per cent. Reducing the top tax rates has given significantly higher cash benefit to those higher up the income scale. Reducing the standard rate of tax was worth more to middle and upper income earners than to those paying tax at this standard rate only. Simulations by Callan, Nolan and Walsh (Callan et al., 1998: Figs 2.4, 2.7)[27] show how tax reductions which are entirely in the form of better tax allowances or credits favour taxpayers in the middle income bands. Packages featuring cuts in tax rates favour those in the upper income groups.[28]

The relative priority given to lower rates as against other forms of income tax change can be gauged from the sums of money allocated to the different elements in Budget day tax packages. The table shows how reductions in tax rates have been generally prioritised over other elements.

Table 5.2: Cost of Different Budget Income Tax Changes

Year	Allowances/ Credits	Bands	Standard Rate	Top Rate
1990	—	IR£23m	IR£72m	IR£20m
1991	IR£14m	IR£12m	IR£37m	IR£8m
1998	IR£125m	IR£15m	IR£211m	IR£104m
1999	IR£400m	IR£45m	—	—
2000	IR£201m	IR£310m	IR£205m	IR£157m
2001	IR£540m	IR£278m	IR£208m	IR£163m

Source: Budget booklets, Department of Finance

---

[27] These simulations use the ESRI tax and welfare simulation model, SWITCH.

[28] Tax reductions of whatever kind tend not to benefit the poorest 35 per cent who have little if any taxable income.

High marginal tax rates are often seen as a disincentive to work. Tax reductions for the lower paid, whose incomes are closest to what they might get on welfare, are probably the more effective way of improving work incentives. This is best achieved by increased personal allowances. The controversial move in Budget 2000 towards individualisation was designed to address the particularly acute high marginal tax rates being experienced by married women and by single people on average earnings.

5.3.4 Expenditure Taxes

Taxes on expenditure are generally regressive (CSO 1973, 1980, 1987). In a global world of mobile consumption (even more so with e-commerce), there is narrowing scope to target the wealthy through taxing luxury items. Indeed, our special taxes on discretionary spending bear heavier on the poor, who pay a disproportionate share of their income through taxes levied on tobacco and drink.

Table 5.3 below shows how direct and indirect taxes cancel each other out to take a broadly similar total, hovering around 40 per cent, from all but the very poorest who pay somewhat more.

Table 5.3: Direct and Indirect Taxes Combined, as a Ratio of Direct Income, 1987 (standardised household composition)

IR£	> 50	50-70	70-90	90-130	130-170	170-210	210-250	250-300	300-350	350-400	400-450	450-520	520+
Inc. taxes	-.020	.054	.053	.098	.156	.185	.200	.217	.249	.262	.285	.277	.298
Exp. taxes	2.55	.547	.382	.297	.251	.203	.190	.169	.157	.147	.140	.120	.097
Total	2.53	.601	.435	.395	.407	.388	.390	.386	.406	.409	.425	.397	.395

Source: Derived from Table E, CSO 1987

5.3.5 Company Taxation

Ireland's corporate tax regime has undergone major changes, from one with nominally high tax rates but widespread tax write-offs to one which has low tax rates, fewer tax shelters and one of the highest shares of tax revenue from business in the EU. That in turn reflects a high profit share in our economy which rose from 28 per cent in 1990 to 38 per cent by 2000. Our 10 per cent tax rate on manufacturing profits has been a major inducement to foreign-owned firms to locate in Ireland. Under EU rules on state aids, special tax subsidies of this kind are no longer allowed. In substitution we have secured EU agreement to a corporation tax regime which will feature, by January 2003, a 12.5 per cent tax on trading profits and a 25 per cent tax on non-trading profits. The banks, supermarkets and the retail sector generally are among the beneficiaries of the substantial cuts in company taxation which are being effected to bring down tax from the previous 32 per cent rate. An understanding reached with the social partners, that countervailing measures would be taken to claw back some of this windfall from the banking sector, appears to have been quietly dropped. A tax rate of 12.5 per cent on corporate income, compared to a standard tax rate on personal income of almost double that, offers a clear incentive to minimise tax by incorporation as a company, for those in a position to arrange their affairs this way.

5.3.6 Capital Taxation

The three main kinds of capital taxes are stamp duties on the sale of property, capital gains tax and capital acquisitions tax (CAT replaced the earlier estate duties). The property boom that began in the mid-1990s has led to fast growth in revenue from stamp duties based on higher property values.

CAT is part of the package of taxes, which included wealth tax, introduced in the mid-1970s to substitute for previous death duties. It is charged on the total value of gifts or inheritances received, subject to thresholds which are low for unrelated people or more distant relations, but are generous within the immediate family or for passing on a family farm or business. CAT was cut to 20 per cent in Budget 2000, at an estimated full year cost of IR£46 million. Probate tax was abolished in 2001, at a cost of IR£30m. As major property or assets may change hands just once in a generation, lowered capital taxes result in a long-term loss of revenue.

Capital gains tax is levied on the sale of assets at a higher price in real terms than they were bought. Sale of the family home, the exchange of one business asset for another, and small capital gains are exempt. The tax on capital gains was halved in the 1999 Budget to 20 per cent. As with incorporation, some people may be able to organise their affairs to take their returns as capital gain rather than income and take advantage of the lower rate.

Capital gains tax on the sale of development land was cut to 20 per cent on the recommendation of the first Bacon Report (1998) on house prices, to encourage the release of land for building.[29] Development levies recoup only a tiny fraction of the costs incurred by public authorities in servicing land (a legal obligation for councils once land is zoned for development), let alone the long run costs incurred in the provision and maintenance of infrastructure and facilities for a new community. The actions of public authorities have enormously enhanced the value of development land, yet only a minimal share of those costs is charged against the owners as unearned capital gains.

While the tax treatment of income usually attracts greater public attention, the increasingly generous treatment of capital wealth is becoming a significant feature of Ireland's tax system. As wealth is far more unequally distributed than income, this policy shift is likely to lead to further divergence in command over resources in our society.

5.3.7 Taxation — Some Conclusions

The public debate around tax cuts has focused on the relative merits in restructuring the tax code of cuts in tax rates versus adjustments to tax bands or allowances. This debate has to some degree diverted attention from other regressive aspects of our tax code and from changes taking place which favour the rich. Expenditure taxes are regressive and special tax reliefs blunt the progressive intention of the income tax system. Substantial reduction in taxes on profits, capital gains and property transfers favour the accumulation and concentration of capital.

---

[29] The Bacon proposal was for a temporary reduction in capital gains tax for a four-year period, with a subsequent reversion to a 60 per cent rate, to discourage land hoarding. The Finance Bill 2001 proposes making the lower 20 per cent rate a permanent change.

5.4 SOCIAL PARTNERSHIP AND THE SHAPING OF THE TAX AND WELFARE SYSTEMS

Social partnership has been an important ingredient in the recovery of the Irish economy from the depths it reached in the 1980s and of Ireland's modern economic miracle. Falling unemployment and rising real incomes have been significant factors in reducing poverty.

The background to Ireland's modern social partnership was a crisis in the public finances. The economic slump that hit Europe in the wake of the oil price crises of the 1970s ended the post-war period of steady economic progress and full employment. Ireland's problems of adjusting to the economic downturn of the 1980s were particularly difficult, as previous economic policies had left an overhang of national debt. This debt problem was compounded by high interest rates, leading to a crisis in the public finances that forced further contraction in the economy. The attempts in the early 1980s to get to grips with the debt crisis were intended both to cut spending and raise taxes. But as higher interest rates drove up the cost of servicing the national debt, and unemployment soared, public spending rose rather than fell, so that effectively it was on the tax side that the burden of adjustment in public finances was carried (Honohan, 1999). Higher taxation in turn drove up the tax wedge, helping to contribute to rising unemployment (Barry and Bradley, 1991).

5.4.1 Tax and Pay Trade-offs

A trade-off between pay moderation and reductions in income tax has been at the core of Ireland's modern social partnership arrangements, which began in 1987 with the Programme for National Recovery (PNR). Centralised negotiations between trade unions, employers and government have been conducted on the basis of net rather than gross pay, to be delivered by a combination of moderate pay rises and tax cuts. Any process that has tax reduction at its heart is likely to give less weight to spending commitments that might compete with tax cuts for available resources. While some significant new commitments around welfare improvements and other social programmes have been written in to agreements, more often the social exclusion measures have consisted either of broad statements, of measures already in the pipeline, or of undertakings to study issues. Other than those already on the way, social welfare commitments did not feature very strongly until Partnership 2000 (Government of Ireland, 1996) and subsequently the Programme for Prosperity and Fairness (PPF; Government of Ireland, 2000).

5.4.2 Specific Agreements on Tax and Welfare Change

The first partnership deal, the 1987 PNR, had its main focus on tackling the debt crisis and reducing inflation. While new social welfare elements were brief and vague,[30] the PNR had a specific commitment to a IR£225 million income tax reduction package over three years, to include IR£70 million extra for the pay as you earn (PAYE) allowance. There were also commitments to increase the share of tax revenue from corporate profits and from capital taxes. In the event, the reductions in personal income tax delivered over that period were estimated to total IR£800 million, roughly three times the amount promised (Government of Ireland, 1991: 15). On social policy, this first agreement was thin and lacking in detailed provisions, the main element being a commitment to improve the real value of social welfare benefits to an unspecified level.

The 1991 Programme for Economic and Social Progress (PESP) was a far more detailed document. On social welfare, it promised to protect weekly rates against inflation, and to reach the Commission on Social Welfare's priority rates by 1993. On the tax side, it promised a IR£400m reduction in income tax, through cutting the standard rate and moving to a single top rate of tax. A striking element of the PESP in terms of distributing society's resources was an extraordinarily detailed set of commitments on additional staffing ratios in education (Government of Ireland, 1991: 30-4), reflecting the strength of

---

[30] These commitments were to maintain the real value of welfare benefits, to review FIS, to improve social welfare appeals and to liaise with voluntary organisations. There was also a commitment, already in the pipeline, to introduce social insurance for the self-employed.

teacher union negotiators on the Irish Congress of Trade Unions (ICTU) team.

The 1994 Programme for Competitiveness and Work (PCW) traded tax cuts for a moderate pay deal. Its social commitments largely echoed those already outlined in the Government's programme or in the National Development Plan. Its formal tax commitment was to help those on low and middle incomes. During the negotiations on the PCW in early 1994, the social partners were presented with a detailed set of possible income tax packages, in advance of the budget, and how they would impact on different specimen families. The final tax proposals agreed with the social partners, and incorporated in the 1994 Budget, reflected the desire to have a package which would be attractive to union members in the skilled worker category, a group whose votes would be important in voting through a new pay deal. Thus the final package agreed involved somewhat higher increases in the tax bands, and slightly lower increases in personal allowances, than other options under considera-tion.[31]

The 1996 Partnership 2000 deal was the first where the so-cial and community pillar was a party to the negotiations.[32] This pillar argued strongly that for welfare recipients, annual in-creases in welfare payments were analogous to securing pay increases. Tax reductions of IR£900 million were accompanied by a promise of an extra IR£525 million in social spending. Tax cuts on double the scale promised were actually implemented. The shape and not just the size of the promised tax cuts became a contentious issue between government and the social part-ners in 1998 and again at the end of 1999, during negotiations on the subsequent PPF. The social partners argued strongly that the balance of the tax package should be tilted more towards

---

[31] The tax package implemented had increases of IR£525 in the single tax band compared to IR£425 in the C7 tax package, and IR£375 in the more re-distributive C4 package. The single tax allowance went up by IR£175 rather than IR£225 provided for in the C4 tax package: Department of Finance pa-pers held by author.

[32] Some of those in the community pillar have argued that they were only partly included in the process: cf. Crowley (1999).

the lower paid. They welcomed the introduction of tax credits in 1999 as a positive move in this direction.

The Programme for Prosperity and Fairness (Government of Ireland, 2000) promises a tax reduction package worth IR£1,500 million and a social inclusion programme on the same scale. The acceleration of inflation even as the programme was signed underlined the basic need to maintain the real value of welfare payments as well as link them to earnings growth in society. The PPF has commitments to "substantial progress towards a target of IR£100 a week for the lowest rates of social welfare", and to move towards administrative individualisation of the social welfare code. The wording of the commitment to a IR£100 a week welfare rate is somewhat equivocal. It remains to be seen whether concerns about work incentives, which have been so central an influence on recent welfare policy, will surface in relation to this commitment. Such concerns could be addressed through improving child benefit or in-work payments rather than by diluting this commitment.

Personal incomes grew slower than the rate of economic growth over the period since the first partnership agreement. This slower growth in personal incomes has fuelled some of the "payback time" pressure for increased tax cuts. Total wages grew slower than overall growth, so that the profit share has increased. Within the wage sector, a significant share of the growth accrued in the form of more jobs rather than in personal incomes. Special pay increases for public sector workers over and above the standard private sector terms have shifted the balance of incomes between the sectors.[33]

5.4.3 The Shaping of the Tax Changes

Some of the national agreements have contained commitments to specific tax changes; others have just specified the amount to be spent on tax reduction without spelling out the form it might take. Negotiations usually involved more detailed discussion of the tax reductions planned for the coming year, with the re-

---

[33] Average gross earnings in the public sector grew by 72 per cent from 1988 to 1999 compared with 54 per cent for private sector workers in both industry and financial services.

maining years of each agreement sketched out in more general terms. The income tax reductions since 1987 have mainly taken the form of lower tax rates, with the result that gains from these tax packages have been somewhat biased towards the better off. The net impact of tax and welfare changes on the distribution of income over the period is now examined.

5.5 THE IMPACT OF WELFARE AND TAX POLICIES ON REDISTRIBUTION

Our choice of social welfare model is one that offers basic protection at a fairly modest level, while earnings-related pensions are left to the private market. We reduced an already low share of taxes in national income as a central feature of national pay bargaining. The result is that redistribution through the tax and welfare system is modest in its scale. Growth in welfare spending and in income taxes as a share of national income such as occurred in years of large scale unemployment during the 1980s are associated with increasing redistribution of income from rich to poor.

The main sources of information on income distribution in Ireland are the household budget surveys conducted in 1973, 1980, 1987 and 1994/5, and the household surveys by the Economic and Social Research Institute (ESRI) in 1987 and annually since 1994. This section presents the findings of CSO and ESRI researchers on developments over these intervals.[34]

5.5.1 How Effective Are the Tax and Welfare Systems at Redistributing Income?

The Gini coefficient is a standard summary measure of inequality. To summarise the effects of taxes and welfare on redistribution, Table 5.4 shows the percentage change in Gini coefficients as one moves from market income to gross income and after tax income. The table should be read across. In 1994 the Gini coefficient for gross income was a quarter lower than for direct

---

[34] Since 1998 the ESRI team have published annual analyses of the impact of tax and welfare changes using a model constructed to simulate social welfare and income tax changes (the SWITCH model) which is based on actual rather than hypothetical families.

income, as a result of the equalising effect of the welfare system. The Gini coefficient for disposable income showed a further fall of 7 per cent. The table shows how the welfare system
plays a much stronger role in reducing inequality than the tax
system. While the combined contribution of both welfare and
tax policies to equality was lower in 1997 than it had been in
1994, it remained well above their combined contribution in
1980. The preliminary figures for 1998 suggest that lower welfare spending (with lower unemployment) and lower taxes
have sharply curtailed the redistributive impact of the tax and
welfare system.

*Table 5.4: Reductions in Inequality in Moving from Direct
to Gross to Disposable Income 1980-97 (as measured by
changes in Gini coefficients)*

Study	Year of Data	% Reduction through Welfare System	% Reduction through Income Taxes	% Combined Reduction
Murphy (1984, Table 5)	1980	17.7	5.3	23.0
Callan and Nolan (1992), Table 4	1987	n.a.	10.0*	n.a.
Nolan et al. (2000), Table 3.2	1994	25.3	8.0	33.3
Nolan et al. (2000), Table 3.2	1997	22.2	8.2	30.4
Nolan et al. (2000), Table 3.12, 3.11	1998	19.6	6.2	25.8

*This shows the percentage reduction from gross income; the other figures
show the percentage reductions from direct income

5.5.2 Redistribution over Individual Periods — Research Findings

1973-80

The 1970s, which were an expansionary period for welfare policy, saw an improvement in overall equality in spite of greater inequality in market incomes (Rottman and Reidy, 1988: 137). Between 1973 and 1980, growing welfare payments, fairly static child benefits and the increasingly progressive impact of tax and PRSI deductions effectively redistributed income away from those with work and from families with children towards the elderly (ibid.: 136-48).

1980-87

The 1980 to 1987 period was marked by a dramatic rise in unemployment, which increased welfare transfers. A growing share of GNP was taken in tax, in order to pay for higher welfare spending and high interest rates on the national debt, and to begin the budgetary adjustment process. This high tax, high welfare spending combination had the effect of redistributing more income from rich to poor (Callan and Nolan, 1999b: 174). This did not signal any golden age, since real disposable incomes actually fell in this period and unemployment soared. During this period the burden of adjustment to economic downturn was more evenly shared in income terms, although not in terms of holding a job.

1987-94

Between 1987 and 1994[35] social welfare incomes improved faster in real terms than incomes from employment. The fastest increases were for the unemployed and other short-term claimants who had started off on the lowest rates, while pensions grew marginally relative to inflation.[36] Personal income taxes fell.

---

[35] The policy intervals discussed reflect availability of data, not necessarily key turning points in policy.

[36] Prices rose by 20 per cent, old age pensions 29 per cent, long-term unemployment assistance by over 60 per cent and unemployment benefit by 44 per cent.

The bottom fifth of the income distribution respond to welfare but not to tax changes. The pattern of tax changes affects the balance of gains or losses between middle income and top income households. So 1987 to 1994 shows a U-shaped pattern of gains, where the bottom fifth of households benefited from welfare increases ahead of earnings, the middle income group experienced disimprovement relative to a benchmark of indexation to earnings, and the top third of households benefited disproportionately from the pattern of tax cuts (Callan et al., 1999b: Fig. 2.1).[37]

From 1994 to 1998, tax changes benefited the top half of the income distribution fairly evenly. Welfare payments, although they grew faster than inflation in these years, did not keep up with changes in earnings (Callan et al., 1999b: Fig. 2.3).[38] The growth from 1994 to 1997 in the number of households who were below conventional poverty lines reflects this relative disimprovement for the poorest households.[39]

1999-2000

Callan and Nolan (1998) make the point that the relative size of the tax and welfare packages within a given Budget envelope has a significant impact on whether the poorest income groups (dominated by welfare recipients) lose out in relative terms. As the public finances moved into surplus in the late 1990s, the size of the budget tax reductions became steadily more generous in absolute terms and relative to the cost of budget welfare improvements (Callan et al., 1998: 33-4).

The introduction of tax credits in the 1999 Budget had a positive effect. All but the poorest 20 per cent of households

---

[37] Between 1994 and 1997, the bottom fifth of the income distribution improved by over 6 per cent against the benchmark. The top tenth of households also fared 6 per cent better than under the benchmark, with smaller gains for those a little lower on the income ladder.

[38] The top half had gains of about 4 per cent relative to earnings, with highest gains on middle incomes. Relative to the benchmark, the bottom fifth of households fell back by 2 per cent.

[39] Using conventional poverty lines set at 40 per cent, 50 per cent, and 60 per cent of average disposable household income, adjusted for household composition: Callan et al., 1999a: Table 3.3.

showed gains relative to an earnings benchmark. Middle income families did relatively better than others (Callan et al., 1999b: Fig. 2.5).[40]

Budget 2000, which dwarfed all previous budgets in its scale with a tax and welfare package totalling over IR£1.6 billion, redistributed resources systematically upwards. Gains for the poorest fifth of households were under 1 per cent, while gains for the top fifth were over 4 per cent (Callan, 1999). Significant upward distribution of income tax changes, combined with changes in welfare at a slower rate than earnings, widened the dispersion of disposable incomes.[41]

5.6 CONCLUSIONS

5.6.1 Increased Dispersion in Economic Boom

Recent economic change is widening the dispersion of market incomes. Two examples are the knowledge economy and what is happening to wealth. Ireland's move from a manufacturing economy to a skill and information-based service economy has increased the demand for highly skilled and educated workers and reduced the demand for unskilled production workers. This has altered the relative rewards from skilled and unskilled work. Since 1987, there has been an increase in Ireland's already high level of earnings dispersion (Callan and Nolan, 1999b: Table 8.2).[42]

The sustained economic boom from 1994 onwards has facilitated an accumulation of wealth. A faster growth in profits,

---

[40] The largest gains were in the middle of the distribution, averaging 3 per cent against the benchmark

[41] The ratio between announced allocations on Budget day to extra tax cuts and welfare increases is an interesting indicator. From 1987 to 1997, the cost of income tax packages ranged between the same scale as the welfare packages, to twice the welfare package. In 1998 the tax package was almost three times the welfare package; in 1999 and 2000, around five times the welfare package.

[42] In 1994, the top 10 per cent full time employees in Ireland earned 4.06 times the amount earned by the bottom 10 per cent. This ratio had increased from 3.67 in 1987. Between 1994 and 1997, the position of the lowest paid workers improved against the median, while higher paid workers continued to pull away: Nolan, Maître, O'Neill and Sweetman, 2000, Table 8.

increasing their share in national output, has also contributed to wealth accumulation. In general, asset values, particularly of property, have risen significantly. Capital accumulation in today's boom has consequences for the future distribution of resources and access to income. Inherited wealth is likely to grow in importance in the future in a society with growing wealth, high rates of home ownership, rapid asset price inflation, and smaller families. The sums of money which people stand to inherit on the sale of the parental home after their parents die are now very substantial due to the combination of high house prices and smaller family size. While widespread home ownership will help disperse such gains reasonably broadly across the community, the wealth gap between home-owning and renting families is set to widen substantially (see Chapter 7).

The tax and welfare systems need to counteract these trends towards increasing wealth and earnings dispersion, or greater inequality in final income will be the result.

5.6.2 Welfare Strategy

Welfare payments must at a minimum be indexed to prices if their real value is to be maintained in inflationary times. Unless welfare rates are also index-linked to overall earnings in the economy, the relative position of welfare recipients becomes eroded during periods of economic growth. As Callan and Nolan (1999a) argue, the most appropriate benchmark to use in judging tax and welfare change is one where tax allowances, tax bands and welfare rates are all indexed to increases in earnings, and relative shares are unchanged.

There has been a concern that gains in welfare rates relative to earnings would worsen replacement rates for welfare recipients who are on the labour market. This concern may be more appropriately addressed by changing the underlying benefit structure rather than continuing to develop a two-tier approach to increases in welfare rates. Buoyant revenue creates an ideal opportunity to phase in changes in the structure of the welfare and tax system which could support a generous welfare regime alongside the maintenance of work incentives. Here are some examples.

As consistently shown by the ESRI, the poor take-up of Family Income Supplements is a key element in maintaining high replacement rates (Callan and Nolan, 1999b, Table 8.2).[43] An automatic entitlement via the tax system, whether in the form of an earned income tax credit or a refund of unused tax credits would be a clear improvement for a scheme that misses two-thirds of its target audience.

The formula used to calculate rent allowances for private sector tenants under supplementary welfare results in any additional income for the tenant being matched by a corresponding reduction in the rent allowance. A IR£10 increase in income means a IR£10 fall in rent allowance, leaving the tenant no better off. This is equivalent to taxing any extra earnings at 100 per cent and constitutes the strongest disincentive to earnings anywhere in the tax and welfare systems. In contrast, the differential rent formula used by the main local authorities in relation to their own tenants means that a IR£10 increase in income will generally result in rent going up by IR£1. The size of the rent allowance poverty trap seems to be both inefficient and inequitable.

A disproportionately high share of larger families are welfare dependent, reflecting partly real or perceived unemployment and poverty traps in the system.[44] The support for children from the state via public services and the tax and welfare codes falls far short of equalising the financial burden between larger families and others (Carney et al., 1994).

Adequate levels of child benefit direct resources towards families with children, in a way that is neutral as between families with two earners, one earner and no earner. Child dependant allowances in the welfare code have been frozen at IR£13.20 a week since 1994 and have been eroding quietly at a slow

---

[43] In 1994, the top 10 per cent of full-time employees in Ireland earned 4.06 times what was earned by the bottom 10 per cent. This ratio had increased from 3.67 in 1987. Between 1994 and 1997, the position of the lowest paid workers improved against the median, while higher paid workers continued to pull away (Nolan et al. (2000), Table 6.1).

[44] A quarter of families of four or more children are welfare-dependent, a third in five child families and two-thirds in families with six or more children: DSCFA 1998.

pace through inflation. Rather than continue this slow death, a strategic decision could be taken and implemented over a number of years to replace them in full with generous child benefit increases, supplemented by designated child support for lower income families which is independent of the parents' source of income. Taxing child benefit is another option for targeting.

Ireland's national pensions strategy sees a major role for private pensions, despite the evidence that less than half the workforce have occupational pension cover and such cover will not become compulsory. This contrasts with generous state earnings-related pension schemes in countries like Sweden which have created a genuinely egalitarian tax and transfer system. If we were to develop a state earnings-related pensions tier it would bring about a substantial change in the degree to which the state redistributes income.

5.6.3 Tax Reform

Tax and welfare policies are important agents of income redistribution but the systems have developed in separate and often contradictory ways (Government of Ireland, 1996). Although individual policy elements are often scrutinised for their impact on different income groups, there is little evidence of any integrated planning by successive governments to redistribute income in a concerted way through dovetailed tax and welfare policies. Redistribution is far from being an explicit policy goal of the tax system. That issue is not driving the agenda when VAT, company taxes and capital taxes are being decided, and has not been foremost in planning income tax reductions. Whether explicitly recognised or not, however, the scale of tax change put in place over the period of social partnership has reallocated a significant share of Ireland's growing income. Too often the tax policy mix has disproportionately favoured those at the top of the income distribution.

Tax reform in Ireland has often been seen as synonymous with tax reduction. The tax marches in late 1979 and early 1980 had as their ostensible focus the unfair share of overall tax being paid by PAYE workers compared to other sectors. However, it would be simplistic to see this tax protest as focused only on the distribution of tax and not primarily on its level.[45]

5.6.4 Rebalancing within the Tax System

Until the move into budget surplus in the late 1990s, significant reductions in income tax were only seen as achievable if funded by higher taxes elsewhere. In its first report in 1993, the Tax Strategy Group considered that reduced personal income taxes could be achieved either through widened expenditure taxes, increased property taxes, or through a broadened income tax base, curtailing discretionary allowances (Department of Finance, 1993: 1-6).[46]

Value Added Tax

As the fall of the government in January 1982 was popularly attributed to the VAT changes introduced in the abortive Budget,[47] there has been little political appetite since then to extend the VAT base to the remaining VAT-free items of food and children's clothing. There have also been the practical concerns that increasing taxes on spending could drive up inflation, or erode the tax base through incentives to cross-border shopping. While the ESRI has argued that trading higher energy taxes for lower payroll taxes would benefit both the environment and the economy (FitzGerald and McCoy, 1992), Ireland, although a net importer of energy, has been reluctant to support carbon energy taxes on a Europe-wide scale or to go this route alone. The highly effective road blockades in protest at high oil prices and high taxes on fuel which took place throughout Europe in September 2000 render it less

---

[45] The popularity in the 1980s of car stickers saying AXE TAX seemed to have caught a public mood

[46] The Tax Strategy Group, which had its inaugural meeting in November 1993, brought together senior civil servants in Finance, Revenue, Enterprise and Employment and Social Welfare, along with political advisers, to review tax options prior to the budget and the finance bill. Its policy papers since 1998 are posted on the Department of Finance's website, under "Publications".

[47] According to the then Taoiseach, Garret FitzGerald, (*The Irish Times*, 9 September 2000), it is a myth that VAT on children's shoes was the cause of the Budget collapse. However, the myth endures.

likely that either Ireland or the rest of Europe will enthusiastically adopt such green taxes in the short term.

Ireland generally has adopted a gradualist rather than a big bang approach to tax reform. The option of switching taxes from income to property has been suggested from time to time as a potential way of achieving significant reductions in income taxes (Honohan and Irvine, 1987; NESC, 1986: 285; Callan, 1991). The changes to residential property tax made in the 1994 Budget[48] could be seen as an initial testing of the waters in relation to such a shift. That measure, which raised IR£15 million, provoked a sustained outcry which led ultimately to the total abandonment of residential property tax in 1997.

The failure of this relatively timid bid at restructuring the tax system illustrates the problems of securing political support for redistributive tax changes with significant numbers of losers as well as winners, particularly where the losers are a clearly identifiable and articulate group. The concept of net gain, when one tax is increased to fund tax reductions elsewhere, is little appreciated by public opinion. Although any increased property tax bills in 1994 would have been more than cancelled out for the vast majority affected through lower income taxes, the public debate never engaged around net gains but concentrated exclusively on the increase in property tax.

This example also illustrates the resistance to taxes that are collected in a lump sum rather than deducted at source, and to taxes on the family home. Rates, water charges and residential property tax have all been abolished following well-organised opposition, as had the earlier wealth tax. The widespread dilution of capital acquisitions tax in the 2000 Budget followed a campaign focused on hardship cases of inheritance of the family home, which could have been tackled through very limited change.[49]

One fundamental structural change in the income tax system that has taken place was the introduction of tax credits in place

---

[48] The income and house value thresholds were lowered, and the tax rate raised.

[49] Budget 2000 cut CAT 20 per cent at an estimated full year cost of IR£46 million.

of tax allowances from 1999. This change, which had been under consideration for some years, was made easier by the buoyant tax receipts which made it possible to compensate higher rate taxpayers for any cash losses which a move to the new system might have otherwise entailed.

Increasing tax credits is the fairest way to distribute resources across all taxpayers, whereas cutting headline rates of tax favours those on highest incomes the most. The continuing vogue for introducing new tax expenditures (such as investment in wind energy, nursing homes or multi-storey car parks) distorts the tax system, favours the better off and moves the system farther away from the comprehensive definition of income favoured by the Commission on Taxation.

5.6.5 Taxes on Property and Wealth

Income tax policy is invariably the main focus for public debate on tax. There has been little public commentary on the rapid erosion of the capital tax system which has been taking place. The absence of any property or wealth tax, the halving of capital gains tax and the erosion of capital acquisitions tax leaves Ireland with one of the most lenient capital tax regimes in Europe. Unearned windfall gains such as from land rezoning are taxed considerably lighter than earned income, although substantial public costs are incurred in the process. The tax treatment of property and wealth facilitates its concentration. While in the short term, capital tax revenues may rise from a short term increase in disposals arising from the changes in the capital tax regime, in the long term the potential yield from any given asset has been severely cut.

The generous treatment of capital wealth is in contrast to the decline experienced in welfare payments relative to other incomes. The scale of welfare improvements relative to earnings has a key role in determining whether the poorest households hold their relative position or see it disimprove. In the longer term, if the current policy of setting welfare increases above price increases but below earnings growth were to continue, the gap between rich and poor will further widen. The ESRI's Medium-Term Review 2000 (Duffy et al., 1999: 34), suggests that personal disposable incomes will rise by 3.5 per cent a year in real terms between 2000 and 2005. That should be the minimum annual target for real welfare increases over that period. On recent evidence, our system of taxes and transfers is being further skewed upwards in favour of those on highest incomes.

5.6.6 Unique Opportunity

While prosperity alters the distribution of income and wealth, the scale of revenue generated also offers unprecedented possibilities for change. It is much harder to win support for redistribution in a near-zero growth environment where gains for one group involve actual cash losses for others. When growth is abundant, redistributing its fruits offers quite a painless way to achieve a more egalitarian result. Had a positive approach towards higher redistribution taken place during the 1990s, a decade where Irish national income grew by 70 per cent, a major shift in income distribution could have been achieved. With the economy expected to experience a gradual return to more moderate growth rates, such an opportunity for redistribution may not readily occur again.

That opportunity has not been well used since the boom began, with resources being redistributed upwards rather than more equally (Callan et al., 1999b: 34; Callan, 1999). Welfare increases that lag behind earnings, and tax reductions focused on the wealthier, are serving to widen not to narrow the gap between rich and poor. The unique opportunity to tilt the system in the direction of those on lower incomes has been wasted. The skew upwards may not be easily reversed as the economy slows down. It is also a harder political task to take away gains which have been given.

Ireland's current prosperity offers a unique opportunity to improve the scale and scope of our welfare system, to get the structure of our welfare and tax systems right, to narrow the gap between rich and poor, promote fairness, and reduce poverty. It is time to place these issues on the national agenda.

References

Atkinson, Anthony B., Lee Rainwater and Tim Smeeding (1995), *Income Distribution in OECD Countries: Evidence from the Luxembourg Income Study*, Paris, OECD

Bacon, Peter and Associates (1998), *An Economic Assessment of Recent House Price Developments*, Dublin, Government Publications

Barry, Frank and John Bradley (1991), "On the Causes of Ireland's Unemployment", in *Economic and Social Review*, Vol. 22, no. 4, July, pp. 253-86

Beveridge, William (1942), *Social Insurance and Allied Services*, Cmd. 6404, London: HMSO

Breen, Richard, Damian Hannan, David Rottman and Christopher T. Whelan. (1990), *Understanding Contemporary Ireland*, Dublin, Gill and Macmillan

Callan, Tim (1991), *Property Tax: Principles and Policy Options*, Dublin, ESRI

Callan, Tim and Brian Nolan (1992) "Income Distribution and Redistribution: Ireland in Comparative Perspective" in Goldthorpe, John and Whelan, Christopher T. (eds.), *The Development of Industrial Society in Ireland*, Oxford, Oxford University Press

Callan, Tim, Brian Nolan and Christopher T. Whelan (1996), *A Review of the Commission on Social Welfare's Minimum Adequate Income*, Dublin, ESRI Policy Research Paper 29

Callan, Tim, Brian Nolan, John Walsh (1998), "Income Tax and Social Welfare Policies" in *Budget Perspectives*, Dublin, ESRI

Callan, Tim and Brian Nolan (1999a), *Tax and Welfare changes, Poverty and Work Incentives in Ireland 1987-94*, Dublin, ESRI Policy Research Paper 34

Callan, Tim and Brian Nolan (1999b), "Income Inequality in Ireland in the 1980s and 1990s" in Barry, Frank (ed.), *Understanding Ireland's Economic Growth*, Basingstoke, Macmillan

Callan, Tim, Richard Layte, Brian Nolan, Dorothy Watson, Christopher T. Whelan, James Williams, and Bertrand Maître (1999a), *Monitoring Poverty Trends*, Dublin, ESRI, DSCFA and Combat Poverty Agency

Callan, Tim, Brian Nolan, John Walsh and Richard Nestor (1999b), "Income Tax and Social Welfare Policies" in *Budget Perspectives*, Dublin, ESRI

Callan, Tim (1999), "Biased Budget towards Better off Marks Return to Earlier Policy" *The Irish Times*, 2 December

Carney, Claire, Eithne Fitzgerald, Gabriel Kiely and Paul Quinn (1994), *The Cost of a Child*, Dublin, Combat Poverty Agency

Central Statistics Office, *Household Budget Surveys* (1973, 1980, 1987, 1994/5), Cork

Central Statistics Office (1995), *Redistributive Effects of State Taxes and Benefits on Household Incomes in 1987*

Clancy, Pat (1995), *Access to College: Patterns of Continuity and Change*, Dublin, Higher Education Authority

Commission on Social Welfare (1986), *Report of the Commission on Social Welfare,* Dublin, Government Publications

Commission on Taxation (1982), *First Report of the Commission on Taxation: Direct Taxation*, Dublin, Government Publications

Crowley, Niall (1999), "Partnership 2000 — Empowerment or Co-option?" in Kirby, Peadar and Jacobson, David (eds.), *In the Shadow of the Tiger*, Dublin, DCU Press

Department of Finance, various years Budget Booklets, Dublin, Government Publications, various years Finance Accounts, Dublin, Government Publications

Department of Finance (1998, 1999) Tax Strategy Group Papers, Department of Finance website: www.irlgov.ie/finance

Department of Finance (1999) *Report of the Budget Strategy for Ageing Group*, Dublin

Department of Finance website: www.irlgov.ie/finance/pubstag

Department of Social Welfare (1996), *Social Insurance in Ireland*, Dublin, Government Publications

Department of Social Welfare (1997), *Actuarial Review of Social Welfare Pensions*, Dublin, Government Publications

Department of Social Community and Family Affairs (various years), *Statistical Information on the Social Welfare Services*, Dublin, Government Publications

Duffy, David, John FitzGerald, Ide Kearney and Diarmaid Smyth (2000), *Medium-term Review 1999-2005*, Dublin, ESRI

European Union (1999a), *Communication on a Concerted Strategy for Modernising of Social Protection*, Luxembourg, Commission of the European Communities

European Union (1999b), *Employment Guidelines 1999*, Luxembourg, Commission of the European Communities

FitzGerald, John and Danny McCoy, eds, (1992), *The Economic Effects of Carbon Taxes*, Dublin, ESRI

Förster, Michael and Michele Pellizzari (2000), *Trends and Driving Factors in Income Distribution and Poverty in the OECD Area*, Paris, OECD Labour Market and Social Policy occasional paper no. 42

Government of Ireland (1996), *Report of the Expert Working Group on the Integration of the Tax and Social Welfare System*, Dublin, Government Publications

Government of Ireland (1997), *Sharing in Progress — the National Anti-Poverty Strategy*, Dublin, Government Publications

Government of Ireland (1999), *Report of Working Group examining the Treatment of Married, Cohabiting and One-parent Families under the Tax and Social Welfare Codes*, Dublin, Government Publications

Government of Ireland — national agreements:

      (1987) *Programme for National Recovery*

      (1991) *Partnership for Economic and Social Progress*

      (1994) *Programme for Competitiveness and Work*

      (1996) *Partnership 2000*

      (2000) *Programme for Prosperity and Fairness*

Dublin, Government Publications

Honohan, Patrick and Ian Irvine (1987), "The Marginal Social Cost of Taxation", *Economic and Social Review*, vol. 19, no. 1

Honohan, Patrick (1999), "Fiscal adjustment and disinflation in Ireland" in Barry, Frank (ed.), *Understanding Ireland's Economic Growth*, Basingstoke, Macmillan

International Labour Office (1999), "Inquiry into the Changing Cost of Social Security 1994-96", www.ilo.org/public/english/protection/socsec/publ/css/cssindex.htm

Korpi, Walter and Joakim Palme (1998), "The Paradox of Redistribution and Strategies of Equality" *American Sociological Review*, vol. 63, October, pp. 661-87

Layte, Richard, Tony Fahey and Christopher Whelan (2000), *Income, Deprivation and Well-being among Older Irish People*, Dublin, National Council for Ageing and Older People

Levitas, Ruth (1998), *The Inclusive Society? Social Exclusion and New Labour*, Basingstoke, Macmillan

Mishra, Ramesh (1999), *Globalization and the Welfare State*, Cheltenham, Edward Elgar

Murray, Charles (1984), *Losing Ground: American Social Policy 1950-1980*, New York, Basic Books

Murphy, Dónal (1984) "The Impact of State Taxes and Benefits on Irish Household Incomes", *Journal of the Statistical and Social Inquiry Society of Ireland*, xxv, pp. 55-120

National Economic and Social Council (1986), *A Strategy for Development 1986-90*, Dublin, NESC

National Pensions Board (1998), *Securing Retirement Incomes — Report of the National Pensions Policy Initiative*, Dublin, Government Publications

Nolan, Brian and Christopher T Whelan (1999), *Loading the Dice? A study of Cumulative Disadvantage*, Dublin, Oak Tree Press/Combat Poverty Agency

Nolan, Brian, Bertrand Maître, Donal O'Neill and Olive Sweetman (2000), *The Distribution of Income in Ireland,* Dublin, Oak Tree Press

O'Connell, Philip and David Rottman (1992), "The Irish Welfare State in Comparative Perspective" in Goldthorpe, John and Whelan, Christopher T. (eds.), *The Development of Industrial Society in Ireland*, Oxford, Oxford University Press

OECD (1999), *Revenue Statistics 1965-1998*, Paris, OECD

Revenue Commissioners (1997), "Effective Tax Rates for High Earning Individuals" (press release)

Reddin, Mike (1978), *Universality and Selectivity: Strategies in Social Policy*, Dublin, NESC

Rottman, David and Mairéad Reidy (1988), *Redistribution through State Social Expenditure in the Republic of Ireland, 1973-1980*, Dublin, NESC

Shaver, Sheila (1998), "Universality or Selectivity in Income Support to Older People? A Comparative Assessment of the Issues" in *Journal of Social Policy*, vol. 27 no. 2, pp. 231-34

Smyth, Emer (1999), *Do Schools Differ?,* Dublin, Oak Tree Press

Tansey, Paul (1998), *Ireland at Work: Economic Growth and the Labour Market 1987-97,* Dublin, Oak Tree Press

Townsend, Peter (1979), *Poverty in the United Kingdom*, Harmondsworth, Penguin

Chapter 6

Public Spending on Education, Inequality and Poverty

Peter Archer

6.1 INTRODUCTION

The main purpose of this chapter is to examine how public spending on education impacts on inequality: to what extent does such spending contribute to inequality and to what extent does it counteract inequality? Particular, but not exclusive, attention will be given to inequalities of social class or socioeconomic background. In other words, a focus will be on the impact of public spending on the "cycle of poverty" (Conference of Major Religious Superiors, 1992; Combat Poverty Agency, 1995). This cycle occurs because of three features of Irish society: (a) people's status and income are largely determined by their paid employment; (b) employment prospects are increasingly determined by educational credentials; and (c) educational attainment and achievement are closely related to social background (social class of origin). These three features, especially the second and third, will be discussed in more detail later.

Dunne (1995: 70) described the cycle of poverty in the following terms.

> Even when schooling has replaced more traditional mechanisms as the dominant agency of social selection, it confirms the biases of these earlier mechanisms: children from poorer families still tend to do less well in school and to remain poorer themselves as adults.

The term "educational disadvantage" is used widely and will be used here to describe children and young people from poor families, whose socioeconomic background means they derive less benefit from their schooling than other young people. It is acknowledged that this falls short of a formal definition of educational disadvantage and fails to reflect the full complexity of the phenomenon (Kellaghan, 1999).

In order to assess the impact of public spending on educational disadvantage and more generally on the phenomenon described by Dunne (1995) as quoted above, a major part of the chapter will analyse *trends in public spending on education,* particularly during the 1990s. Before this, it is necessary to discuss a number of issues by way of providing a broad context:

- *The meaning of equality* as it applies to education;

- *Inequalities in the current education system,* including the social and economic consequences of these inequalities.

Sections dealing with these two issues will be followed by a section on *standard approaches to the relationship between public spending on education and inequality.* This section will contain a critique of some aspects of the thinking that seems to have underpinned the policies of Irish governments on the use of public spending on education to reduce social inequalities. That thinking was most evident during the 1960s, 1970s and 1980s when, along with other aspects of social spending, there was "a shift away from *selectivity,* or provision on a means-tested basis, towards *universalism,* or general provision without reference to means" (Kennedy, 1975: 19, emphases in original). A reversal of the trend towards a universalistic approach became apparent in government policy statements on public spending on education in the 1980s. The word used to describe the emerging approach was "targeting". Thus, policy statements referred to the need to direct or target additional resources, as these became available, to schools and students where need was greatest. The analysis of trends in public spending on education, in the fifth section of this chapter, will relate, to a large extent, to the principle of targeting. In the final section, some general conclusions will be drawn and some alternative approaches to public spending policy will be considered.

6.2 THE MEANING OF EQUALITY

The concept of equality (often described as "equality of educational opportunity") has been a prominent part of discourse on education in Ireland for almost half a century. The concept began to achieve this prominence in the wake of the First and Second Programmes for Economic Expansion and the publication of the report of the *Investment in Education* team in 1965 (*Investment in Education,* 1965). Equality has also been a major theme of educational research within a wide range of disciplines (e.g., economics, philosophy, political theory, psychology and sociology) for most of the twentieth century. Despite the attention it has received, a variety of meanings have been and continue to be attached to the term "equality".

The absence of a shared understanding of equality in relation to education and other aspects of social policy has frequently been addressed. Baker (1998: 21) referred to the "many different types of 'equality'" and argued that "it is not enough to demand 'equality', we need to know what kind of equality we want". Greaney and Kellaghan (1984: 4) noted that the term "'equality of opportunity' . . . is often used in a vague sense or in a way that makes it difficult or impossible to ascertain whether or not a policy designed to promote equality is successful". Kleinig (1982: 117) put the problem of definition colourfully when he described equality "as referentially incomplete, and until it is made clear by reference to what equality is being invoked or rejected, its invocation or rejection amounts to little more than political sloganeering". Although there is no widely accepted definition there is agreement on what constitutes the main approaches to defining equality. A number of types of definition can be considered.

6.2.1 Access

According to Greaney and Kellaghan (1984: 5), equality of opportunity has traditionally ". . . been interpreted to mean that all children — irrespective of characteristics such as race, creed, social class, gender, financial resources, place of residence, or other irrelevant criteria — should have equal *access* to educational facilities."

By focusing on access, attention is directed to the elimination of barriers. Some barriers could be legal, when for example, members of particular racial groups are prohibited from attending certain institutions or when types of education are available only to members of one religious denomination. In the current education system legal barriers are not very significant. There are, however, other non-legal factors that can constitute real barriers for some groups. These include financial factors such as fees or the fact that some families cannot afford the expense of continuing in education. They also include various forms of direct and indirect discrimination, some of which will be described in the Section 6.3. Recent work on access to adult and community education (e.g., Bailey and Coleman, 1998; Ronayne, 1999), has developed a categorisation of barriers that prevent poor Irish adults from availing of opportunities in adult and community education. This categorisation has already contributed to the development of new outreach strategies in adult literacy provision (Bailey and Coleman, 1998).

6.2.2 Participation

A more ambitious definition of equality uses *participation* rather than access as the criterion. According to this definition, equality is achieved when the composition of the student population, in terms of race, creed, gender, social class etc., at all levels of education, reflects the composition of the general population. There is inequality when particular groups are under-represented or over-represented. According to Lynch (1999: 291) "equal participation assumes the pre-existence of equal formal rights and opportunities and equality of access". She noted that when participation is the criterion for equality, policies need to "go beyond the protection of formal rights and the prevention of discrimination as they actively intervene to *enable* and *encourage* participation" (emphasis added).

6.2.3 Achievement

The third definition of equality goes beyond access and participation and uses achievement or outcome as the criterion. This implies that equality will not be reached until differences are eliminated between groups in society in terms of performance (e.g., on public examinations or standardised tests of achievement). Measures to bring about this kind of equality may "require not uniformity of treatment (as when access is the criterion of equality) but additional educational resources in favour of certain groups of children" (Greaney and Kellaghan, 1984: 6). They may also need to include more radical change, according to some commentators. For example, McCormack and Archer (1998a: 24-5) argued that one of the main reasons why children from lower socioeconomic families "under-perform" on public examinations is because "the mainstream curriculum at second level is largely irrelevant to the needs, interests and talents of many disadvantaged students". They advocate changes in the curriculum and assessment that would affect the educational experiences of all students and not just disadvantaged students. Kellaghan, Weir, Ó hUallacháin and Morgan (1995: 64-5) raised similar issues in the course of discussing the need to address "the role that structural problems in the system may be playing in the maintenance, and probably in the creation, of disadvantage". Kellaghan et al. also suggested that measures were needed that went beyond positive discrimination where, by design, the main impact is on the group being targeted. As well as assessment reform, they referred to the need for "system-level action relating to the selection practices of schools and policies of allocating students to classes within schools".

In education policy discourse in Ireland, there has, in recent years, been a move away from definitions of equality based on access and participation towards achievement or outcome. While some programmes to combat disadvantage have focused on participation (e.g., preventing early school leaving), most have sought to go further and raise the achievement of disadvantaged students so that they can derive more benefit from the education system. An earlier draft of what became the Education (1998) Act contained the following object: "to promote equality of access to and participation in education." Following debate in the Oireachtas and elsewhere, the words "and to promote the means whereby students may benefit from education" were added.

6.2.4 Equality in a Wider Context

Several writers have identified limitations in the study of equality based on definitions involving access, participation and achievement. Greaney and Kellaghan (1984), for example, recognised that conventional definitions of equality of educational opportunity presupposed the desirability of a meritocratic society. They went on to cite Young's (1961) satirical work which described an imaginary meritocracy where social stratification was more rigid and less amenable to change. Kellaghan (1985: 112) made a related point when he noted that attempts to assess equality have "neglected forms of achievement other than scholastic ones" (e.g., a person's capacity to "enjoy the culture of his or her society and to participate in its affairs").

Kleinig (1982: 129) is one of many philosophers of education to identify weaknesses in conventional approaches to equality definitions. He noted that "equality of educational opportunity" as it applied to schooling, "abstracts access from, on the one hand, grossly discrepant social conditions, and, on the other, a social order which, statistically, requires the perpetuation of these discrepancies." More recently, researchers at the Equality Studies Centre at University College Dublin (Baker, 1998; Lynch, 1999) have challenged what they describe as "liberal" conceptions of equality (of which access, participation and outcome are central components). These researchers have put forward an alternative perspective which they describe as radical egalitarianism. Baker, for example, argued for more ambitious equality targets. He argued that it is not sufficient to accept "the liberal assumption that major inequalities are inevitable and that our task is simply to make them fair" (Baker, 1998: 31). According to Baker, society must work towards eliminating major inequalities and that "the key to this much more ambitious agenda is to recognise that inequality is rooted in changing and changeable social structures, and particularly in structures of domination and oppression." The structures to which Baker refers include capitalism, patriarchy and racism which combine with other factors to produce a set of unwritten rules by which status, wealth and power are allocated.

The implications of this radical approach to equality are not clear. One view is that tackling inequalities in education is of little use unless there is also a commitment to eliminate more basic inequalities in society (i.e., status, wealth and power). Lynch (1999: 287) argued that "the pursuit of liberal equality policies can be a mere distraction from the business of equality in a more substantive sense". According to Lynch, these policies can result in:

> . . . gain for the relatively advantaged within the marginalised or excluded group who are selected out into more privileged positions. However, the myth of liberalism is that the selection or success of the few will become the pattern for the many (ibid.: 300).

These policies can also result in the phenomenon of "uprooting": the tendency for individuals from disadvantaged communities who acquire qualifications to move to other areas. In these circumstances, the benefits derived from education are lost to the disadvantaged community which is deprived of potential leaders (Lovett, 1988).

Other commentators have also addressed inequalities in education in the context of wider structural inequalities (e.g., Dunne, 1995; McCormack and Archer, 1995; O'Sullivan, 1989). Not all have been as dismissive of policy initiatives within education as Lynch (1999). Dunne (1995: 71), for example, recognised that the present stratification of Irish society was "dysfunctional" and "indefensible" on a "moral-political basis". He suggested that it might be difficult to justify attempts to bring about greater fairness in the methods for assigning people to strata within an unjust stratification. However he conceded:

> Even if one inclines (as I do) to this more radical analysis, one must still acknowledge that it is the present system, deeply entrenched, and pervasive in its effects, that indi-

viduals involved in education — pupils, their parents, and
their teachers — must now contend with. And it is hard to
argue that, individually, they ought to act as if it did not exist
— or that, so long as it does, it is not preferable that an ad-
mittedly limited and compromised ideal of "equity" should
not be pursued (ibid.: 71).

The remainder of this chapter proceeds on the premise that
equality can be pursued within education by raising levels of
educational attainment and achievement of students from
poorer backgrounds. Some limitations and dangers are acknowledged. In particular, it is acknowledged that it may not
be possible to break the link between educational qualifications and social background without addressing the stratified
nature of society. Lynch and O'Riordan (1996: 17) pointed out
that "those who own and control superior resources, in the economic realm in particular, are always in a position to use their
extra resources to circumvent or challenge equality strategies
designed for disadvantaged groups". Some examples will be
mentioned later.

There are also dangers in focusing exclusively on raising
the educational standards of disadvantaged students. It may,
for example, give rise to unrealistic expectations of the contribution which education can, on its own, make to combating
poverty. It may also reinforce false impressions about the nature of poverty by implying that the causes are individual characteristics (the "failure" to benefit from the education offered)
rather than society's structures.

The next section contains a description of inequalities in
education, followed by analyses of the impact of public spending policies on socioeconomic inequalities in participation and
achievement. In the concluding section, radical definitions of
equality will be considered again in the context of a brief revisiting of some of the questions raised above.

6.3 Inequalities in the Current Education System

Before dealing with socioeconomic inequalities of participation
and outcome, we will comment briefly on access and inequalities related to disability, ethnicity and gender.

Considerable progress has been made in removing formal barriers to education through school building programmes and national and EU legislation and directives. However, a number of forms of indirect discrimination are still in place. Lynch (1999: 290), for example, argued that without facilities for blind and deaf students (e.g., a signing interpreter or a Brailling service), in effect, "a rule exists that all people must be able to hear or read print to attend the school or college in question".

Another form of indirect discrimination identified by Lynch is the effect of schools' admissions policies on Travellers. Because they are nomadic, Travellers cannot choose a school before their children are ready to enrol and are prevented from sending their children to a school that operates a waiting list or the principle of "first-come, first-served".

Gender inequalities in education are complex and appear to be changing rapidly and there have been calls for a more critical approach to the definition and treatment of gender inequality (Lewis, 1998; O'Sullivan, 1999). Because several comprehensive reviews exist (e.g., Lewis, 1998; Lynch, 1999), it is sufficient to note a few points. First, the tendency for girls to perform better than boys on almost all subjects in public examinations has grown during the 1990s. Secondly, although fewer examination subjects are gender-specific, girls are still underrepresented in some (e.g., physics and applied mathematics). Thirdly, in international surveys of achievement, differences between genders in performance have been declining in many countries including Ireland. However, one difference remains prominent in Ireland: more boys than girls experience reading difficulties. Fourthly, few gender differences were found in the International Adult Literacy Survey (Morgan et al., 1997). Finally, and perhaps most significantly, early school leaving is much more common among boys than girls. For example, about 65 per cent of young people who leave school without a qualification (i.e., the most vulnerable in the labour market) are male. A similar percentage of those who leave with a Junior Certificate are male.

6.3.1 The Extent of Socioeconomic Inequality

In terms of participation, it is useful to look at two extremes: early school leaving and participation in third level education. Analysis of the annual school leavers' surveys (see, for example, McCoy, Doyle and Williams, 1999) indicates that virtually all of those who leave with no qualifications are from working class or small farm families — 50 per cent where the father is unemployed. Several analyses of early school leaving have appeared recently. These include Combat Poverty Agency (1998); Eivers, Ryan and Brinkley (2000) and Ryan (1999). Young people from poorer backgrounds are also grossly under-represented in third level institutions, especially universities. Clancy and Wall (2000), in their study of third level entrants for the Higher Education Authority, reported participation rates in third level education of approximately 20 per cent for those from lower working class backgrounds compared with over 80 per cent for those from upper middle class backgrounds. The situation in Institutes of Technology appears to be somewhat better than universities but overall the disparities are enormous.

There are also significant differences in benefit derived from a given amount of schooling between social class groupings. Research indicates that differences in achievement are evident early in a child's school career (e.g., Martin, 1979). Large gaps between the achievement of children from poor backgrounds and other children have been observed in the evaluations of programmes for disadvantaged children (e.g., Kellaghan, 1977; Kelly and Kellaghan, 1999; Weir, 1999). Kellaghan (1999: 20) has described these gaps as follows:

> Very early on, difficulties will emerge in learning to read and write. Given this weak start, it is hardly surprising that the achievement gap between children from advantaged and disadvantaged backgrounds tends to widen as children progress through school.

Students from disadvantaged backgrounds do not, on average, perform as well as others in the Junior and Leaving Certificate public examinations (Hannan et al., 1996; Higher Education

Authority, 1995; Smyth, 1999). For example, Hannan et al. (1996) found significant social class differences at both levels. Surprisingly, perhaps, the relationship between social class and Leaving Certificate performance remained significant even after Junior Certificate performance was taken into account. An implication of findings such as these is that spending priorities in relation to inequality need to go well beyond measures to improve access and participation.

6.3.2 The Nature of Socioeconomic Inequality

The relationship between educational participation/achievement and social background is well established. However, a number of questions remain about the nature of that relationship. For example, it may be that it is not linear in that disparities are most pronounced at the extremes of a distribution of participation and achievement in second level schools. There is some basis for this hypothesis in a table in a report of a Technical Working Group on the Future of Higher Education (Higher Education Authority, 1995). This shows disparities between the highest and lowest socioeconomic groups at each of a number of "transition" points (leaving school early, obtaining at least five grade Ds at ordinary level Leaving Certificate, obtaining varying numbers of Grade Cs on higher level etc.). Large disparities are evident at the early school leaving transition point and at the point where students receive large numbers of "honours" (grade C or higher). These data may indicate that the education system has become more successful than it was in retaining young people from poor backgrounds in school and, having retained them, ensuring that many achieve a minimally satisfactory examination performance. However, these data could also help to explain why so few students from poor backgrounds achieve the kind of Leaving Certificate that leads to prestigious and well paid careers, via third level courses where entry is restricted to those who do particularly well under the points system.

Another set of questions relates to identifying reasons for the socioeconomic disparities described above. Some can be regarded as systemic, including the academic focus of curriculum and examinations and selective enrolment and streaming practices.

Financial factors may also contribute to the under-performance of children from poor families. School costs such as books, trips and "voluntary" contributions can be a disincentive to continuing in school. On the basis of interviews with teachers, Lynch and Lodge (1999) reported that whether a school sought a voluntary contribution and, if so, the level of the contribution were significant issues for some parents when deciding about their children's education. The fact that voluntary contributions vary (Association of Secondary Teachers in Ireland, 1996) may also be relevant here. Schools with low levels of contribution are likely to have fewer resources than those with large levels, unless there are compensatory public payments. As a result, the quality of education for poor children may suffer since there will be more of them in schools with a low voluntary contribution.

Another relevant financial factor is access to extra tuition, especially in the run-up to the Leaving Certificate. Recent studies (Gleeson, 1995; Humphries and Jeffers, 1999) indicate that many Leaving Certificate students avail of such tuition. These studies contain evidence of significant differences between socioeconomic groups in terms of their use of extra tuition. Dowling (1991) also found that university students from lower socioeconomic groups were less likely than others to have availed of extra tuition in their preparation for university entrance.

6.3.3 The Consequences of Socioeconomic Inequality

The most obvious consequences of socioeconomic inequalities relate to the labour market. A recent annual school leavers' survey (McCoy, Doyle and Williams, 1999) confirms previous findings on the very different employment experiences of school leavers with varying educational qualifications. Almost 42 per cent without a formal qualification were unemployed one year after leaving school, compared with about 18 per cent of those who left after Junior Certificate and less than 5 per cent of those with a Leaving Certificate. Better qualified leavers also fare better in terms of unemployment duration and earnings.

Poverty is also strongly related to educational qualifications. Using data from a 1994 national survey of adults, Nolan and Whelan (1999) found that about 20 per cent of those with no educational qualifications are in poverty. This declines to 12.5 per cent for those with the equivalent of a Junior Certificate and to just over 6 per cent for those with a Leaving Certificate. Approximately 1 per cent of adults with a third level qualification was in poverty. In a report of an earlier survey conducted in 1987 (Nolan, Callan, Whelan and Williams, 1994), these four percentages were found to be somewhat higher but the same general pattern was observed. A feature of the earlier survey, which appears not to have been replicated, was the description of a group of adults in poverty in terms of their educational qualifications. According to the earlier survey, 75 per cent had no qualifications, 19 per cent had the equivalent of a Junior Certificate, 4 per cent had a Leaving Certificate and the remaining 2 per cent had a third level qualification.

The consequences of the absence of educational qualifications are not confined to the economic sphere but are associated with substance abuse, crime and lone parenthood.

6.4 STANDARD APPROACHES TO THE RELATIONSHIP BETWEEN PUBLIC SPENDING ON EDUCATION AND INEQUALITY

As Hyland (1999: 1) points out, the following quotation from the second Programme for Economic Expansion, published in 1963, encapsulates much of Government thinking behind education policy over several decades.

> Improved and extended educational facilities help to equalise opportunities by enabling an increasing proportion of the community to develop their potentialities and to raise their personal standards of living. Expenditure on education is an investment in the fuller use of the country's primary resource — its people — which can be expected to yield increasing returns in terms of economic progress.

In the 1960s and 1970s, the thinking behind this quotation was clearly seen in measures to increase participation at second and third levels. Most of the investment in these measures was "universalistic" (Kennedy, 1975) or "undifferentiated" in that it involved making resources available to schools to provide additional places and to encourage young people and their families to avail of these places. In a review paper, Sheehan (1982) noted that there were only two types of government expenditure which discriminated directly in favour of "disadvantaged groups". These were means-tested maintenance grants or student aid for third level students and the school transport scheme, limited to students whose home was more than a specified distance from the nearest school. In fact, Sheehan could have mentioned some other schemes (e.g., free books) but his substantive point was basically valid.

The case for undifferentiated investment to boost participation seems to be based on a number of linked propositions, including the following:

- Increased participation in education improves the stock of human capital and, thereby, contributes to economic growth;

- Increased public spending on education results in increased participation;

- Greater participation improves the likelihood that people who might otherwise have difficulties in the labour market will obtain formal educational qualifications and access to jobs.

It is important to acknowledge that none of these propositions is concerned with the economic benefits that accrue to individuals as a result of participation in education, although there is a substantial body of evidence to suggest that these benefits are very significant. A recent study by the Organisation for Economic Cooperation and Development (OECD), based on data from 25 countries, established a clear relationship between length of time in full-time education and performance in the labour market. It is noted (OECD, 1998: 54) that "those with higher levels of education are more likely to participate in the labour market, face lower risks of unemployment, and receive on average higher earnings." On average, individuals with less than upper secondary education were at risk of spending more than twice as much time unemployed as third level graduates. This gap was much larger in a group of countries, including Ireland, which at the time (1995) were experiencing above average unemployment.

In terms of income (earnings), the OECD study also shows large benefits of education to individuals. The size and nature of the relationship between income and education varies across countries, age groups and genders. In Ireland, the differential is somewhat larger than the average for all countries. In almost all countries women are shown to benefit more than men from remaining longer in education in terms of income. Many studies examined the relationship between income and years of schooling rather than highest qualification received as used in the OECD study. Walsh (1998: 11) suggests that these studies reveal an average estimate of "the rate of return to a year's additional schooling" of between 6 and 9 per cent. A recent estimate for Ireland (Callan & Harmon, 1997), at 8 per cent, is within this range.

The three propositions outlined above will now be considered in turn.

6.4.1 Increased Participation in Education and Economic Growth

There is empirical evidence for the long-held belief in a link between the overall level of education of a population and economic growth (Martin, 1998; Walsh, 1996; 1998). However this evidence merely shows a link between two variables. It does not prove the causal connection implied in our first proposition (that increased participation in education leads to economic growth). In fact, the relationship may operate in the opposite direction. A period of growth enables a country to spend more on education and encourages individuals to avail of opportunities to continue in education.

Also relevant in this regard is Murphy (1993: 9), who argued that data from the UK and elsewhere showed that "higher education has been expanded well beyond that threshold, where further expansion could be reasonably regarded as an investment and precondition for national prosperity." Murphy's position was that while investment in education can lead to economic growth, there is a point at which such investment, especially at third level, becomes wasteful. A similar conclusion was reached almost a quarter century earlier in Berg's (1970) book, *Education and Jobs: The Great Training Robbery*.

6.4.2 Increased Investment Leads to Increased Participation

The second proposition is also widely accepted. It is frequently asserted (and even more frequently assumed) that the huge growth in enrolment at second and third levels in Ireland since the 1960s can be attributed to increased government expenditure on education. In fact this is only partly true. Fitzgerald (1998: 37) summed it up as follows: "To a significant extent the policy of investment in education has reflected the changing aspirations of the population at least as much as it has changed those aspirations."

Tussing (1978) attempted to quantify the impact of a series of expensive government measures in the 1960s to increase access to and participation in second level. He examined changes in participation rates in second level schools between 1963 and 1974 and used regression analysis to evaluate the effect of the increased state investment brought about by the introduction of free education and the expansion of school transport in 1967-68. He found there were increases in school enrolments significantly above an existing trend of increasing participation. Tussing argued that the increases (i.e., those in excess of the existing trend) could be attributed to the "free education" measures. He went on to estimate that, by 1974, there were 20,000 post-primary students who were there as a result of the increased investment of resources by the state in the1960s and 1970s.

However, only about a quarter of the overall increase in participation between 1966 and 1974 can be attributed to increased investment. A further 60,000 students enrolled in that period for reasons assumed to be unrelated to the extra state support. Tussing argued the main effect of free education was to create a "windfall" for families whose children would have attended post-primary school anyway. Similar findings were reported by Hyland Associates (undated) in a study of the school transport scheme. In this study 30,000 students were estimated to have enrolled as a result of the transport scheme and other aspects of free education. However 90,000 students were using free transport to post-primary schools at the time.

As can be seen from Table 6.1, participation in non-compulsory schooling since the mid-1970s has continued to grow at least until 1995-96. At the same time spending also continued to grow. As Fitzgerald (1998: 35) pointed out: "Even in the 1980s, when many other sectors suffered severe cut-backs, the education system received privileged treatment". It is not possible to draw any conclusions about the extent to which the participation increases from 1975 onwards are the result of increased spending because the kind of analysis done by Tussing and Hyland has not been repeated. However, it is likely that other factors were more important than state spending in the decisions of growing numbers to remain in school. The shortage of jobs for school leavers in the late 1970s and throughout the 1980s was probably a critical factor.

Table 6.1: Estimated Percentage of Persons Receiving Full-time Education by Age for School Years 1964-65, 1974-75, 1984-85 and 1994-95 to 1997-98

Year	Age					
	14	15	16	17	18	19
1964-65	65.7	51.4	37.7	24.8	8.0	2.4
1974-75	97.9	82.4	66.6	45.2	25.3	13.9
1984-85	99.4	94.4	80.3	63.3	39.7	23.6
1994-95	100	95.7	91.1	81.9	63.6	47.5
1995-96	99.8	96.1	89.8	78.3	60.6	44.5
1996-97	100	96.2	91.8	80.6	63.0	47.7
1997-98	99.8	97.2	91.3	81.3	61.4	48.4

Source: Department of Education Annual Statistical Reports for the years mentioned.

6.4.3 The Impact of Increased Participation on Inequality

The third proposition outlined earlier was that "greater participation improves the likelihood that people who might otherwise have difficulties in the labour market will obtain formal
educational qualifications and access to jobs". The linkages
between socioeconomic background, educational performance
and performance in the labour market have been demonstrated
already. If our third proposition is valid, then it ought to be possible to show that current levels of inequality are less than they
were before the growth in participation in education.

Investment in Education (1965) revealed a number of inequalities and deficiencies in the education system. For example, based on the 1961 census of population, it showed that 15
to 19-year-olds with parents in higher socioeconomic groups
were four to five times more likely to participate in post-
primary education than those whose parents were unskilled
manual workers. The disparity in third level participation was
"as great as 40 to 1" according to a recent revisiting of the
original report by one of its authors (Lynch, 1998: 5).

The issue for this chapter is whether the dramatic expansion
that has occurred since *Investment in Education* has reduced inequalities and, if so, to what extent? This has received a good
deal of attention, especially in the past 15 years (e.g., Conference of Major Religious Superiors, 1988; Greaney and Kellaghan, 1984, 1985; McCormack and Archer, 1998b; Raftery and
Hout,1985; Smyth, 1999; Whelan and Hannan,1999). Findings
are mixed with regard to whether inequality reductions have
occurred or not. Some indicate that the scale of the disparities
revealed by *Investment in Education* has been reduced. For example, the findings of Clancy and Wall (2000) on differential
rates of third level enrolment suggest that, while lower socioeconomic groups are still grossly under-represented, the disparities are much less than they were in 1961. It should be
noted, however, that Clancy and Wall's procedures are different from those reported in *Investment in Education*.

In addition, Whelan and Hannan (1999) found no significant
reduction in disparities in third level entry between three
groups of adults in a 1994 national survey. The three groups

were those born between 1930 and 1939, between 1940 and 1954 and between 1955 and 1969. One might expect lower disparities in the last group since they were young enough to benefit from the increased investment from the 1960s and were presumably part of the participation growth. Whether improvement has occurred since 1980 is also unclear. Clancy's (1995) surveys of third level entrants suggest a reduction in inequalities between 1980 and 1992. However, Smyth (1999: 282) concluded, on the basis of data from the Annual School Leavers' Surveys from 1979 to 1994, that "the effects of social class background on third level participation do not appear to have changed substantially over the period".

In their study, Whelan and Hannan (1999: 303) found no evidence for "the existence of any trend towards equality of educational opportunity although the period covered was associated with a substantial expansion in participation rates". The authors argued that their findings are consistent with research from other countries which shows that expansion per se, except when it takes place in the context of the saturation of demand from privileged groups, does not lead to a reduction in inequalities (Raftery and Hout, 1993). McCormack and Archer (1998b: 24) suggested that, in Ireland, "saturation of demand" has effectively occurred in relation to primary schooling and junior cycle at second level and that the percentage of upper and middle class young people who "take the Leaving Certificate is now in excess of 90 per cent. As a result further increases in Senior Cycle completion rates would relatively quickly bring about saturation."

An examination of changes in levels of inequality needs to take account of other changes that may have taken place in the labour market and in society more generally. For example, in 1980 there was very little difference in terms of getting a job between an Intermediate (Junior) Certificate and a Leaving Certificate. Recent school leavers' surveys indicate that someone with a Leaving Certificate is now twice as likely to get a job as someone with a Junior Certificate. Since 1980, the chances of getting a job with no qualifications have gone from half that of someone with a Leaving Certificate to less than a quarter. These kinds of rises in the level of education required to access employment may have counterbalanced any positive effects of increased participation in terms of equality. There is, as yet, no evidence about the impact of recent improvements in the labour market on the perceived and actual value of educational qualifications.

So far in this chapter three propositions have been examined. While there is some support in the literature for each of the three propositions, it is clear that, in each case, several other factors need to be considered. On this basis, a policy that relied on undifferentiated increased investment in education is unlikely to have a major impact on inequality. Therefore, there seems to be a need for a more differentiated approach to public expenditure. In particular, if poverty and removing inequality are priority issues, spending needs to be targeted at those who benefit least from the present system. The next section analyses attempts to implement a policy of targeting.

6.5 TRENDS IN PUBLIC SPENDING IN THE 1990s

Two types of targeting will be considered. The first derives from the social class disparities in participation in non-compulsory education described earlier. As long as such disparities exist, state educational spending is inherently regressive. A report by the National Economic and Social Forum (NESF, 1997: 56) illustrated this regressivity:

> . . . using per capita costs for different levels of education, the £11,400 spent by the education system on a child who leaves after primary school and the £15,850 incurred on behalf of a child who leaves after two years of secondary school is in sharp contrast to the £37,525 spent by the State on behalf of a student who completes a four year programme at third level.

These differences in expenditure reflect not only differences in the duration in full-time education, but the fact that per capita costs rise significantly from first to second to third level. The case for targeting resources to the primary sector is reinforced by the belief that early intervention to *prevent* problems developing is preferable to later intervention to *solve* problems.

A second kind of targeting relates to the allocation of resources *within* sectors. As we have seen, simply improving access to schooling for disadvantaged students does not necessarily result in greater equality, even if more do participate. If students from disadvantaged backgrounds are to achieve at average levels, it is not sufficient that they receive the same treatment as every other student; instead there is a case for *positive discrimination*.

Since the 1980s governments have committed themselves to the two types of targeting discussed above. In 1984 the government launched a Programme for Action in Education which included the following: ". . . the funding of National Schools will be a major priority of the Minister and Government in the allocation of the resources available for education. In addition, special funding should be directed to disadvantaged areas (p. 14)." Similar statements appear in various government policy documents and national agreements since then.

6.5.1 Targeting across Sectors

Government spending on the three main sectors of education for 1999 is estimated in the following table.

Table 6.2: Government Expenditure (Capital and Current) on Education in 1999 (IR£)

	Primary Level	Second Level	Third Level	Office of the Minister	Total
Total	861m	1015m	658m	196m	2,730m
Per Capita	1,900	2,900	4,000		

It is clear from the per capita figures that public spending is still regressive. Expenditure on a third level student is over two and a half times the expenditure on a primary student and almost 70 per cent higher than a second level student. The OECD report, *Education at a Glance* (OECD, 2000), shows that a similar spending pattern exists in many education systems. However, the report also shows that there is a good deal of variation between systems in how they allocate resources across the sectors. It is of some interest, therefore, to compare the allocations in Ireland with those in other countries. OECD (2000) contains a number of such comparisons for 1997 data which suggest that, in comparison with other OECD countries, primary education in Ireland has a relatively low priority. For example, in one analysis per student expenditure at second and third levels relative to expenditure per primary student was examined. Second level expenditure per student was, on average across countries, 1.4 times higher than at primary level while third level expenditure was 2.4 times higher than primary expenditure. The figure for second level expenditure in Ireland was close to the OECD average of 1.4 but that for third level in Ireland was over 3.0 and was the second highest of the countries in the analysis (only Mexico, with a figure of 5.0, has a substantially higher differential).

It is important to place Ireland's pattern of expenditure on education relative to patterns in other countries in the context of some other international comparisons. For example, the age profile of the youth population in Ireland is more like that of under-developed countries than other OECD members. In 1998, 16 per cent of the Irish population was aged 5 to 14 years old and 9 per cent was aged 15 to 19, compared to OECD means of 13 per cent and 7 per cent respectively. The size of the school-going cohort is, of course, an important determinant of spending. The fact that, in Ireland, this group, although falling in size, is still relatively large impacts on a number of indicators of public spending. For example, it helps to explain why, on indicators related to overall expenditure, Ireland is placed close to the OECD average, even though on indicators related to per capita expenditure, Ireland tends to be below average.

In the context of making inferences about policy priorities from expenditure figures, it is necessary to consider the possibility of a relationship between a country's expenditure pattern and its relative wealth (e.g., its gross domestic product or GDP). It is possible, for example, that less developed countries tend to direct disproportionate amounts of their educational spending to third level, perhaps in the belief that this will speed up the process of economic development. Table 6.3 contains information relevant to the issue of the relationship between patterns of expenditure and a country's wealth as measured by its GDP.

Table 6.3: Expenditure per Student as a Percentage of GDP per Capita

	Primary Level	Second Level	Third Level
Ireland	12	19	39
OECD mean	19	26	45
Ireland's rank	Last of 23	Last of 22	16th of 24

Source: OECD (2000)

Table 6.3 confirms the relatively low priority assigned to spending on primary education. Thus, while Irish expenditure per student relative to GDP per capita on third level education is close to the OECD mean and 16th of 24 countries, its per capita expenditure on primary and secondary education relative to GDP is the lowest of all the 14 countries in the analysis.

These international comparisons do not reflect the prioritisation of primary education expressed in official policy documents in the context of goals and objectives related to tackling inequality and disadvantage. However, it would be unfair to base conclusions about the prioritisation of primary education on international comparisons without examining spending patterns in Ireland over time as well as between countries. Table 6.4 attempts this examination. The first three rows of Table 6.4 are from an information leaflet, *Key Education Statistics 1987/88-1997/98,* issued by the Department of Education and Science (undated). The fourth row contains the ratio of third level per student expenditure to primary per student expenditure.

Table 6.4: Per Student Expenditure 1990 to 1998 (IR£, 1998 prices)

	1990	1991	1992	1993	1994	1995	1996	1997	1998
Primary	1072	1136	1260	1350	1438	1477	1552	1690	1786
2nd Level	1811	1892	1963	2136	2254	2290	2376	2604	2645
3rd Level	4130	3887	3898	3932	3947	3905	4209	4749	4016
Ratio of 3rd to Primary	3.9:1	3.4:1	3.1:1	2.9:1	2.7:1	2.6:1	2.7:1	2.8:1	2.2:1

It is clear that there have been important shifts in spending patterns during the 1990s. In particular, third level per student expenditure declined (by almost 3 per cent), while per student expenditure increased substantially at the other two levels (by about 67 per cent in the case of primary education and 46 per cent in the case of second level education). The ratios in Table 6.4 reveal the scale of the shifts. In 1998, the cost to the state of a third level student was 2¼ times that of a primary school student. However, in 1990, a third level student was almost 4 times more expensive. The shifts have largely been part of a consistent and sustained trend. Per student expenditure at third level increased by almost 8 per cent in 1996 and almost 13 per cent in 1997 but then fell by almost 15 per cent in 1998 to IR£4,016, which is only IR£111 more than the 1995 figure. Otherwise there is little variation from year to year over the 1990s. In contrast, per student expenditure on primary education increased every year by between 3 and 11 per cent.

Before the data in Table 6.4 can be interpreted as evidence of a deliberate attempt to redress previous inequities in funding and thereby honour commitments to prioritise primary education, there are a number of other factors to consider. During the 1990s, enrolment in primary schools fell by 17 per cent (from 552,182 in 1989-90 to 460,845 in 1997-98). Over the same period, enrolment in third level colleges increased by 134 per cent (from 64,137 to 104,439). The fall in primary school enrolment was due almost entirely to the fact that recorded births peaked in 1980 and then declined sharply every year until very recently. The increase in third level enrolment can be attributed to: (a) the fact the relevant age cohorts were increasing in size (for almost all of the period, third level entrants would have been born before the 1980 peak in births); and (b) the fact that the percentage of school leavers going on to third level more than doubled.

Not surprisingly, changes in total expenditure over the 1990s reveal a very different picture to that in Table 6.4 which dealt with per capita expenditure. Between 1990 and 1998, expenditure increased by 71 per cent at first level, 88 per cent at second level and 134 per cent at third level. The trends in total expenditure are difficult to reconcile with a policy of prioritising primary education unless one takes account of the concurrent enrolment changes.

To conclude, there is evidence of a deliberate effort during the 1990s to shift resources towards primary education. At the same time, however, there were pressures to increase spending in the other sectors, most notably to create large numbers of new third level places in response to rapidly growing demand. The system seems to have responded by making a number of choices: to protect primary spending from the effects of falling enrolments, thereby increasing unit (per capita) costs and to achieve economies of scale in relation to third level spending.

6.5.2 Targeting within Sectors

Here, a second type of targeting which involved allocating additional resources to those students, schools, families and communities believed to be in greatest need (i.e., a form of positive discrimination) will be examined. It may be useful to first make some general observations about how some of the extra money available to education was spent during the 1990s.

In 1998 public expenditure on primary education was IR£361.5 million more than it was in 1990. Almost 80 per cent of the extra money was spent on teachers' salaries and superannuation. This resulted in the recruitment of 670 extra teachers (an increase of 3.3 per cent) and improved pay rates. While the number of extra teachers may seem modest, the fact that student numbers were declining allowed significant progress to be made in reducing the student-teacher ratio (i.e., the ratio of students to teachers in the system as a whole). This ratio, which was 27.2 in 1989-90 fell by between 0.4 and 0.8 every year to 21.8 in 1997-98. The extent of the change emerges when figures for 1989-90 and 1997-98 are compared. Between 1989-90 and 1997-98 average class size fell from 30.8 to 26.1. More significantly, classes of more than 40 students fell from 3.4 per cent of the total to less than a fifth of 1 per cent, while classes with *less* than 30 students almost doubled from 37 per cent to 69 per cent.

Second level expenditure in 1998 was IR£480.5 million more than it was in 1990. Over 72 per cent of this figure was spent on teachers' salaries and superannuation, with an extra 2,318 teachers employed. However, because second level enrolments increased between 1990 and 1998, there was little change in the student-teacher ratio. It was 17.5 in 1998 compared to 18.1 in 1990.

Targeting of educational spending was relatively rare until the 1980s. In 1984 the government began to designate some schools as "disadvantaged" on the basis of the number of students from poor families as assessed by indicators such as unemployment and possession of a medical card. Additional resources were allocated to these schools, initially to use as they saw fit. In later years there were more focused interventions. These included the Home–School–Community Liaison scheme, additional staff to reduce the student-teacher ratio, Early Start, Breaking the Cycle, appointment of teacher-counsellors and, more recently, the 8 to 15-Year-Old and Stay in School initiatives to discourage early school leaving and the new programme announced in January 2001 ("Giving Children an Even Break by Tackling Disadvantage"). There was also an attempt to discriminate positively in favour of designated schools in terms of resources that all schools are entitled to avail of, or at least apply for (e.g., capitation grants, remedial teaching and the psychological service).

Designation of schools has been a central part of government policy to combat disadvantage since 1984 along with some other elements. These include curriculum innovations, especially at second level to cater for the needs of much wider abilities and interests among students and schemes to target individuals rather than schools (free books, school meals and the Back to School Clothing and Footwear Scheme). At third level there is support for students from low income families and some public funds are available to increase participation rates in third level by young people from disadvantaged backgrounds. Finally, outside the formal school system, the Department of Education and Science provides various second chance initiatives for early school leavers (e.g., Youthreach and VTOS, the Vocational Training Opportunities Scheme) and for other adults who did not benefit from their schooling (e.g., the Adult

Literacy and Community Education Scheme). Murphy (2000) provides a description of many of these initiatives.

Ideally, one would wish to examine the overall costs of strategies to tackle disadvantage and relate these to other aspects of public spending on education. It would be interesting, for example, to calculate the proportion of total education expenditure that is targeted and examine whether this proportion has changed over time. Unfortunately, the available data do not permit this kind of exercise. The European Social Fund (ESF) Programme Evaluation Unit (1997) was able to estimate the annual costs of a number of specific schemes to tackle disadvantage at IR£43 million or about 2 per cent of total educational spending. The schemes included were: Early Start, Home–School–Community Liaison, teacher counsellor posts, concessionary teaching posts, extra capitation grants and the book grant and rental schemes. In addition, 60 per cent of the cost of providing remedial teaching was included in the estimate. The ESF Evaluation Unit acknowledged that it was not possible to quantify changes in the amounts of money targeted. However it did note that "the development of new initiatives and expansion of older programmes" indicate that targeted expenditure "has been rising steadily since the early 1990s" (p. 71).

Since these estimates were made a number of significant new initiatives have been introduced. Breaking the Cycle, which precisely targets resources on the most seriously disadvantaged schools, has been operating since 1996-97. More recently two schemes to prevent early school leaving (the 8 to 15 Year Old and the Stay in School initiatives) were introduced. Finally, in January 2001, the Minister for Education and Science announced a new initiative entitled "Giving Children an Even Break by Tackling Disadvantage" (Department of Education and Science, 2001). Like previous initiatives, schools with the heaviest concentrations of disadvantage are targeted through an increased staff allocation. In addition, however, schools are being provided with finance to allow them to provide supports to disadvantaged children in all schools, irrespective of the number of other disadvantaged children in these schools. This will be done using a "sliding scale" based on an estimate of the number and percentage of disadvantaged children in each school.

It is not possible to determine what proportion of the extra resources available during the 1990s was allocated to disadvantaged schools. Some evidence does exist, however, on whether the policy of targeting succeeded in bringing about a situation in which designated schools are better off than other schools in terms of various kinds of resources (i.e., ensuring "positive discrimination" in favour of designated schools).

A report by Kellaghan, Weir, O hUallachain and Morgan (1995: 17) showed that, at least up to 1993, the effect of the schemes had not, in fact, been positive discrimination. Rather it seems that the effect was simply to close the gap in terms of income and resources between schools in disadvantaged areas and other schools. Thus, Kellaghan et al. report that:

> In analyses of the findings of a National Reading Survey that was carried out in 1993, class sizes were virtually identical in designated and non-designated schools and little difference was found in the number of books available per pupil in the two kinds of school. No major difference emerged either between designated and non-designated schools in relation to having a professional library for teachers, access to a photocopier, or availability of computers for pupil use. However, while remedial services were found to be available in just over two-thirds of non-designated schools, over 96 per cent of designated schools had such services.

It is not possible to say whether measures introduced since 1993 have made a difference to the relative positions of designated and non-designated schools.

Attention has also been drawn to inconsistencies in government efforts to implement positive discrimination in schools' capitation grants (e.g., McCormack and Archer, 1995). In 1992, the capitation grant for disadvantaged primary schools was IR£45 compared to IR£28 for other primary schools (i.e., a premium of 61 per cent). By 1994, the value of the premium on disadvantaged schools had fallen to 45 per cent when the grants were IR£55 and IR£38. The 1995 and 1996 budgets reversed the erosion, bringing the grants to IR£75 and IR£45 (i.e., a premium of 67 per cent). However since 1997, there appears to have been a policy of maintaining the absolute difference between the two grants at IR£30. This means that the value of the premium has again fallen. The grants for 2000 were IR£94 and IR£64, a premium of just 47 per cent. It should be noted that these comparisons of capitation grants to disadvantaged and other schools take no account of the recent initiative ("Giving Children an Even Break") which involves financial allocations to schools based on the number of disadvantaged children in the schools.

One aspect of public expenditure on third level education, over the 1990s, arguably runs counter to the principle of targeting. In 1990, IR£60.9 million, out of a total of IR£292.3 million, was allocated to "student support" (20.8 per cent). Student support is made up, almost entirely, of means-tested grants and scholarships and is, therefore, targeted to students from low income families. Between 1990 and 1994, the percentage of the total spent on third level education allocated to student support rose to almost 25 per cent but since 1994 it has fallen. In 1999, 15.1 per cent of the total went to student support and estimates for 2000 indicate a further fall to 12.3 per cent. The main reason for this decline was the abolition of tuition fees. This decision necessitated an increase in the allocation to third level institutions and resulted in a reduction in the amount allocated to the means-tested schemes.

6.6 SUMMARY AND CONCLUSION

This chapter has demonstrated the role that education plays in maintaining inequalities in society and how it transmits poverty from one generation to the next. Young people who leave education with little or no qualifications come mainly from poor families and are likely to remain poor as adults. This cycle of poverty occurs because society is highly stratified, largely on the basis of occupational status, with large disparities in income and prestige.

The particular focus of the chapter is on public spending on education rather than the education system as a whole. Its main purpose was to examine the extent to which such spending contributes to inequality and the extent to which it can counteract inequality. Therefore, it has only dealt in a superficial way

with some very significant issues about the relationship between education and the wider economy and society.

Public spending on education contributes to inequality because it is regressive in the sense that the state spends much
more on the education of better off young people (who tend to
remain in the system) than it does on young people from poorer
families (who tend to leave the system early). Another factor
which contributes to inequality is that such spending must be
supplemented by local voluntary contributions. Relying on local contributions fails to take account of the reality that there is
little scope for voluntary fund raising in disadvantaged areas as
well as variations, between areas, in terms of running costs due
to vandalism, higher insurance etc.

With regard to the potential of public spending to counteract inequality, two broad approaches were considered. The
first approach, described as universalistic or undifferentiated,
is partly based on three propositions, the evidence for which
was found to be at best mixed.

First, while there is a clear link between investment in education and economic growth, it is not always possible to distinguish cause and effect. There may also be a point of diminish-
ing returns for state investment beyond investment in basic
levels of education.

Secondly, while increased participation in education can be
stimulated by government making extra money available (e.g.,
by abolishing fees), it seems that other factors are more important when individuals decide whether to stay in school or
not. In addition, it appears that the main beneficiaries of this
kind of increased spending are families who would otherwise
have paid for their children's education.

Thirdly, increased participation in education seems to impact on the scale of inequality only in the context of saturation
of demand from more advantaged groups (i.e., when the participation rate of the more advantaged groups approaches 100
per cent).

The second approach to public spending considered involves a move away from universalism towards targeting resources to schools and students where need is greatest. There
has been growing awareness of the need for a more targeted

approach to expenditure decisions, reflected in policy statements which promised to prioritise primary education (targeting across sectors) and to discriminate positively in favour of educationally disadvantaged students (targeting within sectors). It is too soon to assess the impact of the new approach on levels of inequality but some questions arise about how fully this approach has actually been implemented.

Figures published by the OECD (2000) show that, compared to other countries, Ireland allocates relatively few resources to primary education. When account is taken of the large decline in primary enrolment and the large increase in third level participation during the 1990s, it is clear that some progress was made in shifting resources towards primary education.

In addition, although significant expansion of special measures to tackle disadvantage has occurred, it is not clear how much of the extra resources available during the 1990s have been targeted. It is likely that a significant proportion of the additional resources has been spread evenly across the system.

At least until 1993, the various primary level schemes to combat educational disadvantage had not resulted in genuine positive discrimination for schools designated as disadvantaged. However, these schemes did succeed in bringing the income and resources of schools in disadvantaged areas up to the level of those in other areas.

There is a need for more research and evaluation on the two types of targeting with which much of this chapter has been concerned. However, the case for continuing to pursue a policy of targeting to tackle inequality would seem to be justified. There is, in fact, some basis for believing that both types of targeting will become easier to achieve and more likely to have an impact. Demographic changes could relieve the pressure to increase investment in third level education and sustained economic growth would enable the shift of resources to primary education to continue. At the same time the additional resources being allocated to special schemes to tackle disadvantage in the future have the potential to bring about genuine positive discrimination. Another development that may facilitate the targeting of resources to disadvantaged schools is a series of decisions to reduce the reliance of schools on local fund raising. The Department of Education and Science is now willing to pay for a larger proportion of schools' capital costs and has frozen the contribution that it expects local communities to make to schools' running costs.

While the continued commitment to targeting is important, there are limitations to this approach. One such limitation arises from a realisation of the extent to which advantaged groups in society can deploy superior resources to maintain their advantage. Thus, better off families may respond to targeting by increasing what they spend on their children's education, either directly (e.g., through extra tuition for these children) or indirectly (e.g., through contributions to schools to help them improve their facilities). This may point to the need for more radical changes in the funding of education. In particular, there may be a value, from an equality perspective, in revisiting the issue of fees for third level education.

Another limitation of the policy of targeting is that it can hope to address only a small part of inequality. This is true in two senses. In the first place, some of the reasons for inequality are systemic and include aspects of curriculum, assessment and procedures such as selection and streaming. Tackling these aspects of the education system has some cost implications. It needs increased investment in research and development and in-career development for teachers. However, these costs could never represent more than a tiny fraction of the overall education budget. Therefore, the most important implications of promoting systemic change are not financial; they relate to changes in attitudes and in established practices and structures.

Perhaps, the most fundamental limitation is one described in the earlier section on "The Meaning of Equality" where it was acknowledged that any action to address inequality in education must be seen in the context of efforts to address structural inequality in the wider society. Educators have a role in dealing with the wider inequality in society that goes beyond designing strategies to maximise the benefit disadvantaged children derive from their schooling. They can try to ensure that public expectations about what can be achieved by educational measures to tackle inequality are realistic. Thus, they have a responsibility to point out unrealistic goals set by government strategy or a National Partnership Agreement. Ideally this should go beyond simply calling for educational strategies to be integrated with other social policy measures (taxation, housing etc.). It should explain why such policy integration is necessary and it should identify measures in other areas of social policy that are necessary from an educational perspective.

The creation of a more equal society can be advanced by more analysis and debate about the purposes of education, the relationship between education and the wider society and the implications of the fact that educational credentials are so important in the labour market and elsewhere. Multidisciplinary initiatives such as the present volume will hopefully make a valuable contribution to this analysis and debate.

References

Association of Secondary Teachers in Ireland (1996), *Staffing, Funding and Facilities in Irish Second-level Schools,* Dublin, ASTI

Bailey, Inez and Ursula Coleman (1998), *Access and Participation in Adult Literacy Schemes,* Dublin, Aontas

Baker, John (1998), "Equality", in Healy, Sean and Brigid Reynolds (eds), *Social Policy in Ireland: Principles, Practice and Problems,* Dublin, Oak Tree Press

Berg, Ivar (1970*), Education and Jobs: The Great Training Robbery,* Middlesex, Penguin

Callan, Tim and Colm Harmon (1997), *The Economic Return to Schooling in Ireland,* Centre for Economic Research, Working Paper (WP97/23), University College Dublin

Clancy, Patrick (1995), *Access to College: Patterns of Continuity and Change,* Dublin, Higher Education Authority

Clancy, Patrick and Joy Wall (2000), *Social Background of Higher Education Entrants,* Dublin, Higher Education Authority

Conference of Major Religious Superiors (1988), *Inequality in Schooling in Ireland,* Dublin, CMRS Education Commission

Conference of Major Religious Superiors (1992), *Education and Poverty: Eliminating Disadvantage in the Primary School Years,* Dublin, CMRS Education Commission

Combat Poverty Agency (1995), Foreword, in Kellaghan, Thomas, Susan Weir, Seamus Ó hUallacháin, and Mark Morgan, *Educational Disadvantage in Ireland,* Dublin, Combat Poverty Agency/Department of Education/Educational Research Centre

Combat Poverty Agency (1998), *Educational Disadvantage and Early School Leaving,* Dublin

Department of Education (1966), *Tuarascáil Statistiúil: Statistical Report for 1964-65,* Dublin, Stationery Office

Department of Education (1977), *Tuarascáil Statistiúil: Statistical Report for 1974-75, and 1975-76,* Dublin, Stationery Office

Department of Education (1984), *Programme for Action in Education,* Dublin, Stationery Office

Department of Education (1986), *Tuarascáil Statistiúil: Statistical Report for 1984-85,* Dublin, Stationery Office

Department of Education (1996), *Tuarascáil Statistiúil: Statistical Report for 1994-95,* Dublin, Stationery Office

Department of Education (1997), *Tuarascáil Statistiúil: Statistical Report for 1995-96,* Dublin, Stationery Office

Department of Education and Science (1991), *Tuarascáil Statistiúil: Statistical Report for 1989-90,* Dublin, Stationery Office

Department of Education and Science (1997), *Tuarascáil Statistiúil: Statistical Report for 1996-97,* Dublin, Stationery Office

Department of Education and Science (1999), *Tuarascáil Statistiúil: Statistical Report for 1997-98,* Dublin, Stationery Office

Department of Education and Science (2001), *Giving Children an Even Break by Tackling Disadvantage,* Dublin, Stationery Office

Department of Education and Science (undated), *Key Education Statistics 1987-88 to 1997-98,* Dublin, Stationery Office

Dowling, Teresa (1991), "Inequalities in Preparation for University Entrance: An Examination of the Educational Histories of Entrants to UCC", *Irish Journal of Sociology, 1,* pp. 18-30

Dunne, Joseph (1995), "What's the Good of Education", in Hogan, Padraig (ed.), *Partnership and the Benefits of Education,* Maynooth, Educational Studies Association of Ireland

Eivers, Eemer, Eoin Ryan and Aoife Brinkley (2000), *Characteristics of Early School Leavers: Results of the Research Strand of the 8 to 15-Year-Old Early School Leaving Initiative,* Report to the Department of Education and Science, Dublin, Educational Research Centre

European Social Fund Programme Evaluation Unit (1997), *Preliminary Evaluation: Preventive Actions in Education,* Dublin, Department of Enterprise and Employment

Fitzgerald, John (1998), "The Way We Are: Education and the Celtic Tiger", *Issues in Education,* 3, pp. 35-44

Greaney, Vincent and Thomas Kellaghan (1984), *Equality of Opportunity in Irish Schools,* Dublin, Educational Company of Ireland

Greaney, Vincent and Thomas Kellaghan (1985), "Factors Related to Level of Educational Attainment in Ireland", *Economic and Social Review,* 16, pp. 141-156

Gleeson, Jim (1995), "Preparing for the Leaving", University of Limerick, unpublished paper

Hannan, Damian F., Emer Smyth, John McCullagh, Richard O'Leary and Dorren McMahon, (1996), *Coeducation and Gender Equality: Examination Performance, Stress and Personal Development,* Dublin, Oak Tree Press

Higher Education Authority (1995), *Interim Report of the Technical Working Group of the Steering Committee on the Future Development of Higher Education,* Dublin, Higher Education Authority

Humphries, Eilis and Gerry Jeffers (1999), *Pointing to the Future: Some Second-level Students' Perceptions of the Points System,* report on behalf of Transition Year Support Team to the Commission on the Points System, Dublin, Stationery Office

Hyland Associates (undated), *Consultants' Report on the School Transport Scheme,* Dublin, Department of Education

Hyland, Aine (1998), "The Economic Return on Education", paper presented to a seminar organised by the Statistical and Social Inquiry Society of Ireland, 19 February

Investment in Education (1965), *Report of the Survey Team Appointed by the Minister of Education* in October 1962, Dublin, Stationery Office

Kellaghan, Thomas (1977), *The Evaluation of an Intervention Programme for Disadvantaged Children,* Windsor, NFER Publishing

Kellaghan, Thomas (1985), "The Child and the School" in Greaney, Vincent (ed.), *Children: Needs and Rights,* New York, Irvington

Kellaghan, Thomas (1999), "Educational Disadvantage: An Analysis", paper presented at Inspectors' Conference, Killarney, December

Kellaghan, Thomas, Susan Weir, Seamus Ó hUallacháin and Mark Morgan, (1995), *Educational Disadvantage in Ireland,* Dublin, Combat Poverty Agency/Department of Education/Educational Research Centre

Kelly, Donal and Thomas Kellaghan (1999), *The Literacy and Numeracy Achievements of the First Cohort of Early Start children (1994-95) When They Were in Second Class (1998-99)*, Dublin, Educational Research Centre

Kennedy, Finola (1975), *Public Social Expenditure in Ireland,* Broadsheet No. 11, Dublin, Economic and Social Research Centre

Kleinig, John (1982), *Philosophical Issues in Education,* London, Routledge

Lewis, Mary (1998), "Gender Inequality in Ireland 1980-1997: An Educational Perspective", *Administration,* 46, pp. 3-18

Lovett, Tom (1998), "Community Education and Community Action", in Tom Lovett (ed.), *Radical Approaches to Adult Education: A Reader,* London, Routledge

Lynch, Kathleen (1999), *Equality in Education,* Dublin, Gill and Macmillan

Lynch, Kathleen and Anne Lodge (1999), "Essays on Schools", Chapter 8, in Kathleen Lynch, *Equality in Education* Dublin, Gill and Macmillan

Lynch, Kathleen and Clare O'Riordan (1996), *Social Class, Inequality and Higher Education,* Dublin, Equality Studies Centre, University College Dublin

Lynch, Patrick (1998), "Societal Change and Education: Investment in Education Revisited", *Issues in Education,* 3, pp. 3-7

McCormack, Teresa and Peter Archer (1995), "Christianity, Social Justice and Education", *Studies in Education,* 11, pp. 23-36

McCormack, Teresa and Peter Archer (1998a), "Inequality in Education: The Role of Assessment and Certification" in CORI, *Inequality in Education: The Role of Assessment and Certification,* Dublin, Education Commission of the Conference of Religious of Ireland

McCormack, Teresa and Peter Archer (1998b), "A Response to Patrick Lynch's Revisiting of Investment in Education", *Issues in Education,* 3, pp. 17-33

McCoy, Selena, Audrey Doyle and James Williams (1999), *1998 Annual School Leavers' Survey,* Dublin, Economic and Social Research Institute/Department of Enterprise, Trade and Employment/Department of Education and Science.

Martin, John P. (1998), "Education and Economic Performance in the OECD Countries: An Elusive Relationship?", paper presented to a seminar organised by the Statistical and Social Inquiry Society of Ireland, 19 February 1998

Martin, Michael O. (1979), "Reading and Socio-economic Background: A Progressive Achievement Gap?" *Irish Journal of Education,* 13, pp. 62-78

Morgan, Mark, Brendan Hickey and Thomas Kellaghan, with Anne Cronin and David Millar (1997), *Report to the Minister for Education on the International Literacy Survey: Results for Ireland,* Dublin, Stationery Office

Murphy, Brian (2000), *Support for the Educationally and Socially Disadvantaged: An Introductory Guide to Government-funded Initiatives in Ireland*, Education Department, University College, Cork

Murphy, James (1993), "A Degree of Waste: The Economic Benefits of Educational Expansion", *Oxford Review of Education*, 19, pp. 9-31

National Economic and Social Forum (1997), *Early School Leaving and Youth Unemployment*, Forum report no. 11, Dublin

Nolan, Brian, Tim Callan, Christopher T. Whelan and James Williams (1994), *Poverty and Time: Perspectives on the Dynamics of Poverty* Paper no. 166, Dublin, Economic and Social Research Institute

Nolan, Brian and Christopher T. Whelan (1999), *Loading the Dice? A Study of Cumulative Disadvantage,* Dublin, Oak Tree Press

OECD (1998), *Human Capital Investment: An International Comparison,* Paris

OECD (2000), *Education at a Glance: OECD Indicators,* Paris

O'Sullivan, Denis (1989), "The Ideational Base of Irish Educational Policy" in Mulcahy, Donal G. and Denis O'Sullivan (eds.), *Irish Educational Policy: Process and Substance,* Dublin, Institute of Public Administration

O'Sullivan, Denis (1999), "Gender Equity as Policy Paradigm in the Irish Educational Policy Process", *Economic and Social Review,* 30, pp. 309-36

Raftery, Adrian and Michael Hout (1985), "Does Irish Education Approach the Meritocratic Ideal? A Logistic Analysis", *Economic and Social Review,* 16, pp. 115-40

Raftery, Adrian E. and Michael Hout (1993), "Maximally Maintained Inequality: Expansion, Reform and Opportunity in Irish Education 1921-75", *Sociology of Education,* 66, pp. 41-62

Ronayne, Tom (1999), "Reaching the Socially Excluded", paper at the tenth annual conference of VTOS coordinators, Dublin, Department of Education and Science

Ryan, Clare (1999), "Early School Leaving: A Sharing of Responsibility", *Issues in Education,* 4, pp. 45-54

Sheehan, John (1982), "Education, Education Policy and Poverty" in Joyce, Lorraine and Anthony McCashin (eds.), *Poverty and Social Policy,* Dublin, Institute of Public Administration

Smyth, Emer (1999), "Educational Inequalities among School Leavers in Ireland 1979-1994", *Economic and Social Review,* 30, pp. 267-84

Tussing, A. Dale (1978), *Irish Educational Expenditure, Past, Present and Future,* paper No. 92, Dublin, Economic and Social Research Institute

Walsh, Brendan (1996), "The Contribution of Education to Irish Economic Growth: A Survey", Department of Economics, University College Dublin, mimeo

Walsh, Brendan (1998), "The Economic Return to Education", paper presented to a seminar organised by the Statistical and Social Inquiry Society of Ireland, 19 February 1998

Whelan, Christopher T. and Damian F Hannan (1999), "Class Inequalities in Educational Attainment among the Adult Population in the Republic of Ireland", *Economic and Social Review,* 30, pp. 285-308

Weir, Susan (1999), *An Analysis of the Application Variables Used to Select Schools for the "Breaking the Cycle" scheme*, Dublin, Educational Research Centre

Young, Michael (1961), *The Rise of the Meritocracy 1870-2033*, London, Pelican Books

Chapter 7

Housing and Inequality in Ireland

P.J. Drudy and Michael Punch

7.1 INTRODUCTION

Despite considerable progress over the last few decades, significant inequalities persist in Ireland. The distribution of income has shown minimal change since the 1970s and a significant minority of the population still live in relative poverty or experience disadvantage of various kinds (see, for example, Collins and Kavanagh, 1998; Nolan et al., 1998; Pringle, et al., 1999; Drudy and Punch, 1999; Johnston and O'Brien, 2000). This group includes the unemployed, those on low pay, people with few or no educational qualifications, those with mental and physical disabilities, Travellers and refugees.

It is increasingly recognised that poverty cannot be defined in unidimensional terms. It is not simply a question of low incomes. However, low incomes are always closely associated with circumscribed opportunities for participation in a range of social and cultural activities and access to good quality housing appropriate to needs. There seems to be a clear association between housing and poverty. The international evidence suggests that being unable to access accommodation appropriate to particular needs and at reasonable cost is one of the realities of "living in poverty". Those in the lower socioeconomic groupings are more likely to be living in lower value properties, in worse conditions and in the poorest environments with lowest levels of public and commercial services. Indeed, this group may be excluded from housing altogether (Forrest and Murie, 1995; Lee and Murie, 1997). Furthermore, in countries where the housing system is dominated by the market provision of accommodation, those on low incomes are increasingly channelled towards a residualised social rented sector (Balchin, 1996; Kemeny, 1995). This may be associated with unsatisfactory dwellings and an environment lacking support services and amenities normally available to more advantaged communities (Lee et al., 1995). Consequently, this latter sector may become unnecessarily and unfairly stigmatised as well as residualised. Powerlessness within the housing system is also a fact of life for poorer households, who experience insecurity, vulnerability and a relative lack of choice (Ravetz, 1980).

The situation is starkly different for other households who are "living in affluence" and have maximum choice in securing a home in terms of location, housing tenure and size and quality. Multiple home ownership is an option for some, including properties abroad. Housing is also regarded by some as a lucrative investment opportunity rather than as a "social good" providing shelter and a home — one of the fundamental determinants of the quality of life of all citizens. In examining inequalities in the housing system as a whole, it is important to keep in view the relations between all its parts, including the market and non-market elements, provision for rent or for owner occupation and the qualitative variation in terms of standards and choice afforded different households and communities.

In this chapter we focus on whether housing — one of the most fundamental requirements of any population — can contribute to levels of inequality. A number of earlier studies have provided detailed estimates of housing subsidies (e.g. Blackwell, 1988). The intention here is to complement this work and to examine in broad outline the differential emphasis of public policy on the various components of the Irish housing system. First, we examine the nature of housing policy in relation to the various tenures, owner occupation, private rented, and social housing. Second, we describe some recent trends and difficulties in housing provision and highlight the links to policy. Arising from the above, we finally set out a number of fundamental changes which are required if we are to move towards an equitable housing system.

7.2 HOUSING POLICY IN IRELAND

The Irish housing system is dominated by owner occupation. Almost 80 per cent of households now own their own home (see Table 7.1). This is the highest proportion in the European Union. The preoccupation with ownership may derive to some extent from difficult historical experiences and a related high regard for the security attached to property ownership. However, the main factor influencing a high rate of owner-occupation has been a whole range of government incentives aimed almost exclusively at homeowners over the last four decades. Whether such incentives are justified in either efficiency or equity terms is open to serious question, as we examine below.

Table 7.1: Occupancy by Tenure, 1961-97

	1961	1971	1981	1991	1997*
Local Authorities					
000s	124.6	112.6	111.8	98.9	92.7
Per cent	18.4	15.5	12.5	9.7	7.8
Privately Rented					
000s	116.3	96.7	90.3	81.4	131.5
Per cent	17.2	13.3	10.1	8.0	11.0
Owner Occupation					
000s	404.6	499.7	667.0	808.4	944.9
Per cent	59.8	68.8	74.4	79.3	79.3
Other					
000s	30.9	17.4	27.0	31.0	22.8
Per cent	4.6	2.4	3.0	3.0	1.9
Total					
000s	676.4	726.4	896.1	1,019.7	1,191.9
Per cent	100	100	100	100	100

Source: *Census of Population,* 1961-1991; McCashin, 2000, based on Special Tabulations of the 1997 *Labour Force Survey.*

Note: The trend after 1991 is indicative rather than precise since the Census and Labour Force Survey use somewhat different definitions.

At the same time, the proportion of accommodation provided for rent either by private landlords or local authorities has declined significantly. The privately rented sector had declined to about 8 per cent of the total (from 42 per cent in 1946) by 1991. However, this tenure expanded to about 132,000 households by 1997 (an increase of 50,000 in a six-year period), increasing to 11 per cent of the total. The number of houses being rented from local authorities has dropped consistently between 1961 and 1997 — from 125,000 to 93,000 — and now represents a mere 7.8 per cent.

7.2.1 Owner Occupation

Government support to owner occupation has been consistent over many years to the extent that it has in fact become the predominant housing policy. Preoccupation with this sector in three reports commissioned by the government confirms this (Bacon, 1998, 1999, 2000). The bias towards supporting private home ownership has manifested itself most clearly in the failure to impose a tax on "imputed" income (the equivalent of a rent paid by an occupier to an owner). This bias is reflected in a number of key policies:

- Remission of rates on new housing prior to 1978; residential rates abolished since 1978;

- A residential property tax introduced in 1984 was abolished in 1994;

- No capital gains tax on sale of principal residence;

- No stamp duty on new housing for owner occupation;

- Mortgage interest relief;

- Cash subsidies to first-time buyers;

- Significant discounts to local authority tenants to encourage owner occupation; very favourable terms on local authority mortgages;

- Surrender grant offered in the 1980s to encourage local authority tenants to move out of public housing;

- Shared ownership and affordable housing schemes designed to encourage owner occupation with public assistance.

7.2.2 Privately Rented Sector

It has long been recognised that this part of the housing system has been neglected by policymakers. As noted earlier, the privately rented sector declined significantly in Ireland up to 1991. Since then it has increased. Nevertheless, it has been described as the "forgotten sector" in the sense that little real attention has been paid to it in terms of policy or development in order to achieve a system appropriate to the needs of both landlords and tenants. This is in stark contrast to the situation in a range of European countries where privately rented accommodation plays a central and honourable role (see Balchin, 1996; Kleinman, 1996; Drudy et al., 1999). The main policies of relevance to this sector are summarised below:

- Limited rent control operated in Ireland up to 1982 when the courts abolished it on the grounds that it was unconstitutional. No rent regulation has existed since that time;

- Section 23 and Section 27 income-tax allowances to encourage the construction of accommodation (mainly apartments) for letting;

- Supplementary welfare allowance payments covering a proportion of rental expenses incurred by tenants who cannot be otherwise accommodated;

- Tax relief to tenants (currently up to IR£750 per person annually);

- Mandatory rent books, minimum notice to quit (one month), minimum standards of accommodation since 1992;

- Registration of rented accommodation (currently being contested in the courts).

7.2.3 Social Housing

In the Irish housing system, the term "social housing" refers to residences provided on a non-market basis for those who are low incomes, disadvantaged and marginalised groups such as Travellers and refugees as well as those suffering from family breakdown or violence, drug and alcohol addiction. Others who are marginalised in relation to the market system include those with physical or mental disabilities and those inappropriately placed in institutions. The main housing providers for these groups are local authorities, housing associations, housing co-operatives and, to a lesser extent, local community development organisations. A number of policy orientations characterise this sector:

- Construction of public housing for low-income households, often in "segregated" developments;

- The sale of public housing for owner occupation;

- Differential rent scheme in operation, whereby rental levels are related to circumstances.

- Housing maintenance remains the responsibility of the relevant local authority;

- Housing allocation by way of a "list" system based on level of need. Points are awarded for various factors, including over-crowding, homelessness, length of time on the list, etc.

- Some encouragement of voluntary or co-operative housing with support from the Department of the Environment.

7.2.4 Assessing Government Intervention in Housing

In assessing government intervention, particular criteria have long been recognised. Is intervention contributing to efficiency and equity? The most fundamental requirement of a housing system is that those needing housing should have access to it. Does supply satisfy housing need? For example, are there blockages or constraints which inhibit supply and thus maintain prices at levels well in excess of inflation or rises in the price of labour or materials? Is there a mismatch between specific housing supply and needs? Are large five-bedroom houses or holiday homes being built (implying over-housing) at a time when those requiring one-bedroom units are homeless (under-housing supply and needs? Are large five-bedroom houses or holiday homes being built (implying over-housing) at a time when those requiring one-bedroom units are homeless (under-housing)? Does government intervention distort the economy in general by its special treatment of housing? Does such intervention encourage investment in housing of particular kinds (e.g. holiday homes which remain vacant for much of the year) and hence reduce investment in other housing types or in other forms of productive activity? These are some of the efficiency-type questions which arise.

In relation to equity, one particular objective might be to improve the distribution of housing between different groups — the poor as well as the relatively well-off. This would at least imply equality of treatment in the various tenures; that is, policies which are "tenure neutral" and do not unduly favour one over another.

It seems clear that the extent of government intervention to encourage home ownership has been significant. This has been of direct benefit to home owners, but it has also, by stimulating demand, indirectly assisted a whole range of players, including developers, builders, architects, building societies, estate agents and solicitors. However, those who do not have the necessary funding or are not in a position to acquire a mortgage gain little or nothing from this state intervention. Furthermore, a range of serious inequities and inefficiencies have been pinpointed in a number of studies over the last decade (see, for example, Blackwell, 1988; National Economic and Social Council (NESC), 1990, 1993; Fahy, 1999; McCashin, 2000). We deal briefly with some of these.

Homeowners in Ireland have no housing cost in the form of a rent. This is, in effect, a subsidy to the homeowners, often referred to as an imputed income (the rent the occupant would otherwise pay). The principle of equity would imply that this imputed income should be subject to income tax (Callan, 1991; McCashin, 2000). It is also inequitable since homeowners are, in effect, treated significantly better than the tenant in the private rented sector who must pay a rent and receives a minimal tax allowance. As the Commission on Taxation (1982) put it almost two decades ago: "the cost of holding onto accommodation in excess of needs is nil". The lack of a tax on imputed income from owner-occupied property also represents inefficiency since it encourages over-investment and trading up in property and a waste of scarce resources. The failure by successive governments to impose and maintain taxes on property breaches one of the most fundamental tenets of taxation, that is, that all resources and not just income should be subject to taxation. The abolition of domestic rates (rather than an adjustment of them in relation to ability to pay) gave special treatment to homeowners in comparison with those in either the private or public rented sectors. The residential property tax introduced in 1984 — a modest attempt to deal with these problems — was abolished in 1994 (under pressure from an influential group of property owners).

The absence of capital gains tax on residential property has further encouraged home ownership (often well above needs) as well as trading up. With significant price rises in recent years, the modest capital gains tax (reduced to only 20 per cent since 1997) has further encouraged investment and speculation in residential property in the clear knowledge that large (and unearned) profit could be made by short-term trading. The absence of a property tax allied to the particularly generous treatment of capital gains has encouraged speculative investment on a substantial scale and has undoubtedly contributed to the escalation of house prices in recent years.

At the same time, serious inequities have for long accompanied mortgage tax relief. While there has been some recent attempts to phase out tax relief, it still remains and for several decades tax allowances were granted at the highest marginal rate, so that the greatest benefit went to those on the highest incomes who took on sizable mortgages for the most expensive properties. Not only was this practice inequitable between homeowners (borrowers at different levels), it gave a significant subsidy to home ownership while no such subsidy was available to those in the private rented category. This special treatment is likewise inefficient in that it encourages investment and speculation in particular types of housing and above needs and leads to an imbalance in the tax system favouring property.

Cash grants to first time buyers (first introduced in 1977) have also been highly questionable. Apart from exacerbating inequality between sectors, one of their effects was simply to stimulate the demand and drive up the cost of housing. Such grants are therefore of little benefit, even to recipients, as they are simply absorbed by developers or builders in the form of increased house prices.

The final subsidy worthy of mention here is the discount on the sale of local authority housing to tenants. While this scheme was well-intentioned and had considerable political appeal, the extent of the discount represented a substantial subsidy towards the privatisation of social housing. Over the period 1964 to 1998 alone, some 151,700 local authority houses were built; however, 156,600 were sold to sitting tenants during the same period. Such houses were invariably sold on very favourable terms by local authorities and (apart from a short period) no claw-back has existed to discourage profit-taking on subsequent sale. This is, in effect, the "commodification" of public housing, whereby housing produced for social ends has been privatised and becomes a commodity which may be used for profit-taking as opposed to its primary function of providing shelter.

It is clear from the foregoing that the main preoccupation of government housing policy has been the encouragement of owner-occupation. On the other hand, the private rented sector received little encouragement. Since the 1980s, tenants over 55 years of age received modest tax relief and this was recently extended to all tenants. However, the level of relief has always compared very unfavourably with that offered to owner-occupiers. The main incentives in this sector have been granted to landlords under various sections of the Finance Acts (known as Section 23 and Section 27 reliefs). While these incentives have undoubtedly encouraged the construction of residential property for rent in inner cities and holiday resorts, it can be argued that they have also contributed in an artificial manner to price escalation and have made it all the more difficult for young people to rent or purchase homes.

The mandatory introduction in the early 1990s of rent books, minimum notice to quit, registration of rental accommodation and minimum standards in the private rented sector were welcome, though basic, requirements. However, fundamental inequities persist. For example, owner-occupied and local authority tenants enjoy security of tenure. Private tenants do not. Tenants can be evicted at four weeks' notice with no reason given and the practice of illegal eviction still persists. Owner-occupied and local authority tenants can be relatively assured of the level of repayment or rent. However, no such certainty exists in the private sector, where rents can be increased at frequent intervals by arbitrary amounts. The minimum standards are basic, yet many properties do not meet even these. The regulations created in the 1990s have not been adequately enforced. In 1997, only 3,846 private-rented units, or 3 per cent of the total stock, were inspected. Only a limited proportion of landlords have complied with the registration requirements (Drudy et al., 1999).

7.3 THE CURRENT HOUSING "CRISIS"

The difficulties in housing across all the tenures that have emerged in recent years are so acute that the situation has been described in crisis terms. The first element of the crisis is the failure to develop a vibrant social housing sector, as reflected in a low level of provision and rapidly expanding waiting lists.

As the trends outlined in Section 7.2 show, social housing has played a residual role. The annual social housing output is completely inadequate in the light of increasing needs. For example, in 1998 local authorities built only 2,800 houses, but 43,000 families were on the waiting list in that year compared with only 18,000 in 1987. Despite this, the privatisation of local authority housing has continued unabated, as illustrated earlier. Over the three year period 1996-1998, a total of 8,079 houses were built by local authorities in Ireland. However, 6,429 houses were sold to local authority tenants over the same period at discounted prices. The net gain over the three-year period, therefore, was 1,650 houses. At the same time, the local authorities acquired 1,993 houses at full market price (Government of Ireland, 2000a). From the point of view of both efficiency and equity the sale of public housing is highly questionable, in view of scarce resources and escalating housing need. Over the same period, provision by housing associations and other voluntary bodies dropped from 917 to a mere 485 units.

The 43,000 families on local authority waiting lists in 1998 noted above amounted to at least 100,000 persons. At the same time, an estimated 30,000 persons were in short-term private rented accommodation (subsidised by the state at a cost of more than IR£100 million per annum). Estimates from representative organisations suggest that at least 5,000 homeless and about 7,000 Travellers need accommodation. In addition, it is estimated that up to 12,000 refugees or asylum seekers now enter the country each year. A significant number of people (including those with mental disabilities and addiction problems) live in unsatisfactory institutional settings. We estimate therefore that in 1998 at least 150,000 persons were in serious housing need. There is no evidence to suggest that the situation has improved since then.

Furthermore, the local authorities have pursued, until recently, a policy of concentrating low income families in particular geographical areas. As an example, considerable numbers were relocated from the inner city of Dublin to the periphery of the city where some estates contain up to 90 per cent local authority tenants. Similar policies were carried out in other cities. At the same time, very little residential building took place in the inner cities. The surrender grant of the 1980s had the adverse effect of denuding some local authority estates of those who were employed on relatively high incomes and their replacement with further low income families.

The placing of problem tenants in particular flat complexes or estates further exacerbated the difficulties. The end result — still with us today — was a concentration of low income families in a poor physical environment with high levels of unemployment, educational disadvantage and a range of social problems, including drug abuse. This has led to the regrettable and erroneous impression that to live in local authority housing is somehow to have failed. Furthermore, the segregation of the poor into local authority housing may be worsening, as evidenced by household budget figures, which show a steady residualisation of the sector in terms of the relative income levels of tenants (see also Nolan and Whelan, 1999).

It is important to keep in mind that segregation of this kind is not inherent to social housing and must be understood in its broader context. There is evidence to suggest that segregation and inequality are integral elements in market-driven housing systems. Those from the lower social classes are excluded or displaced from the highly valued areas through the prohibitive cost of housing, rapidly escalating land prices and the lack of non-market options. These élite residential areas are thereby ring-fenced from invasion by the poor or other "undesirable" social groups, who must then seek accommodation elsewhere. In effect, this distinction between highly valued "good" areas and stigmatised "bad" areas underpins the broad price differentials evident across the housing market. In this market model, access and housing choice depend on ability to pay. As a result, the poorest groups have the least choice and end up in the least desirable locations, while the richest can access the more exclusive areas, where property prices are highest to begin with, and there is strong expectation of steady future increases. This begs the question as to whether inequality and segregation to some extent prop up the housing property market — what are the socioeconomic relations between the segregated IR£1 million-per-house enclave and the inner city ghetto or the peripheral deprived urban neighbourhood?

A representative of the Irish Auctioneers and Valuers Institute put the case for segregation:

> In future, people will speak of pre- and post-1999 developments . . . whether they live in mixed developments or are among the lucky few residing in segregated private schemes. Of course, we don't approve of such snobbish attitudes — publicly. Privately, however, most of us will con-

tinue to do what we have always done — pay considerably more to be among the latter group (Cooke, 1999).

Despite an increase in the provision of private-rented accommodation (much of it influenced by government incentives referred to above), significant difficulties remain for private tenants. The sector is almost completely unregulated and this has engendered many problems for tenants and was partly responsible for a generally negative perception of the rental option. In effect, the vulnerability, variable quality and poor value for money associated with rental has meant that households are encouraged to get out of this sector and into home ownership if at all possible. The ongoing problems associated with renting a home have long been highlighted by housing agencies such as Threshold (see O'Brien, 1982). Little has changed in recent years, and tenants regularly experience difficulties through rent uncertainty, illegal evictions, deposit retention, low quality, unfit dwellings in terms of fire and safety and other problems (Drudy et al., 1999). Alongside these traditional problems, further tensions have been generated through escalating rents (Downey, 1998). It now seems that rental increases in recent years have tracked house price increases, leading to a "crisis of rented affordability" (McCashin, 2000). This is a serious concern, particularly as a viable rental option is likely to become increasingly important both socially and economically as greater levels of vulnerability and flexibility are introduced to labour markets through increases in temporary and part-time work arrangements (see MacLennan and Pryce, 1996).

A similar crisis exists for those who are attempting to purchase their homes. The aspiration for owner occupation has become increasingly difficult to achieve due to the alarming escalation of house prices in recent years. The average new house price for which loans were approved for the country as a whole increased from IR£57,281 in 1994 to IR£116,970 in 1999 — an increase of 104 per cent. Over the same period, the average new house price in Dublin increased from IR£64,575 to IR£152,414 or 136 per cent. Some other areas of the country have also experienced significant increases. It is clear that a predominant pattern has emerged of accelerating house prices since 1994. Thus, for the country as a whole, new house prices increased by 4 per cent between 1993 and 1994, but the annual rate of increase escalated to 23 per cent between 1997 and 1998, reducing to an increase of 19 per cent between 1998 and 1999 (Government of Ireland, 1995, 1999a, 1999b and 2000). It is important to point out that the apparent proportionate improvement in the recent period still represented an annual increase of IR£18,287 — remarkably similar to the absolute increase of IR£18,177 in the previous period and well above the average industrial wage. While Dublin showed a similar proportionate reduction, average new house prices still increased by IR£25,853 between 1998 and 1999. Furthermore, the proportionate increases in average new house prices between 1998 and 1999 in Cork, Galway, Waterford and Limerick were 26 per cent, 17 per cent, 22 per cent and 17 per cent respectively. These represented significant increases on the previous year and confirm a worsening in house price increases in these areas (Government of Ireland, 2000a). Separate data produced by the Irish Permanent Building Society in association with the Economic and Social Research Institute support this conclusion (Irish Permanent Building Society, 2000).

It is clear therefore that there were exceptional price increases over the period since 1994 and there is no consistent sign of stabilisation. How do these increases compare with other price indices? Figure 7.1 provides evidence for this. Up to 1994, new house prices increased broadly in line with the consumer price index, house building costs (labour and material costs) and average industrial earnings. Since 1994, however, house prices have diverged significantly from these other indices and have increased at a much faster rate than house building costs over the period in question.

Figure 7.1: Trends in Private New House Prices, Earnings, House Building Costs and Consumer Prices

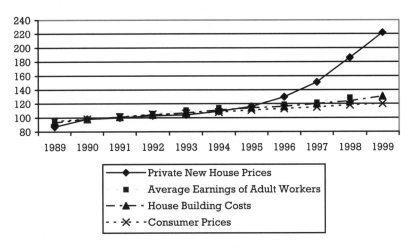

Source: *Annual Housing Statistics Bulletin*, 1999

Thus, in the owner-occupied category, escalating prices in recent years have placed home ownership beyond the reach of a large proportion of young people who have a fundamental problem of affordability. Many income earners who could traditionally purchase a home are now simply unable to do so. The problem is particularly apparent in the changing trends in the social class of house buyers (see Table 7.2). Those from the professional classes make up an increasing proportion of house buyers (as evidenced by the occupations of those receiving loan approval). Representation of those from all other classes declined steadily since 1994.

Table 7.2: House Buyers by Social Class (% share)

Year	Professionals, Managers Employers	Non-manual Workers	Skilled/Semi-skilled Manual Workers	Unskilled Manual Workers	Farmers, Fishers
1994	37.7	26.5	26.5	7.3	2.0
1995	41.9	24.1	24.2	6.6	3.2
1996	44.3	23.3	23.2	6.4	2.8
1997	52.2	19.5	20.3	4.4	3.7
1998	52.9	22.0	19.9	3.4	1.8

Source: Annual Housing Statistics Bulletin, 1998

The factors accounting for these large price increases may be summarised briefly. Various market factors — demographic, economic and social — have resulted in significant increases in the demand for housing. At the same time, the supply of housing has been inadequate to meet this demand and therefore excess demand has invariably pushed up prices. This excess demand is fuelled by a number of influences. First, low interest rates and the ready availability of significant funding have encouraged large-scale borrowing, thus contributing to further price increases and greater indebtedness.

Second, a considerable number of people have been viewing housing as an investment opportunity, even on a short-term basis. This has placed further upward pressure on house prices and has resulted in a significant decrease in first-time buyers in recent years. The available evidence suggests that an increasing number of purchasers are buying a second residential property (see Table 7.3). In exceptional cases, buyers purchase entire blocks of houses. In the current environment, such buyers can purchase for speculative purposes on the assumption of accruing large capital gains, modest capital gains tax payments (illustrated above), high rents and little regulation during the period the property is held. The recent increase of 2 per cent in capital gains tax suggested in the third Bacon report (2000) will have virtually no effect if the trend in house price escalation illustrated above persists.

Table 7.3 shows that the proportion of new house buyers who are already owner-occupiers has increased significantly between 1994 and 1998 — from 36 to 50 per cent of the total. While some of these may consist of purchasers moving to another home in a new location, it seems that a high proportion consists of second home owners, investors or speculators. At the same time, it may be noted that the proportion of buyers who were tenants or resident with parents has declined, further indicating that first time buyers are now playing a reduced role in house purchase.

Table 7.3: Previous Tenure of New House Buyers, 1993-98

Year	Owner-Occupiers	Private Rental	Local Authorities	Parents' Residence	Other
1994	35.5	26.4	2.4	33.9	1.9
1995	40.8	24.6	1.3	30.5	2.8
1996	46.4	22.8	1.1	27.3	2.4
1997	52.6	22.9	1.1	21.4	2.0
1998	50.1	23.4	0.7	23.8	1.9

Source: Annual Housing Statistics Bulletin 1998

A third factor of central importance is, in our view, the availability and price of land suitable for housing, together with the servicing of such land with water, sewage, drainage and waste management. Builders, planners and estate agents all agree that the price of land is a major determinant of the rise in house prices. For example, the Irish Home Builders Association has estimated that average site prices in Dublin rose by 200 per cent between 1995 and 1998 and in that year accounted for 36 per cent of the average house price compared to 21 per cent in 1995. Recent land sales indicate that in future the proportion taken up by the price of land could be even higher. These exceptional increases in the price of land inevitably feed into higher houses prices. They are a matter of serious concern.

The availability of land at a reasonable price for housing, especially in the main urban centres, has been a deep cause of concern in Ireland for almost three decades. In the early 1970s, this concern resulted in the establishment of a Committee on the Price of Building Land under the chairmanship of Mr Justice Kenny. The main objective was to find a way to stabilise or reduce the price of building land and to ensure that the community acquired on fair terms the "betterment" element which arises from works carried out by local authorities. The Committee reported to the government in 1973, its main proposal being that local authorities should be able to acquire potential development land designated by the High Court at "existing use value" plus 25 per cent (Kenny, 1973). This proposal inevitably raised objections, and in particular it was argued that it

was an "unjust attack" on property rights and therefore contrary to the Constitution. This view was far from universal, however, on the grounds that the rights of property owners must be
regulated by principles of social justice and the common good
— also set out in the Constitution. In any case, this matter was
never resolved and no action was taken. In the present circumstances, where we face a severe housing shortage, social justice and the common good must surely dictate that land owners
should not accrue huge gains purely as a result of land re-
zoning or planning permission. Such planning permission always carries the responsibility to provide services; yet land
owners may make little or no contribution to these (Dublin Local Authorities, 1999; Drudy et al., 1999).

Fourth, the price increases are so significant that they suggest a monopoly-type situation among developers where supernormal profits are being made. With various constraints affecting
supply in the short term (e.g. lack of serviced land, water, sewage and other facilities), a relatively small number of developers
can hoard serviced land and release it slowly, thus exerting
control over prices and increasing profits from housing. The significant difference between building costs and the price of
housing suggests that supernormal profits are indeed being
made (see Figure 7.1). Successful "models" of affordable housing, which show that the building cost of an average three-
bedroom home in the Ringsend area of Dublin (including the site
cost and builder's profit) should be no more than IR£100,000,
lend credence to this (City Housing Initiative, 1999). Apart from
equity considerations, this represents a diminution of competition and thus a serious inefficiency in the system.

Finally, it is important to note that there are direct links between the policy orientation set out in detail above and the
range of difficulties in the various housing tenures and the ensuing inequalities. The preoccupation with owner occupation
and the related failure to develop vibrant social and private
rental alternatives have been central to the problem. Mortgage
tax relief, the abolition of residential rates, stamp duty remission on new houses and first-time buyer grants were intended
to reduce the cost of housing for owner-occupiers. In reality,

however, they contributed to increasing demand for housing and thus to higher house prices, adding to the affordability problem even for relatively well-off purchasers (O'Connell and Quinn, 1999). The failure over many years to address the fundamental problem of land prices or the taxation of residential property, including capital gains, had similar effects.

Furthermore, the tax reliefs provided to investors in rental property in inner city areas, seaside resorts and in many towns throughout the country are inherently regressive since they can only benefit those with sufficient incomes to incur tax liability. Those who have low incomes are disqualified from sharing in these benefits as they do not have the necessary capital to become investors in property development in the designated areas or to become owner-occupiers once the schemes are completed. This problem has generated conflict in recent years both in the inner city areas and in seaside towns, where the indigenous populations find themselves excluded from the benefits and even "displaced" as escalating land and property prices make it impossible for their children to establish homes in the local area. The possibility that the viability of some communities, both rural and urban, may come under threat in this way highlights one of the more damaging effects of the uneven treatment of housing.

7.4 CONCLUSION

In this chapter we have pointed to a number of serious inequities in the housing system. This raises a fundamental question: should housing be regarded as a commodity as well as a home and thus a mechanism for profit-making by landowners and developers and for personal investment by those with sufficient capital to do so? Alternatively, should it function primarily as a "social" or "merit" good which provides accommodation appropriate to need at a reasonable price and which ought to be available to everybody as a "right"? It seems clear that the latter aim is not being achieved and government policies have consistently favoured a market-led approach which, in effect, facilitates and even encourages the commodification of this vital requirement. This approach is replicated to a large extent in

Britain, but is markedly different to that pursued in a range of other European countries where more balanced and equitable policies pertain (Barlow and Duncan, 1994; Kemeny, 1995; Balchin, 1996; Lee and Murie, 1997). Furthermore, various European countries have given the right to housing either legislative or constitutional status (e.g. Portugal, 1976; Spain, 1978; Netherlands, 1982; Belgium, 1995; Finland, 1995). Irish agencies and trade unions concerned with housing issues (e.g. Combat Poverty Agency, Threshold, Simon Community, the Irish Commission for Justice and Peace, the Civil and Public Service Union and SIPTU—Services Industrial Professional and Technical Union) also stress the need to treat housing as a fundamental human right (CPSU and SIPTU, 1998; Irish Commission for Justice and Peace, 1998; Combat Poverty Agency, 1999; Drudy et al., 1999).

A number of important conclusions and policy implications can be drawn from this chapter. Major changes need to take place in relation to the non-market sector which has been relegated to a residual position. It is entirely unacceptable that, in a relatively affluent society, a large number of our people still have inadequate housing or none at all. There is therefore an urgent need for an expanded construction programme of social housing by all non-profit providers — including local authorities, housing associations, co-operatives and other voluntary and community development organisations. As illustrated in this chapter, the record in recent years in providing social housing has been very poor in relation to needs. The precise reasons for this are not entirely clear, but it is a matter of urgency that a radical change should occur. The *National Development Plan, 2000-2006* includes a number of proposals relating to housing requirements. These include the provision of 5,000 local authority houses per annum over the period 2000-2006 (Government of Ireland, 2000b). Furthermore, there is a strong case for broadening the base of social housing provision as has happened in other European countries in order to give it the status it deserves. This would involve a new role for social housing in providing "general needs" housing for the middle classes as well as for its traditional clients. The financial surplus generated from renting to middle-income residents could cross-subsidise the costs of providing housing for poorer households (MacLaran, 2000). Unfortunately, there has been little interest in achieving this to date.

> Denying any "general needs" housing role to the public sector effectively protects the market sectors. Vital interests are at stake: landowners, developers, builders, landlords, mortgage financiers and the plethora of property professions. All do well from rapidly rising prices. Our TDs must be told that the urban environment doesn't exist as a quarry to be mined by property and development interests. People's lives are being seriously damaged by their failure to act (MacLaran, 2000).

A fundamental policy shift is also required to address the extent of segregation in Ireland which is unacceptable and badly out of line with what is happening in other countries. Sadly, such segregation is supported by some groups on the dubious grounds that it "protects property values". It is now clear that the policy pursued to date by some local authorities of concentrating high proportions of social housing in particular areas is deeply flawed. The Dublin Docklands Development Authority (1997) has pledged in its *Master Plan* to ensure that 20 per cent of the housing in Dublin docklands will be in the social category. The outcome of this remains to be seen. It may also be noted that under existing legislation (see Section 38 of the Local Government Planning and Development Act of 1963), this objective can be achieved. The recent Planning and Development Act, 2000 has a similar aim.

Reform in the privately rented housing sector is long overdue in the interests of both landlords and tenants. A privately rented sector which offers fair rents (indexed for inflation and relevant improvements), good quality and reasonable security of tenure (as is the case in many other countries) could play a central role in the housing system, to meet a range of needs. Regular inspections of rental accommodation to ensure quality control and adherence to agreements should be the norm. Anything less would be inadequate. This would be in the interests of both landlords and tenants and would encourage the provision of a wider range of rental accommodation in the long term. We reject the assertion that a fair rent (which provides for a normal profit to the landlord) represents an extreme type of rent control which could militate against landlords and hence reduce the supply of rental accommodation further. Despite regular and unquantified claims about the alleged dangers of rent regulation, the experience in other countries simply does not support this view. Regrettably, the majority view of the Commission established by the government to make recommendations on the private rented sector concluded that rent levels should continue to be dictated by the market, although this view was rejected by agencies such as Threshold (Commission on the Private Rented Residential Sector, 2000).

The continuing escalation in house prices is a matter of serious concern. It is important to stress that the level of price increases in recent years identified in this chapter could have the overall effect of slowing down or seriously compromising the considerable economic progress achieved in Ireland over the last decade. The exceptional increases must inevitably give rise to significant wage demands and inflation, as evidenced by demands in the building industry and concerns expressed by trade union leaders. Indeed, the generally favourable international perception of Ireland's economy could be irrevocably damaged unless serious action is taken as a matter of urgency. There is of course the questionable argument that existing home owners have gained significantly from price increases. We reject such a justification. Against this is the more tenable logic that those who have struggled to purchase homes in recent times have taken on large and often excessive loans. If interest rates were to rise further (and there are clear indications that they may), the level of indebtedness could become unsustainable for many.

How can we deal with the problem of escalating house prices? Will increasing the supply of housing alone resolve the problem? While an increase in supply of owner-occupied housing may stabilise or reduce prices in the long term, much more immediate direct intervention is essential (as in the case of rents above) to ensure fair prices are charged in view of the current monopoly-type situation where exceptional (supernormal) profits are being made by developers. Indeed, a significant increase in supply over the last few years has been accompanied by accelerating house prices. A fair price certificate should be provided for all new housing for sale. We must stress that this is entirely different from the concept of "reasonable" value (based on the market) which was briefly introduced in the past. The fair price certificate would be based instead on agreed criteria such as the quality of the property and closely linked to building costs, land costs, levies and a reasonable profit for the developer and builder.

A considerable re-orientation of current policy (which is both inefficient and inequitable) is required to reduce the highly favourable treatment of owner-occupation in comparison with the other tenures in Ireland. The introduction of a property tax to capture "imputed income" is essential. This would be accompanied by mortgage tax relief at the standard rate in order to allow for the expenses (interest repayments) associated with property ownership, but not stamp duty which would represent double taxation. A further key change would be the introduction of a capital gains tax on the sale of residential accommodation. It may be noted that such taxes have been proposed by a range of bodies over several decades, including the Commission on Taxation and the National Economic and Social Council.

The price of land is central to the rise in house prices and rents. Since land is one of the critical resources required for housing, whether for sale or for rent, the state has a duty to acquire sufficient land at a reasonable cost for this purpose. A significant programme of state acquisition of land should therefore commence without further delay. Such land can then be released in an orderly fashion to private and social housing providers in response to requirements. Land being acquired by the state for such housing purposes (whether for social or private housing) should be acquired at existing use value plus a reasonable addition for compensation and disturbance — a proposal made over 25 years ago by Mr Justice Kenny, but largely ignored on dubious constitutional grounds since that time. One further alternative is a substantial land tax or a capital gains tax on unearned price increases. At present we are in the absurd situation where actions taken by the state on behalf of the community (e.g. via re-zoning, planning permission or the provision of infrastructure) simply result in enormous profits to landowners who bear none of the costs of residential development. By contrast, policies in a number of countries abroad have long succeeded in dampening or eliminating the speculative element in relation to the provision of housing through the practice of public land banking and the subsequent allocation on a rational basis of sites for development by both market and non-market providers (see Barlow and Duncan, 1994; Kemeny, 1995; Balchin, 1996).

In view of the multiple problems identified, it is now clear that housing can no longer be treated simply as a market commodity or as an investment like stocks and shares. Rather it should be seen as a social good and a fundamental right. In order to achieve this, policies must be implemented to ensure that every person has affordable, secure, good quality accommodation appropriate to their needs. Such a basic need as housing can not be left largely to the market. There is thus a case for direct government intervention to ensure that fair prices are charged for all new housing and fair rents charged for all rental accommodation. Reasonable security of tenure is also essential in the private rented sector. We must also deal with the problem of land prices once and for all.

There is a need for a holistic and co-ordinated approach to ensure equality of status and treatment of the various housing tenures and social groups, leading to an integrated housing system. Such a system would involve both "market" and "non-market" providers of housing for sale and rent — non-profit voluntary, co-operative and community organisations as well as local authorities, private developers and institutions, such as building societies, pension funds, trade unions, universities and credit unions. This could ensure well-managed good quality rental housing appropriate to the diverse needs of the population offering a viable alternative to owner-occupation. Social housing could also be a major competitor to owner-occupied and privately rented housing as in other countries, thus improving affordability, quality and diversity. Housing could be a critical component in community development efforts, in combatting social exclusion and in furthering a comprehensive regional, urban and rural strategy. This balanced approach involving an expanded role for the non-market production and allocation of housing and a fair deal for households, whether they own or rent their homes, will lead to a less unequal society.

References

Bacon, Peter, et al. (1998), *An Economic Assessment of Recent House Price Developments*, Report to the Minister for Housing and Urban Renewal, Dublin,

Bacon, Peter, et al. (1999), *The Housing Market: An Economic Review and Assessment*, Report to the Minister for Housing and Urban Renewal, Dublin

Bacon, Peter, et al. (2000), *The Housing Market in Ireland: An Economic Evaluation of Trends and Prospects*, Report to the Department of the Environment and Local Government, Dublin

Balchin, Paul (ed. 1996), *Housing Policy in Europe*, London, Routledge

Barlow, James, and Simon Duncan (1994), *Success and Failure in Housing Provision: European Systems Compared*, Oxford, Pergamon

Blackwell, John (1988), *A Review of Housing Policy*, NESC Report No. 87, Dublin

Callan, Tim. (1991), *Property Tax: Principles and Policy Options*, Policy Research Paper No. 12, ESRI, Dublin

City Housing Initiative (1999), *Community Development Through Housing*, Ringsend Action Project presentation paper, Dublin

Collins, Micheal, and Catherine Kavanagh (1998), "For Richer, for Poorer: The Changing Distribution of Household Income in Ireland, 1973-94" in Healy, Sean and Reynolds, Brigid, *Social Policy in Ireland: Principles, Practice and Problems*, Dublin, Oak Tree Press

Combat Poverty Agency (1999), *Submission to Cross-Department Team on Homelessness*, Department of the Environment, Dublin

Commission on the Private Rented Residential Sector (2000), *Report*, Dublin, Stationery Office

Commission on Taxation (1982), *First Report: Direct Taxation*, Dublin, Stationery Office

Cooke, Alan (1999), quoted in *The Irish Times,* 14 October

CPSU and SIPTU (1998), *Affordable Accommodation: A Trade Union Issue and Human Right,* Dublin

Downey, Daithi (1998), *New Realities in Irish Housing,* CRUBE, Dublin Institute of Technology, Dublin

Drudy, Patrick J. Chairman (1999), *Housing: A New Approach,* Report of the Housing Commission, Dublin, Irish Labour Party

Drudy, Patrick. J., and Michael Punch (1999), "The Regional Problem, Urban Disadvantage and Development", *Trinity Economic Papers,* Trinity College, Dublin

Dublin Docklands Development Authority (1997), *Dublin Docklands Area Master Plan,* Dublin

Dublin Local Authorities (1999), *Housing in Dublin,* Dublin

Fahey, Tony (ed., 1999), *Social Housing in Ireland: A Study of Success, Failure and Lessons Learned,* Dublin, Oak Tree Press

Forrest, Ray, and Alan Murie, (eds., 1995), *Housing and Family Wealth: Comparative International Perspectives,* London, Routledge

Government of Ireland (1995), *Annual Housing Statistics Bulletin,* Dublin, Stationery Office

Government of Ireland (1999a), *Annual Housing Statistics Bulletin,* Dublin, Stationery Office

Government of Ireland (1999b), *Action on House Prices,* Dublin, Government Information Office

Government of Ireland (2000a), *Housing Statistics Bulletin,* March Quarter, Dublin, Stationery Office

Government of Ireland (2000b), *National Development Plan, 2000-2006,* Dublin, Stationery Office

Irish Commission for Justice and Peace (1998), *Re-Righting the Constitution: The Case for New Social and Economic Rights,* Dublin

Irish Permanent Building Society (2000), *House Price Index,* 26 July 2000, in association with the ESRI, Dublin

Johnston, Helen and Tracey O'Brien (2000), "Planning for a More Inclusive Society: An Initial Assessment of the National Poverty Strategy", Dublin, Combat Poverty Agency

Kemeny, Jim (1995), *From Public Housing to the Social Market: Rental Policy Strategies in Comparative Perspective,* London, Routledge

Kenny, Justice (1973), *Report of the Committee on the Price of Building Land*, Dublin

Kleinman, Mark (1996), *Housing, Welfare and the State in Europe*, Cheltenham, Edward Elgar

Lee, Peter, et al. (1995), *The Price of Social Exclusion*, London, National Federation of Housing Associations

Lee, Peter, and Alan Murie (1997), *Poverty, Housing Tenure and Social Exclusion*, Bristol, Policy Press

MacLaran, Andrew (2000), "Middle Class Social Housing: Insanity or Progress?", *Cornerstone: Magazine of the Homeless Initiative*, issue 5, April

MacLennan, Duncan, and Gwilym Pryce (1996), "Global Economic Change, Labour Market Adjustment and the Challenges for European Housing Policies", *Urban Studies*, Vol. 33, No. 10, pp. 1849-66

McCashin, Anthony (2000), *The Private Rented Sector in the 21st Century: Policy Choices*, Dublin, Threshold & St. Pancras Housing Association

National Economic and Social Council (1990), *A Strategy for the 1990s: Economic Stability and Structural Change*, NESC Report No. 89, Dublin

National Economic and Social Council (1993), *A Strategy for Competitiveness, Growth and Employment*, NESC Report No. 96, Dublin

Nolan, Brian, Christopher T. Whelan, and James Williams (1998), *Where Are Poor Households? The Spatial Distribution of Poverty and Deprivation in Ireland*, Dublin, Oak Tree Press

Nolan, Brian and Christopher T. Whelan (1999), *Loading the Dice: A Study of Cumulative Disadvantage*, Dublin, Oak Tree Press

O'Brien, Lance M. (1982), *Private Rented — The Forgotten Sector*, Dublin, Threshold

O'Connell, Tom, and Terry Quinn (1999), "Recent Property Price Developments: An Assessment" in *Central Bank of Ireland: Bulletin*, Dublin, Autumn

Pringle, Dennis G., Jim Walsh, and Mark Hennessy (1999), *Poor People, Poor Places: A Geography of Poverty and Deprivation in Ireland*, Dublin, Oak Tree Press

Ravetz, Alison (1980), *Remaking Cities: Contradictions of the Recent Urban Environment*, London, Croom Helm

Chapter 8

Health Inequalities in Ireland

Eamon O'Shea and Cecily Kelleher

8.1 INTRODUCTION

Variations in health status are not simple to explain or address. Traditionally such variations are understood to be the product of a combination of determinants including genetic or constitutional factors particular to all individuals, personal lifestyle behaviours, the wider social, cultural and physical environment and access to health care services. While the focus of resources and public debate has been mainly on the latter throughout most of this century, particularly in the post-second world war period, most serious analysts across a spectrum of disciplines believe that the contribution of health care to overall patterns of morbidity (or illness) and mortality has always been marginal by comparison with other influences (Black Report, 1980). It is true that revolutions in treatment standards for major illnesses like coronary heart disease (Tunstall-Pedoe et al., 2000), breast cancer (Hermon and Beral, 1996; Schrijvers et al., 1995) and AIDS (Hirshell and Francioli, 1998) have each had a significant effect on mortality rates in recent years but none of these essentially downstream strategies can have affected incidence rates or new cases, and in each instance differential access to services within and between countries has served only to highlight further issues of equity of access to care. Mackenbach (1994) refers to this health care provision strategy as the least fundamental approach to reducing socioeconomic inequalities in health. Indeed, how we organise our health care systems says as much about our sociopolitical priorities as it does about the impact on health status. As Wilkinson points out, in the study of what determines health inequalities we have learned almost as much about society as we have about health (Wilkinson, 1996).

The argument that differences in health status are explained by social inequality is contested. Moreover, that this should be a matter of public policy is an even more challenged position, particularly in Ireland. We are used to thinking of ourselves as a homogenous nation (Kelleher, 1999). While we are familiar with the notion of Irish people being disadvantaged as emigrants to other countries across all social groupings, and we accept too that there are particular groups in Irish society who have long-standing disadvantage (classically, Travellers: O'Donovan et al., 1995), we are far less attuned to the notion of wide-scale inequality or any sense of graduated disadvantage within the country. Yet the international literature supports the hypothesis that variations in health status across social class are relative and graduated (Ben-Shlomo et al., 1996; Blane and Drever, 1998; Davey Smith et al., 1994). Accordingly, measures that reduce that social class gradient are as appropriate for policy intervention as those which seek to identify particularly high-risk groups and target these.

In recent years, research on health inequalities has developed in other countries, particularly the industrialised nations of the EU and the US (Eames et al., 1993; Fiscella and Franks, 1997; Ford et al., 1994; Judge et al., 1998; Pappas et al., 1993; Kawachi et al., 1996). Here in Ireland, however, we have been hampered by a lack of data at individual, ecological and health service utilisation level. This has contributed to official inertia in dealing with both the causes and consequences of health inequalities. There has been concern for some time, formally articulated in the recently published cardiovascular strategy (Department of Health and Children, 1999), that surveillance mechanisms are incomplete and uncoordinated. For instance, while we collect census level data as might be expected, we produce no area level analyses for the population on a routine basis at an official level. Two groups who have worked on area level analyses are researchers in the Small Area Health Research Unit (SAHRU) in Trinity College (SAHRU, 1997) and the Health Information Unit in the Eastern Health Board (Johnson and Dack, 1989; Johnson and Lyons, 1993; Johnson et al., 1994). Preliminary findings from these groups using a variation of standard deprivation indices compiled from a range of social status indicators suggest that area-based variations are certainly apparent in large cities in line with international experience. However, we have a serious problem with regard to the availability of individual-level data; the HIPE (hospital inpatient enquiry) system collects data at incident or case level and does not record individual data (Wiley and Fetter, 1990). There are no large-scale population-based cohort studies in progress in Ireland to date and, until the national health and lifestyle surveys were instituted last year (Centre for Health Promotion Studies, 1999a, 1999b; National Nutrition Surveillance Centre, 1999), we had no systematically collected population level data on health behaviour or health care utilisation.

This chapter deals with some of the critical issues in the health inequality debate. That debate is not as advanced in Ireland as in other European countries and much groundwork needs to be done to identify the critical issues for discussion. This chapter therefore attempts to provide a framework for the future discussion of health inequalities in this country from a theoretical, empirical and philosophical perspective. Although we can learn much from empirical analysis undertaken in other countries, and from comparative public policy analysis, there is a big research agenda to be undertaken in this country before an integrated strategy dealing with health inequalities can be formulated and implemented. In the section that follows the introduction we discuss the problem of causality in the relationship between economic status and health. Does poor economic status lead to poor health or is it the reverse: bad health causes people to slip down the social ladder? This is followed in Section 8.3 by an examination of the literature in health inequalities, with a review of some on the main findings in the international literature on the effect of socioeconomic status on health, together with a report on the limited Irish evidence of mortality differentials by socioeconomic group (SEG). The relationship between income inequality and health is explored in Section

8.4. This is a controversial area with argument and counter-argument put forward on the robustness of the available evidence of a relationship between income inequality and mortality in developed countries. Section 8.5 considers the meaning of equity in health and health care. Equity can be a vague and misunderstood concept and such a loosely formulated objective that it is imperative to provide some philosophical frameworks to anchor the discussion in this area. This is done in Section 8.6. Policy issues in an Irish context are considered in the final section. Although the importance of equity is nowadays acknowledged in policy formulation, the fact is that little has been achieved in the implementation of policies that might address the serious equity problems that exist in both health status in itself and health care provision in this country. This must change if unnecessary deaths are to be avoided in the future.

8.2 ECONOMIC STATUS AND HEALTH: THE DIRECTION OF CAUSALITY

Much evidence of varying merit has been produced on the relationship between economic status and health. For many years, most people accepted that differences in socioeconomic position were responsible for variations in health, although why this occurred often produced debate. In more recent times, attention has turned to the effect that health can have on economic status. The problem of causality was recently examined by Smith (1999) who investigated the association between health and wealth. Using data from the US, Smith compared household wealth with the head of household's self-reported general health status. The study revealed that people reporting excellent health in 1984 had 74 per cent more wealth than those reporting fair or poor health. Moreover, those who reported poor health had considerably smaller absolute wealth growth over a ten-year period. The same differential in reported health status exists using income data rather than wealth data.

The difficulty lies in establishing the direction of the relationship between income/wealth and reported health status. While there is evidence that both household income and wealth have statistically significant positive effects on self-reported health status, even controlling for behavioural influences, the debate about causality is far from closed (Smith, 1999). Health can exert an influence on people's ability to earn money and generate savings, which in turn affects both their economic and social status. Bad health events may reduce the amount of labour supplied and subsequently affect savings. In contrast, healthier people can work longer hours in a week and more weeks in a year, leading to higher earnings. Health effects may also influence future income streams, particularly with respect to social security and pension entitlements.

The relationship between economic status and health accordingly works in both directions. This means that the effect that health has on economic status clearly cannot be ignored. However, it appears unlikely that the main explanation of the association between economic status and health can be attributed to the effect that health has on wealth. To do so would imply, for example, that changes in income distribution are determined mainly by changes in health. That would mean denying the contribution of economic factors like unemployment, taxes, benefits, profits and wage bargaining to income distribution. Wilkinson (1996) adds that the data on class differences in mortality have been thoroughly examined for the effects of reverse causality. Although reverse causality happens to a small extent, it does not account for the bulk of health inequalities. Whatever effect it may have on the economically active population of working age, it has little or no effect on economically inactive children and old people.

8.3 THE EFFECT OF SOCIOECONOMIC STATUS ON HEALTH

There is a long tradition of international research exploring differences in mortality among socioeconomic groups (SEGs) and social classes in different countries. This has mainly focused on males due to methodological problems with the deaths data for females, leading to both inconsistent and fragmented classification of women by socioeconomic group, particularly women outside of the paid labour force. In general, the results of this research show, for all countries, that the more disadvantaged people's circumstances are, the higher is their mortality relative to their more affluent counterparts (Kunst and Mackenbach, 1994; Benzeval et al., 1995). In Britain, mortality rates at all ages were recognised as being between two and three times higher among disadvantaged social groups than in the better-off classes (Black Report, 1980; Whitehead, 1987). Furthermore, throughout the last two decades those variations widened, particularly in the case of the most disadvantaged, which some commentators attributed to the political economy of the period (Davey Smith and Dorling, 1996).

Longitudinal surveys confirm differences in mortality by class for men of working age in Britain (Goldblatt, 1990a). Social gradients in mortality also exist outside of conventional class scales, as demonstrated by Marmot et al. (1984) in their work on mortality differences by occupational grade in the British civil service. Similar gradients exist with respect to housing tenure and car ownership (Goldblatt, 1990b; Blaxter, 1990). Not surprisingly, given the evidence on differences in overall death rates, gradients in mortality by social class exist for nearly all the major causes of death, with the steepest gradients in Britain found in the accident and respiratory categories (Whitehead, 1987). While many particular and rarer causes of death, for example some cancers, show either very little or reverse socioeconomic gradation (Davey Smith et al., 1991), the fact that the big killers like cardiovascular disease show such patterns both explains the width of the gradient and suggests that social forces must be contributory. It is necessary to consider whether such effects are the direct result of material deprivation only or have a more complex psycho-social explanation that assimilates the full experience of relative disadvantage on individuals (Wilkinson, 1996).

One of the most influential studies in the area of health inequalities was the Whitehall study of 17,000 civil servants working in government offices in London between 1967 and 1969 (Marmot et al., 1984; Marmot and Theorell, 1988). The study documented for men a steep inverse relationship between employment grade and poor health outcomes, including mortality from many diseases. What is striking about the study is that such large differences occurred even though the study population excluded not only the poorest without work but also all manual workers. A follow-up study, Whitehall II, examined a new group of British civil servants between 1985 and 1988. The most important finding of Whitehall II is that in the 20 year interval since Whitehall I there had been no reduction (in some cases even a widening) in prevalence and incidence of many diseases. In the 25 year follow-up of Whitehall I men aged 49-64 there was a four-fold higher relative risk of death from all causes of mortality from the lowest to the highest occupational grade (Marmot, 1999).

In contrast to the interest shown in this topic in other countries, the volume of research output on socioeconomic differences in mortality has been low in Ireland. Mortality data are not routinely reported either by small area or according to socioeconomic grouping. The simplest measure of differences in mortality between socioeconomic groups is the crude death rate, which takes no account of the age distribution of the population. This is the ratio of the number of deaths to the number of people at risk expressed as an annual rate. The overall annualised death rate for males for the period 1986-91 in Ireland is 4.1 deaths per year. There is wide variation in the rate across SEGs, ranging from a low of 2.0 in the higher professional group to a high of 5.7 in the unskilled manual group. The difficulty with the crude death rate centres on the fact that the age structure of the population in the various socioeconomic groups is not taken into account in calculating the relative rates. The use of standardised mortality ratios (SMRs) overcomes the difficulties associated with the application of crude death rates. An SMR over 100 means, of course, that the SEG has had more deaths than would be expected on the basis of average age-specific death rates and the SEG's actual age composition.

Nolan's (1990) was the first attempt to examine standard mortality differentials by socioeconomic group using national data for Ireland. Using standard methodology for generating SMRs, Nolan's results revealed substantial differences in mortality across socioeconomic groups. There were significant differentials in SMRs between people in the professional and managerial occupational groups and those in the manual occupational groups. For example, men in the unskilled manual category had an SMR almost three times higher than men in the professional group. Nolan's work was based on 1981 population and mortality data, confined to males between the age of 15 and 64 and limited to aggregate rather than disease-specific death rates.

Continuing this work, O'Shea (1997) looked at male mortality differentials by socioeconomic group for the period 1986-91. He found significant variation in SMRs by socioeconomic group, ranging from 49 in the higher professional group, to 139 in the unskilled manual group, and 268 in the residual category. Both the semi-skilled and unskilled manual categories have an SMR score significantly above 100. All of the other SEGs with the exception of the farm labourer and fishermen category have SMR scores substantially below 100. The results confirm Nolan's findings of significant differences in mortality for males among socioeconomic groups in Ireland. Standardised mortality ratios by socioeconomic group can also be calculated for the most common causes of death for males in Ireland (Table 8.1). Cancers and diseases of the circulatory system account for over two-thirds of all deaths in the country. The third most common cause of death is respiratory disease at 14 per cent. Tussing (1986) cites evidence that these three common causes of premature death, together with injury and poisoning, are most often found among people in lower socioeconomic groups.

Gradients in mortality by socioeconomic group are apparent for all of the four major causes of death referred to above (O'Shea, 1997). There is a sharp class gradient associated with diseases of the circulatory system. Males in the unskilled manual SEG are 2.8 times more likely to die from diseases of the circulatory system (ICD-9 Code 390-459) than males in the higher professional category. The ratio of SMRs between the combined unskilled and semi-skilled manual groups and the two professional groups is just under 2.5:1. The SMR ratio between the unknown category and the higher professional group rises to 4.5 :1.

Table 8.1: Standardised Mortality Ratios for Males (15-64) by Cause of Death by Socioeconomic Group, 1986-91

	Socioeconomic Group	All Cancers	Circulatory System	Injury and Poisoning	Respiratory
0	Farmers, relatives assisting and farm managers	76*	89*	110*	87**
1	Farm labourers and fishermen	93	94	146*	116
2	Higher professional	61*	50*	42*	36*
3	Lower professional	62*	58*	58*	37*
4	Employers and managers	75*	62*	56*	31*
5	Salaried employees	77*	69*	58*	46*
6	Non-manual wage-earners (white collar)	88*	92**	73*	60*
7	Non-manual wage-earners (other)	101	96	67*	77*
8	Skilled manual workers	104	89*	71*	65*
9	Semi-skilled manual workers	126*	119*	94	98
X	Unskilled manual workers	135*	138*	151*	177*
Y	Unknown	197*	227*	367*	363*
	Total deaths	6,450	9,961	3,977	1,451

* 1% level of significance

** 5% level of significance

Source: O'Shea (1997)

The mortality differentials among SEGs arising from diseases of the circulatory system are likely to be due to variations in causal factors known to influence the risk and incidence of heart disease. Altogether, there are approximately 300 risk factors for coronary heart disease (CHD), none of them providing the final piece in the inequality jigsaw (Hopkins and Williams, 1986). However, the three principal risk factors for CHD are smoking, total cholesterol level and raised blood pressure

(Department of Health and Children, 1999). Limited data in an Irish context indicate that of these risk factors, only smoking is significantly class-related (Kilkenny Health Project, 1992). Smoking behaviour is believed to be an important major factor influencing social class differentials in the risk of ischaemic heart disease but of itself does not provide the explanation for the observed socioeconomic variations in mortality (Pocock et al., 1987; Davey Smith et al., 1991). Mortality differentials with respect to heart disease may also be linked to economic factors including the structure of the job market, variations in the level of employment and in the proportion of early retirees among socioeconomic groups (Starrin et al., 1993). Part of the association between social class and cardiovascular illness may also be due to differences in psychosocial work conditions (Marmot and Theorell, 1988; Rosengren et al., 1993). The latter includes an important number of crucial job-related variables such as skill discretion, authority over decisions, social support at work and the ability to deal with stress.

The question of precisely why inequalities in mortality exist remains as yet unanswered. In recent years there has been a focus on early foetal exposure and long-term adult risk (Barker et al., 1989; Barker, 1992, 1997). In exploring the aetiology of heart disease, the most promising avenue may be the exploration of advantage and disadvantage, not just at a point in time, but over the course of a lifetime (Kaplan and Salonen, 1990). Multiple deprivation is very often a lifetime phenomenon, defying both simple behavioural and structuralist explanations for its persistence, but ultimately leading to premature death. Health at middle and later life reflects health at earlier life, right back to life in the mother's womb, in a complex but important way (Lundberg, 1993; Davey Smith et al., 1997, 1998; Kuh and Ben-Shlomo, 1997). This holds, not only for cardiovascular disease but also for other main causes of death, particularly respiratory disease (Barker, 1992). The precise causal relationship between life circumstances at an early age and poor health in adulthood are not yet fully understood. Biological mechanisms (Barker, 1992), lifestyle, such as smoking and physical activity (Blane et al., 1996) and psychological attributes (Bosma et al., 1999) have all been put forward as plausible explanations for the influence of early life factors on adult health. However, more studies, which gather data about infancy, childhood, and adult life, are required to clarify the nature and size of the causal relationships and the various pathways to ill health. Evidence suggests that present, childhood and parental social position all contribute to the development of disease in adult life and a series of elegant cohort analyses by Davey Smith et al. (1998) have shown that these effects may vary in importance depending on the condition in question. Stomach cancer relates to adverse childhood experience, coronary heart disease relates to childhood and adult behaviours but lung cancer is largely attributable to adult smoking. It is regrettable, given that Ireland has such high death rates from CHD and some cancers and has undergone such major socioeconomic changes in the last century that we know so little about the social influences on these disease patterns. One study, comparing two generations of Irish migrants to America with a group at home, produced data consistent with a lifecourse explanation. But the study was quite small and the findings statistically insignificant (Kushi et al., 1986).

Deaths from cancers account for approximately one-quarter of all deaths in Ireland. Males in the lower socioeconomic groups experience higher mortality from cancer than males in professional and managerial socioeconomic groups. Males in the manual categories have an SMR score twice that of males in the professional groups. The ratio of SMRs between the unskilled manual category and the higher professional group is 2.2:1. These results are similar to those found in Britain, where deaths from malignant neoplasms are highest in the lower socioeconomic groups (Leon, 1988; Kogevinas, 1990). However, the data for Ireland do not explore the relationship between socioeconomic position and particular cancers, although we know the association between cancer risk and socioeconomic position varies by type of cancer, by site and over long periods of time, leading to a good deal of heterogeneity in the relationship (Davey Smith et al., 1991). Occupational exposure is likely to be important in this context; some cancers like non-Hodgkins lymphoma are increasing in incidence. Almost certainly there is some kind of environmental explanation and they are higher in certain groups of workers, particularly modern farmers (Kelleher et al., 1999; Hope et al., 1999a).

The major causes of death under the injury and poisoning heading are motor vehicle accidents, accidents at work, murder and suicides. The highest SMRs are found in the unskilled manual group, the farm labourer and fishermen category, while farmers also have an SMR score significantly above 100. Males in the unskilled manual group have an SMR 3.6 times greater than males in the higher professional category. The inclusion of farmers, farm labourers and fishermen in the high risk category is not surprising given the potential hazards they face in their jobs. From the evidence presented above, it is obvious that working conditions play an important role in inequalities in mortality among socioeconomic groups. It follows logically that policies designed to effect an improvement in working conditions for people in vulnerable SEGs would be an important advance in dealing with existing inequalities in mortality.

Mortality rates from respiratory disease are high in Ireland relative to other developed European countries. Tussing (1986) explained the high Irish rate by reference to the particular meteorological conditions that prevail in the country. Historically, tuberculosis rates in Ireland were relatively high. While this may partly explain the high rate in Ireland, it does not account for the large differences in mortality among socioeconomic groups arising from respiratory problems (Table 8.1). The highest SMRs are again found in the unskilled manual and unknown SEGs. The lowest SMRs are in the employers and managers group and the two professional groups. The ratio between the unskilled manual group and the employers and managers group is just under 6:1.

Material circumstances are likely to be a major cause of differences among SEGs with respect to mortality from respiratory causes. Homelessness, poor housing, damp housing and over-crowding are likely to lead to increased respiratory infections with an increasing risk of mortality. Much of the influence of material circumstances on respiratory illness may begin in childhood and lead to premature adult mortality (Robinson and Pinch, 1987). Behavioural tendencies, such as high levels of smoking, may also interact with material circumstances to bring about higher levels of mortality from respiratory sources in some SEGs. An integrated explanation, of material, behavioural and psychosocial factors is also possible (Wilkinson, 1996).

To what extent are these differences in mortality rates according to socioeconomic group replicated when areas associated with deprivation or advantage are examined? Small area differences in SMRs have been studied in Dublin city (Johnson and Dack, 1989), including later work on the socioeconomic determinants of observed differences across areas (Johnson and Lyons, 1993). The variation of SMRs between district electoral divisions in Dublin can partly be explained by variation in socioeconomic factors. A similar association between socioeconomic disadvantage and low birth weight was also established using data for Dublin city and county divided into 322 wards and district electoral divisions. Significant differences in mortality ratios across counties have also been identified in Ireland (Howell et al., 1993). These differences could not, however, be explained in the study either by the Townsend index of material deprivation or by a new Irish index of material deprivation developed for the study. Recent work does show mortality differentials within urban areas in keeping with international experience, though interestingly this pattern did not hold true for rural areas, in part perhaps because standard deprivation indices do not apply in that setting. The fascinating question of whether ill health is associated with indicators of individual affluence, wider community circumstances, or both, therefore remains to be fully explored in an Irish context.

There are now two major datasets that can be used to examine important socioeconomic relationships in health in Ireland. The national health and lifestyle surveys were commissioned by the Department of Health and reported on in 1999 (Centre for Health Promotion Studies, 1999a, 1999b). SLAN, the survey of lifestyles, attitudes and nutrition, was based on a multistage sample drawn from the electoral register at district electoral division; the final sample was 6,539 adults with a response rate of over 61 per cent which is respectable by international standards. The health behaviours in schoolgoing children survey (HBSC) is part of an international project and uses a standard protocol. Pupils were selected through classrooms and were representative of all regions and types of schools. The final sample was 8,487 pupils. For the first time, therefore, we have detailed information on self-reported health status, some health service utilisation and self-reported lifestyle behaviours.

These datasets have been examined, so far, according to self-reported occupation of the respondent or head of household and according to eligibility for general medical services, which in Ireland is a means tested system entitling beneficiaries to comprehensive services, particularly in primary care. Among young people, particularly in primary school and early teens, there are few variations in self-reported lifestyle behaviours according to parents' occupation but such patterns become established by late teens among both boys and girls in relation to common lifestyle factors like smoking, diet and alcohol consumption. In relation to virtually all such lifestyle behaviours there are strong consistent inverse relationships with social class. Similarly, among adults, there are highly significant variations in all common lifestyle behaviours and this is a graduated, not a dichotomous pattern. In other words, rather than a particular proportion of people who are at marked social disadvantage there is a spectrum of risk from the least to the most affluent. To take some examples, while one third of the population are smokers, the range varies from 25 per cent of men in social classes one and two to 38 per cent of men in social classes 5 and 6.[1] For women, the comparable rates are 27 per cent and 39 per cent respectively. Not alone do these rates indicate that there are behavioural differences to be tackled but also that health promotion strategies that do not take account of these variations are likely, ultimately to be unsuccessful. Furthermore there are few strong regional variations. Though some differences exist between the Eastern Health Board and the rest of the country, these effects are eliminated or significantly attenuated when measures of social/economic circumstances are taken into account.

---

[1] Social class in Ireland is measured on a six-point ordinal scale similar to that used in the UK, devised from 12 socioeconomic groups, in turn compiled from 137 job categories taken from the census data.

If one examines the data according to medical card status, marked significant differences also emerge. Those who hold medical cards consistently do worse than non-card holders in every parameter measured, from health care need and utilisation through to smoking and drinking patterns. Respondents were asked to report whether they had ever been told by a doctor that they had various cardiovascular or other conditions. Such self-reported cardiovascular morbidity was also consistently higher for medical cardholders than for non-cardholders. The only exception to this trend related to having been told previously that one had a raised cholesterol (Kelleher et al., 1999), suggesting possibly that primary care coverage for this risk factor is more a matter of demand by the more affluent than the meeting of need. In a previous study Lyons et al. (1996) also demonstrated that the distribution of chronic illness in middle-aged Dublin residents is clearly social class-related. We now plan to examine these effects at small area level to interrelate the patterns of individual, class and area of socioeconomic advantage more closely.

How do these effects translate into health education and health promotion programmes in different settings? Here the evidence from qualitative attitudinal work and intervention data is also interesting. For instance attitudes to risk of heart disease show gender and generation variation (Nic Gabhainn et al., 1999). Men perceive themselves as less susceptible than women and those who are older exhibit more fatalism about risk than younger people and more faith in health care. Class-related patterns of knowledge about risk are not as marked, but there is evidence that those in blue collar occupations express themselves in less comprehensive detail than people who are more affluent. The likelihood that personal development or lifeskills strategies are more finely tuned to the needs of the better educated and more affluent is borne out by the fact that social circumstances played a role in the effectiveness of lifeskills and health promotion programmes in schools (Nic Gabhainn and Kelleher, 1995, 1998, Friel et al., 1999) and in general practice-based programmes for school-going children (Kelleher et al., 1999). In the workplace, many programmes have focused on individualised lifestyle programmes which may be more practicable for workers with more discretion and time to attend. On the other hand, facilitation of environmental or organisational change, even in the case of basic lifestyle-related programmes such as alterations in canteen food or opportunities for exercise, can have an impact when workers are consulted. In one recent study in Ireland in this area, the gain for blue collar women workers appeared to be relatively greater (Hope et al., 1999b).

8.4 INCOME INEQUALITY AND HEALTH

A number of studies have produced controversial evidence that countries with less income inequality enjoy better health. Wilkinson (1996) discusses several such studies that appear to show that people live longer in countries where income differences between the poorest and richest classes are lower. Japan, for example, had the highest life expectancy of any developed country in the late 1980s and the lowest level of income inequality. Sweden had the second highest life expectancy in the world and the second lowest level of income inequality. People in Japan and Sweden live, on average, two or three years longer than people in the US and Britain where income differences are wider. Kennedy et al. (1998) found that individuals living in states in the US with the greatest inequalities in income were 30 per cent more likely to report their health as fair or poor than individuals living in states with the smallest inequalities in income. Similarly, Kaplan et al. (1996) argue that variations in the distribution of income among states in the US are significantly associated with differences in health outcomes and mortality across states. Some researchers have expressed doubt on the existence of any strong relationship between income inequality and health. In a review of published work on the relationship between measures of income inequality and average levels of population health, Judge et al. (1998) identify a number of methodological problems, including the poor quality of some of the income distribution data which cast doubt on the reliability of results in this area. Their overall conclusion is that the existing literature only provides modest support for the view that income inequality is associated with variations in average levels of national health among rich industrial nations. Even if people who live in more egalitarian societies have higher life expectancy this does not necessarily tell us very much, as many factors can affect average life expectancy, including a wide range of cultural, economic and social factors, most of which interact with each other. Concern has also been expressed by Gravelle (1998) that the observed relationship between income inequality and mortality is, in effect, a statistical artefact linked to an underlying individual level relation between income and risk of mortality. However, these differences cannot be explained as statistical artefacts of an underlying individual relation between income and mortality (Wolfson et al., 1999). It seems, therefore that health differences between developed countries reflect, not only differences in wealth, but also differences in income distribution (Quick and Wilkinson, 1991).

The relationship between health and income distribution seems to hold even when other factors such as GNP per capita and medical services are accounted for. Inequality is bad for the health of populations irrespective of the absolute standard of living of that population (Davey Smith, 1996). Income inequality may also matter more than the overall size of the welfare state. Japan and Sweden are at opposite ends of the OECD spectrum in terms of government social expenditure, but both are high achievers in terms of overall life expectancy.

What is it about income equality that positively affects life expectancy? To get a better idea of the answer to this question Wilkinson looked at particular societies that have changed either economically or socially during the 20th century, and describes how the health of their population has responded to change. What matters most in developed countries, he contends, is not absolute income but relative income. Societies with more income equality are more likely to be socially cohesive and, therefore, enjoy a richer and stronger community life. Although people with more social contacts and more involvement in local activities seem to have better health, this is only part of the picture. With income equality the stress associated with relative deprivation is reduced. This reduction in stress levels can have an important impact in reducing death by car-

diovascular and cancer associated illnesses. Moreover, more
equality and the reduction in stress levels associated with a
more egalitarian society are likely to reduce the number of
deaths from alcohol-related diseases, murder and accidents.

A recent paper by Lynch et al. (2000a) points to conceptual
and empirical difficulties with the psychosocial interpretation of
the relationship between income inequality and differences in
health and mortality. The main thrust of their argument is the
failure to adequately relate psychosocial factors to the material
conditions that structure the day to day experience of poor individuals and communities. They also caution against overly
simplistic interpretations of the links between investment in social capital and good health, particularly when these relationships are understood only in terms of horizontal social relations,
without any consideration of the role of vertical, institutional
social relations (political, economic, legal) in determining and
mediating informal social relations. The worry is that too much
emphasis on social capital will distract attention from the need
for public policy intervention to improve the living standards of
poor and impoverished communities within the framework of
full political and economic participation for all citizens (Lynch
et al., 2000b). This debate is essentially about the optimal public policy response to existing inequalities in health, whether
the heaviest weighting should go on interventions to deal with
neo-material conditions or whether more effort should be directed towards investment in social capital. For Wilkinson
(2000), inequality is a barrier to the development of health-
inducing social relations and for that reason investment in appropriate social capital is a key strategy for public health. This
is not a debate that should divide major researchers in this field
or allow policymakers to become complacent about the need
for change. While agreeing that the evidence of the relationship between income inequality and mortality is mixed, the
weight of the evidence suggests clearly that this cannot be ignored as a significant factor in understanding health inequalities across regions and countries.

8.5 EQUITY IN HEALTH AND HEALTH CARE

Up to now we have been examining the various factors that contribute to health inequalities both within and across countries. But there is an even more fundamental question, formulated as follows, that must be addressed before giving any consideration to the implications of all this evidence for public policy: what do we mean by equity in health? This is a searching and complex question, the answer to which we will not be able to give in this chapter but we will try to give some general clarity to the discussion, in the hope of providing some basis for effective policymaking and stimulating more discussion and research in this area in the future.

With that in mind the first issue is to distinguish between equality and equity. Equity involves some concept of fairness or justice in the distribution of a good or service — in this case health or health care. Some groups may deserve more health care resources than others on the basis of need, or because they cannot afford to pay for health care within a market or insurance-based system. Differences in the allocation of resources depend, therefore, on some shared view of social justice, linked to an assessment of need among various communities. The origin of the concern about fairness, or the philosophical and moral framework within which equity is negotiated is very important, as we will see, but it need not detain us at this early stage. Equality is both a narrower and simpler concept than equity, though it too may carry complex normative implications. Equality is concerned only with equal shares, which may or may not be judged fair or ethical. Equality is, therefore, but one particular interpretation of equity, simply that everyone should have the same of whatever is being distributed.

When we think of equity or equality in this area is it in relation to health status, health care, or both? While we all may want a fairer distribution of health the reality is that many of the factors that influence health status lie outside of the health care system. As we have already argued, health care is only one factor in the production of health. Complete health equality therefore, may not be a viable policy objective given the range of endogenous and exogenous factors associated with achieving that goal. The health production function contains many variables (Grossman, 1972), some of which are genetically-based and, therefore, not capable of influence from any public policy source, at least in the short to medium term. Other influences on health are structural in origin. To change them would require fundamental reform in the way the economy is organised, making it unlikely that these changes could occur without serious upheaval and disruption in our society. Coercing people to achieve the same level of health might also undermine important personal freedoms as well as proving financially damaging to both individuals and society. People may like doing things that damage their health and may consider policies that prevent them doing what they want to do to be elitist and/or authoritarian.

On the other hand, a core tenet of the modern health promotion movement is that individuals should be enabled to exert some control over determinants of their health status if they wish to do so (World Health Organisation, 1986), which is a function of both personal development and public policy strategies. While a major social or political shift on this premise alone is unlikely, many more minor strategies are achievable, though requiring cross-sectoral support. For instance, food production and distribution policies, fiscal strategies in relation to alcohol and tobacco and school education programmes are all achievable. A focus on early childhood exposure to risk is now advocated in several countries, as in the case of the UK's policy document on health inequalities (Acheson, 1988) and the recently produced Irish policy document for children (Denyer, Thornton, and Pelly, 1999). In ambitious strategies of this kind health status is treated as a valuable resource to society in and of itself, and its maintenance is at the least an equivalent consideration to other outputs and objectives in determining public policy generally. The goal of complete health equality would require more resources than could ever be made available, since equalisation at the highest possible level of attainable health would be prohibitively expensive, assuming, of course, that we could ever get agreement on what optimal health means, which is highly unlikely. However, there is increasing recognition internationally that cross-sectoral policy initiatives, although methodologically and ethically complex, could have a highly significant role.

Equity in quality and type of health care provision is arguably, therefore, a much more achievable goal (Fisher et al., 1999; Saxena et al., 1999; Weich et al., 1998), even if the limitations of any equalisation in health care on overall health status must be acknowledged. However, even within health care there are different approaches that can be taken to equity criteria. The primary distinction is between horizontal and vertical equity. The former refers to equal treatment of equals with respect to utilisation and access, while vertical equity refers to the unequal treatment of unequals which in the case of health care refers primarily to the progressivity of the financing system. Under horizontal equity the main policy focus has been on two criteria: equal utilisation for equal need and equal access for equal need. To the extent that countries have explicit policy targets with respect to equity, utilisation and access are the usual way in which these targets are formulated (Donaldson and Gerard, 1993).

Utilisation is mainly constrained by financial status so countries that value equal utilisation for equal need, such as Canada, have largely publicly financed systems. Free health care does not, however, guarantee equal utilisation since people's ability to use health care is also related to non-financial variables. Information problems may also persist which prevent people from taking up some health care services, particularly in the area of preventative services. In addition, equality of utilisation fails to take account of the individuality of patient-doctor relationships, particularly with respect to compliance, and the heterogeneity of medical practice for each type of need. Patients differ in how they experience health care interventions and doctors differ in how they practice medicine. There may also be a need for positive discrimination for some groups which goes beyond equality of utilisation. This means that some people should get more than others to simply catch up in terms of measured health. This, in turn, raises the difficult and thorny question of the measurement of need in any formulation of equity.

Equality of access takes account of some of these complexities by simply giving people the opportunity to use needed health care services. Equalising access by class or geographical area may, however, lead to efficiency-equity trade-offs which may prove impossible for policymakers to accept. For example, bringing health services to people living in remote areas may be desirable from an equity perspective, but the cost of achieving this equity goal may be so high as to make it impossible for any government to consider funding spatially equalising health care programmes. Efficiency-based, economies of scale arguments are likely to supersede equity objectives whenever there is a clash between the two. This is not to say that they should, simply that they nearly always do. In addition, equalising access may require investment outside of health care, particularly in the areas of education and transport. This investment may not only have financial ramifications, but may also throw up organisational difficulties which prevent the investment from taking place. For example, many social economy-type transport initiatives designed to reduce access problems in health and health care in remote areas have floundered on bureaucratic inflexibility and intransigence. This also brings up important questions of the valid participation by individuals and groups in decision making about their health care linked to the general nature of the public consultation process, a point highlighted in Ireland recently in respect of the Women's Health Initiative (O'Donovan, 2000).

8.6 PHILOSOPHICAL FRAMEWORKS AND EQUITY IN HEALTH AND HEALTH CARE

When discussing equity in health and health care it is helpful to locate any policy prescriptions within some specified philosophical position. Equity, in philosophical writings usually has a wider meaning than might be suggested by the above discussion, and incorporates concerns about both distributive justice and procedural justice. Although Donaldson and Gerard (1993) have characterised the philosophy debate as less than helpful in terms of aiding our understanding of the role of equity in health and health care, some treatment of philosophical issues is necessary if we are to set priorities for achieving equity. This is particularly true in a country like Ireland where there has never been an explicit debate on what weighting health inequalities should be given in resource allocation decisions both within and outside of the health care system. For example, the absence of health targets in the National Anti-Poverty Strategy is difficult to understand given the weight of evidence on the association between poverty and ill health. One can only conclude that this too reflects an inadequate database on which to make such recommendations and/or a limited conception of the impact of cross-sectoral initiatives on the health of individuals.

While different philosophical theories of justice have been developed, none has focused directly on health and health care issues. It is possible, however, to derive some insight into equity in health and health care from the available literature. There are two broad distinctions within liberal moral philosophy, that between teleological theories and deontological theories. Teleological theories will always justify their decisions in terms of their consequences. Deontological theories justify theories in terms of following the right procedures rather than promoting the best consequences. The best known teleological theory is utilitarianism, while the leading deontological theory is Rawls' theory of justice. Since Rawls' theory developed in 1971, many contemporary political thinkers have been more concerned with deontological theories than with teleological theories, though much of economic thinking continues to be based on a utilitarian calculus.

According to utilitarianism, justice is associated with maximising the sum total of human happiness. The optimal solution in all choice exercises is taken to be the sum total of individual utilities. Sum ranking gives no value to equality; indeed, utilitarianism is prepared to contemplate endlessly sacrificing one person's good in order to maximise the overall good (Kymlicka, 1989). All variables involving choice such as actions, rules, or institutions are judged in terms of their consequences, their contribution to the maxim and ideal. Process and procedures are not important in the utilitarian calculus. Outcomes are all that matters with the latter judged in terms of individual utilities.

One of the most difficult questions for the utilitarian is whether preferences are always synonymous with value. The emphasis here is on revealed-preference utilitarianism where utility is simply a representation of people's choices. Is knowledge of what people choose sufficient to arrive at conclusions about what they regard as valuable? A necessary condition in this regard is that value is equated with choice. People's choice may, however, be constrained by the availability of suitable alternatives. This is particularly true of placement decision making for dependent elderly people. People may choose long stay residential care but only because community care services are so under-developed. At other times it is difficult to define true sovereignty. For example, dependent older people may be forced to live with relatives they do not like on the basis that somebody else has decided that this is where they should live. Another difficulty is that preferences may be based on false beliefs. This may be particularly relevant in the case of non-purchase of needed health care or the purchase of health "bads", such as cigarettes. For that reason, defenders of utilitarianism have claimed that only choices based on full information need be considered in the utilitarian calculus. The dilemma for the utilitarian is that this approach, which is basically one of laundering preferences, undermines the consumer sovereignty ideal, which is itself a major element in the utilitarian framework.

Contractarianism refers to a method of devising principles or rules rather than any particular choice of same. It refers more to a method of arriving at moral judgements than to a substantive moral theory (Hausman and McPherson, 1993). The idea is that rational people, under certain appropriate conditions, can be expected to consent to rules and institutions which guarantee certain moral and political rights in a society in which they expect to live. A particular type of contractarian approach is the Rawlsian theory of justice. Rawls (1971) argued that impartial rational actors making choices behind a veil of ignorance are the best adjudicators of alternative theories of justice. Behind the veil of ignorance individuals are denied access to any information which might allow them to predict their position and/or potential advantages and disadvantages in society. Indeed, individuals are denied knowledge not only of their traits and status but also of their preferences.

Rawls moves away from utility as a measure of the well-being of individuals. Instead he uses the concept of primary goods. The latter include basic liberties such as freedom of thought and association and self-respect, as well as the more tangible elements such as income, wealth, health and education. These primary goods are the means by which individuals can live out any of a number of rational life plans. Denied knowledge of their own likely endowments of primary goods, individuals, behind a veil of ignorance, adapt a risk-averse strategy in agreeing principles of justice. They would seek first to guarantee individual rights and then, subject to this constraint, seek to protect the interests of the least well-off in society through the promotion of just social and economic institutions.

Rawls' theory is based on two principles. First, civil liberties must be distributed equally and secondly, when inequalities exist they must be to the greatest benefit of the least advantaged members of society. When looking at inequalities, Rawls viewed them in terms of inputs as opposed to outcomes. People should have equal access to inputs which they can use to pursue their own health and happiness in whatever way they please. If we look at equality in terms of outcomes, Rawls claims that we would be failing to take into account that different people have a different view about what makes life worth living. Even allowing for the lexicographic representation of the principles defined above in favour of the liberty principle, Rawls' concept of justice as fairness allows for substantial involvement by government in the market. Intervention is necessary to protect the interest of the least well-off in society. Such concern is not merely altruistic. There is a moral basis for supporting institutions and processes that protect the disadvantaged which goes beyond altruism or notions of duty and citizenship.

There is a range of theories which argue that the focal point of welfare economics should be the freedom and opportunity that individuals have. According to Sen (1982) the opportunity aspect of freedom is concerned with our actual capability to achieve. It relates to the real opportunities we have of achieving things that we can and do value. For Sen, differences are the essence of any theory of equality. There are considerable differences among people in their ability to achieve or obtain what they want in life. Equalising resources is necessary to overcome these differences but it is clearly not sufficient. The capabilities of a person to achieve must also be addressed. Capabilities in this case refers to those characteristics of individuals beyond their immediate control. Failures that result from factors which are under the control of individuals should not be compensated against. At least there is no moral imperative which leads one to the view that imbalances in capabilities which result from poor endogenous decision-making should be of interest to society. Only those capabilities beyond the control and sphere of influence of the individual deserve to be recognised and addressed. Equal access in this case can be interpreted as equal availability of resources required to fulfil individual potential.

Le Grand (1991) argues that a distribution is equitable if it is the outcome of informed individuals choosing over equal choice sets. Once again, it is barriers beyond individual control that are a source of inequity in society. These barriers act as constraints on individuals acquiring the same level of capabilities as others; what people do with capabilities once they have them should not be of concern to society. In other words, individuals should not be compensated for poor individual decision-making. Similarly, Cohen (1993) has argued that public policy should be aimed at securing equality of access to advantage. The equality aspect is similar to Le Grand in that Cohen thinks differential advantage is unjust save where it reflects differences in genuine choice on the part of relevant agents. Arneson (1990) argues similarly that society is not obligated to intervene in the distributive process if an individual is responsible for the special need he or she has acquired. It is only if the acquisition and retention of the need is beyond the control of the individual that society must intervene, regardless of the nature of the need.

This approach has interesting implications for people who engage in behaviour which damages their own health. Should people who, with full information, knowingly consume health "bads" be compensated in the form of free health care when they become ill? On the basis of the above theories, the answer on the face of it is negative. But the health choices that people make may be determined by many non-health-related structures and opportunities. They may make such decisions because they face unequal choice sets which force them into the consumption of health "bads" in the first place. Proponents of health education, or indeed education generally, would argue that skills development for helping people to make better choices is empowering in discriminating the most advantageous choice, and, therefore should be part of health investment strategies. Achieving full equality of choice sets will, therefore, require increased investment and positive discrimination in areas outside of traditional health care and health sectors.

8.7 POLICY IMPLICATIONS IN AN IRISH CONTEXT

Traditionally, there has been very little attention paid to the effect of social inequalities on health in this country. Given the absence of much information on existing health inequalities, it is perhaps not surprising to find so little discussion on the causes of socioeconomic mortality differentials (Cook, 1990). Part of the reason for this may have been complacency and myopia among policymakers, stemming from the belief that free health care for the least well-off would serve to mitigate the worst effects of social inequalities in health status. As has been clearly demonstrated in the UK however, even the provision of a comprehensive health care system cannot meet health needs if there are other negative social forces at work (Black Report, 1980; Ben-Shlomo et al., 1996). An analysis of recent public policy documents in Ireland reveals a paradox however. Despite the absence of appropriate evidence-based information and a general lack of practical application there has been an active approach to change in public health policy in published documentation.

In 1986, a document titled "Health: The Wider Dimensions" was published (Department of Health, 1986). This document was arguably unusual in that it explicitly advocated a cross-sectoral approach to health policy, asserting that the health of individuals was determined by a range of different factors outside the control of the traditional health care sector and hence was as much a function of education or employment policy as it was a matter of health service provision. In 1994, a major document was published titled "Shaping A Healthier Future" (Department of Health, 1994). This was a comprehensive collation of documents produced in every area of the health service over the intervening period since "Health: the Wider Dimensions" was published. It similarly advocated a cross-sectoral multidisciplinary approach and reiterated statements in previous documents on the need for an inter-departmental government strategy. In many specific areas since, such as policy on older people (Department of Health and Children, 1998) or in relation to cancer or heart disease a similar line has been taken.

The 1994 document stressed core principles of equity, accountability and access but was not explicit to any degree on disadvantage. The need for health development sectors to highlight areas of disadvantage and specific high-risk groups was mentioned but not expanded upon in detail. This leaves some gaps in public policy as enunciated by these documents. First there is an assumption that there are regional or area effects to disadvantage. However, while we do see some evidence of this in such area-based work as exists, there is no convincing regional evidence that cannot be explained by more specific individual-level analysis. Second, although we operate a two-tier health care service, the precise nature of eligibility and the impact of this on health has not been fully explored. Since Tussing (1986) first described the inequities apparent in the GMS, very little work has been undertaken to highlight why this is so and what policy bearing it has. Yet, as we indicated earlier, considerable variations in health status exist according to GMS status, which may be a function of real social differences, of expressed need and demand or of standards of equitable delivery. Data from the Economic and Social Research Institute (Nolan, 1991) showed a relatively high share of health care expenditure going to the lower income quintiles but this was less than the proportion of people reporting serious illness within these quintiles. However, more sophisticated measures of need would be required before any firm conclusions could be drawn about whether health care was distributed equitably in relation to needs. Third, work on the causes of social variation in mortality continues to be scarce, notwithstanding the promise of new initiatives set out in the recent report of the Cardiovascular Health Strategy Group (Department of Health and Children, 1999).

As indicated earlier, there is little data on variations according to social class grouping at any level, though what data we do have suggest that such inequalities do exist and are similar to other developed countries. In recent years there have been important policy initiatives, but while both the cancer strategy (Department of Health, 1996) and the cardiovascular strategy (Department of Health and Children, 1999) highlight the need to tackle disadvantage and take account of demographic variation, there is little explicit focus on the issue. Despite the fact that class differentials in mortality and morbidity patterns and lifestyle behaviours are known to exist (and the health promotion strategies to tackle common disease patterns like heart disease in various settings have also demonstrated a graduated pattern of effectiveness), there has been little concerted effort to address why or shift the focus in public policy to support the less advantaged or to create targets that narrow inequality beyond more general rhetoric about issues of equity and access.

This is regrettable because it is likely that in a country the size of the Republic of Ireland, currently in a state of rapid economic transition, any public policy measures to narrow gaps, such as universal education, a minimum wage, adequate social welfare, changes in which are linked to average incomes, and concerted area-based community development can be effective in stemming the problem. Why should we wait until things deteriorate to the level of other countries before we do something about it, in a period of unprecedented economic growth? The weight of evidence points to the importance of investment in neo-material conditions in reducing health inequalities within countries. Cultural processes also matter, with more unequal societies less likely to generate and foster supportive social environments, which in turn contribute to higher levels of health inequality. One of our difficulties appears to be a lack of ideological variation in public policy debate. Three of the four main political parties are very similar in terms of policy. In the area of health inequalities, they are prepared to acknowledge geographical but not socioeconomic differentials in health. The core issue for political parties, and for us all, is whether we can call ourselves a decent society when, scarcity of data duly acknowledged, there exist fundamental, but avoidable, differences in health between rich and poor in this country.

8.8 CONCLUSION

The conventional starting point for discussions on causation for health inequalities are the explanations provided by the Black Report (1980). These explanations cover the following areas: measurement error (i.e. the differences are a mere statistical artefact), social selection (poverty results from a poor constitution or ill health), individual behaviour (the individual is responsible for his or her own misfortune), and material and social circumstances. While international research on causal relationships is a long way from providing a consensus on the causes of health inequality, the distinction between behavioural and materialist explanations is increasingly seen as artificial in that they are inextricably linked. What appears to be the most fundamental cause of health inequalities is life circumstances, which contains elements of both behavioural and materialist explanations. While this is about as far as agreement goes, policymakers in this country can learn from the vast amount of published research in the area, as well as from intervention strategies in other countries, such as the Netherlands (Mackenbach, 1994). It is to be hoped that we will see a concerted programme of research and policy innovation with respect to health inequalities in this country in the coming decade.

References

Acheson, D. (Chairman, 1988), *Independent Inquiry into Inequalities in Health Report*, London, Stationery Office

Arneson, R. (1990), "Liberalism, Distributive Subjectivism, and Equality of Opportunity for Welfare", *Philosophical and Public Affairs*, Vol. 56, 158-94

Barker, D.J.P. (1992), *Fetal and Infant Origins of Adult Disease,* London, British Medical Journal Books

Barker, D.J.P., C. Osmond, J. Golding, D. Kuh, and M.J.E. Wadsworth (1989), "Growth in Utero, Blood Pressure in Childhood and Adult Life, and Mortality from Cardiovascular Disease", *British Medical Journal,* Vol. 298, 564-67

Barker, D.J.P. (1997), "Maternal Nutrition, Fetal Nutrition and Diseases in Later Life", *Nutrition,* Vol. 13, No. 9, 807-13

Benzeval, M., K. Judge and W. Whitehead (1995), "Introduction" in Benzeval, Judge and Whitehead (eds.), *Tackling Inequalities in Health: An Agenda for Action,* London, King's Fund

Ben-Shlomo, Y., I.R. White and M. Marmot (1996), "Does the Variation in the Socioeconomic Characteristics of an Area Affect Mortality?", *British Medical Journal,* Vol. 312, 1013-1014

Black Report, (1980), *Inequalities in Health,* Report of a Research Working Group, Sir Douglas Black, Chairman, London, HMSO

Blane, D., C.L. Hart, G. Davey Smith, C.R. Gillis., D.J. Hole and V.M. Hawthorne (1996), "Association of Cardiovascular Disease Risk Factors with Socioeconomic Position during Childhood and during Adulthood", *British Medical Journal,* Vol. 313, 1434-8

Blane, D. and F. Drever (1998), "Inequality among Men in Standardised Years of Potential Life Lost, 1970-93", *British Medical Journal,* Vol. 317, 255

Blaxter, M. (1990), *Health and Lifestyles,* London, Tavistock/Routledge

Bosma, H., D. Van de Mheen. and J. Mackenbach (1999), "Social Class in Childhood and General Health in Adulthood: Questionnaire Study of Contribution of Psychological Attributes", *British Medical Journal,* Vol. 318, 18-22

Centre for Health Promotion Studies, (1999a), *Results of the National Health and Lifestyle Surveys (SLAN),* Health Promotion Unit, Department of Health and Children and Centre for Health Promotion Studies, Galway

Centre for Health Promotion Studies, (1999b), *Regional Results of the National Health and Lifestyle Surveys,* Health Promotion Unit, Department of Health and Children and Centre for Health Promotion Studies, Galway

Cohen, G.A. (1993), "Equality of What? On Welfare, Goods and Capabilities", in Nussbaum, M., and Sen A., eds., *The Quality of Life,* Oxford, Clarendon Press

Cook, G. (1990), "Health and Social Inequities in Ireland", *Social Science and Medicine,* Vol. 31, No. 3, 285-290

Davey Smith, G., D. Leon, M.J. Shipley and G. Rose (1991), "Socioeconomic Differentials in Cancer among Men", *International Journal of Epidemiology*, Vol. 20, No. 2, 339-345

Davey Smith, G., D. Blane, and M. Bartley (1994), "Explanations for Socioeconomic Differentials in Mortality: Evidence from Britain and Elsewhere", *European Journal of Public Health*, Vol. 4, No. 2, 131-144

Davey Smith, G. (1996), "Income Inequality and Mortality: Why are They Related?" *British Medical Journal*, Vol. 312, 987-988

Davey Smith, G., C. Hart, D. Blane, and D. Hole (1998), "Adverse Socioeconomic Conditions in Childhood and Cause Specific Adult Mortality: Prospective Observational Study", *British Medical Journal*, Vol. 316, 1631-35

Davey Smith, G., C. Hart, D. Blane, C. Gillis and V. Hawthorne (1997), "Lifetime Socioeconomic Position and Mortality: Prospective Observational Study", *British Medical Journal*, Vol. 314, 547-52

Denyer, S., L. Thornton, and H. Pelly (1999), *Best Health for Children: Developing a Partnership with Families — A Progress Report,* Dublin

Department of Health (1986), *Health, the Wider Dimensions*, Dublin, Stationery Office

Department of Health (1994), *Shaping a Healthier Future: A Strategy for Effective Healthcare in the 1990s,* Dublin, Stationery Office

Department of Health (1996), *Cancer Services in Ireland: A National Strategy*, Dublin, Stationery Office

Department of Health and Children (1998), *Adding Years to Life and Life to Years, A Health Promotion Strategy for Older People,* National Council on Ageing and Older People

Department of Health and Children (1999), *Building Healthier Hearts: The Report of the Cardiovascular Health Strategy Group*, Dublin

Donaldson, C. and K. Gerard (1993), *Economics of Health Care Financing: The Visible Hand,* London, Macmillan

Eames, M., B. Ben-Shlomo, and M.G. Marmot (1993), "Social Deprivation and Premature Mortality: Regional Comparisons across England", *British Medical Journal*, Vol. 307, 1097-1011

Fiscella, K. and P. Franks (1997), "Poverty or Income Inequality as Predictors of Mortality: Longitudinal Cohort Study", *British Medical Journal,* Vol. 314, 1724-1727

Fisher, B., H. Neve, and Z. Heritage (Editorial), (1999), "Community Development, User Involvement and Primary Health Care", *British Medical Journal*, Vol. 318, 749-50

Ford, G., R. Ecob, K. Hunt, S. Macintyre and P. West (1994), "Patterns of Class Inequality in Health through the Lifespan: Class Gradients at 15, 35 and 55 Years in the West of Scotland", *Social Science and Medicine*, Vol. 39, 1037-50

Friel, S., C. Kelleher, P. Campbell and G. Nolan (1999), "Evaluation of the Nutrition Education Programme of Primary School (NEAPS)", *Public Health Nutrition*, Vol. 2, 549-55

Goldblatt, P. (ed.) (1990a), "Longitudinal Study: Mortality and Social Organisation", *Office of Population Censuses and Surveys*, Series LS No. 6, London, HMSO

Goldblatt, P. (1990b), "Mortality and Alternative Social Classifications" in Goldblatt, P. (ed.) *Longitudinal Study: Mortality and Social Organisation*, OPCS Series LS. No. 6, London, HMSO

Gravelle, H. (1998), "How Much of the Relation between Population Mortality and Unequal Distribution of Income is Statistical Artefact?" *British Medical Journal*, Vol. 316, 382-85

Grossman, M. (1972), *The Demand for Health: A Theoretical and Empirical Investigation*, New York, NBER

Hausmann, D. and M. McPherson (1993), "Taking Ethics Seriously: Economics and Contemporary Moral Philosophy", *Journal of Economic Literature*, Vol. 31, 671-31

Hermon, C. and V. Beral (1996), "Breast Cancer Mortality Rates are Levelling off or Beginning to Decline in Many Western Countries: Analysis of Time Trends, Age-Cohort and Age-Period Models of Breast Cancer Mortality in 20 Countries", *British Journal of Cancer*, Vol. 73, 955-960

Hirshell, B. and P. Francioli (1998), Progress and Problems in the Fight against AIDS, *New England Journal of Medicine*, Vol. 13, 906-08

Hope, A., C. Kelleher, L. Holmes and T. Hennessy (1999a), "Health and Safety Practices among Farmers and Other Workers: A Needs Assessment", *Occupational Medicine*, Vol. 49, 231-5

Hope, A., C. Kelleher and M. O'Connor (1999b), "Lifestyle and Cancer: The Relative Effects of a Workplace Health Promotion Programme across Gender and Social Class", *American Journal of Health Promotion*, Vol. 13, 315-318

Hopkins, P.N. and R.R. Williams (1986), "Identification and Relative Weight of Cardiovascular Risk Factors", *Cardiology Clinics*, Vol. 4, 3-31

Howell, F., M. O'Mahony, J. Devlin, O. O'Reilly and C. Buttenshaw (1993), "A Geographical Distribution of Mortality and Deprivation" *Irish Medical Journal*, Vol. 86, No. 3, 96-99

Johnson, Z. and P. Dack (1989), "Small Area Mortality Patterns", *Irish Medical Journal*, Vol. 82, No. 3, 105-108

Johnson, Z. and R. Lyons (1993), "Socioeconomic Factors and Mortality in Small Areas", *Irish Medical Journal*, Vol. 86, No. 2, 60-62

Johnson, Z., P. Dack and J. Fogarty (1994), "Small Area Analysis of Low Birth Weight", *Irish Medical Journal*, Vol. 87, No. 6, 176-77

Judge, K. (1995), "Income Distribution and Life Expectancy: A Critical Appraisal", *British Medical Journal*, Vol. 311, 1282-85

Judge, K., J.A. Mulligan and M. Benzeval (1998), "Income Inequality and Population Health", *Social Science and Medicine*, Vol. 46, 567-79

Kaplan, G.A. and J.T. Salonen (1990), "Socioeconomic Conditions in Childhood and Ischaemic Heart Disease during Middle Age", *British Medical Journal*, Vol. 301, 1121-3

Kaplan, G.A., E. Pamuk, J.W. Lynch, R.D. Cohen and J.L. Balflour (1996), "Inequality in Income and Mortality in the United States: Analysis of Mortality and Potential Pathways", *British Medical Journal*, Vol. 312, 999-1003

Kawachi, I., G.A. Colditz, A. Ascherio, E.B. Rimm,, E. Giovannucci, M.J. Stampfer and W.C. Willett (1996), "A Prospective Study of Social Networks in Relation to Total Mortality and Cardiovascular Disease in Men in the USA", *Journal of Epidemiology and Community Health*, Vol. 50, 245-51

Kelleher, C. (1999), "Health and the Celtic Tiger: Progress of Health Promotion in Modern Ireland", editorial, *Health Education Research*, Oxford University Press, Vol. 14, No. 2, 151-54

Kelleher, C.C., U.B. Fallon, and E. McCarthy et al. (1999), "Feasibility of a Lifestyle Cardiovascular Health Promotion Programme for 8-15 Year Olds" in *Irish General Practice: Results of the Galway Health Project,* Vol. 14, 221-29

Kelleher, C., J. Newell, C. MacDonagh White, E. MacHale, E. Egan, E. Connolly, B. Delaney, H. Gough, E. Shryane (1998), "Incidence and Occupational Pattern of Leukaemias, Lymphomas and Testicular Cancers in the West of Ireland over an 11 Year Period", *Journal of Epidemiology and Community Health*, Vol. 52, 651-57

Kelleher, C., J. Harrington and S. Friel (1999), "Reported Cardio-vascular and other Morbidity among Adults over 55 years in the General Population: Findings from the Survey of Lifestyles, Attitudes and Nutrition (SLAN)", paper presented at the Faculty of Public Health Medicine Summer Scientific Meeting, Dublin, 8-9 June

Kennedy, B.P., I. Kawachi, R. Glass and D. Protherow-Stith (1998), "Income Distribution, Socioeconomic Status, and Self-rated Health in the United States: Multilevel Analysis", *British Medical Journal*, Vol. 317, 917-21

Kilkenny Health Project, (1992), *Final Report*, Kilkenny

Kogevinas, M. (1990), *Longitudinal Study: Socioeconomic Differences in Cancer Survivors*, 1971-83, OPCS Series LS No. 5, London, HMSO

Kondrichin, S.V. and O. Lester (1999), "I'm Alright Jack in Russia too", *Perceptual and Motor Skills*, Vol. 88, 892

Kuh, D. and Y. Ben-Shlomo (1997), *A Life Approach to Chronic Disease Epidemiology*, Oxford University Press, Oxford

Kunst, A. and J. Mackenbach (1994), *Measuring Socioeconomic Inequalities in Health*, World Health Organisation, Regional Office, Copenhagen

Kushi, L.H., R.A. Lew, F.J. Stare, C.R. Ellison, M. Lozy, G. Bourke, L. Daly, I. Graham, N. Hickey, R. Mulcahy and J. Kevaney (1986), "Diet and 20 Year Mortality from Coronary Heart Disease: The Ireland-Boston Diet-Heart Study", *New England Journal of Medicine*, Vol. 312, No. 13, 811-818

Kymlicka, W. (1989), *Contemporary Political Philosophy: An Introduction*, New York, Oxford University Press

Le Grand, (1991), *Equity and Choice: An Essay in Economics and Applied Philosophy*, London, Harper Collins, Academic

Leon, D.A. (1988), *Longitudinal Study: Social Distribution of Cancer*, 1971-75, OPCS Series LS No. 3, London, HMSO

Lundberg, O. (1993), "The Impact of Childhood Living Conditions on Illness and Mortality in Adulthood", *Social Science and Medicine*, Vol. 36, 1047-52

Lynch, J.W., G. Davey Smith, G.A. Kaplan and J.S. House (2000a), "Income Inequality and Mortality: Importance to Health of Individual Income, Psychosocial Environment, or Material Conditions", *British Medical Journal*, Vol. 320, pp.1200-1204

Lynch, J.W., P. Due, C. Muntaner and G. Davey Smith (2000b), "Social Capital: Is it a Good Investment Strategy for Public Health?", *Journal of Epidemiology and Community Health*, Vol. 54, 404-408

Lyons, R.A., F. O'Kelly, J. Mason, D. Caroll, M. Flynn, K. Doherty, D. O'Brien (1996), "Social Class and Chronic Illness in Dublin", *Irish Medical Journal*, Vol. 89, No. 5, 174-6

Mackenbach, J.P. (1994), "Socioeconomic Inequalities in Health in the Netherlands: Impact of a Five Year Research Programme", *British Medical Journal*, Vol. 309

Marmot, M., M. Shipley, M. and G. Rose (1984), "Inequalities in Death — Specific Explanations of a General Pattern?" *The Lancet*, Vol. 1, 1003-1006

Marmot, M. (1999), "Multilevel Approaches to Understanding Social Determinants" in Berkman L. and Kawachi, I., *Social Epidemiology*, Oxford University Press

Marmot, M. and T. Theorell (1988), "Social Class and Cardiovascular Disease: The Contribution of Work", *International Journal of Health Services*, Vol. 18, No. 4, 659-674

National Nutrition Surveillance Centre, Annual Report (1999), *Dietary Habits of the Irish Population: Result from SLAN*, Dublin and Galway

Nic Gabhainn, S., C.C. Kelleher, A.M. Naughton, F. Carter, M. Flanagan and M.J. McGrath (1999), "Socio-demographic Variations in Attitudes to Cardiovascular Disease and Associated Risk Factors", *Health Education Research*, Vol. 14, 619-628

Nic Gabhainn, S. and C.C. Kelleher (1995), *Evaluation of the North-Western Health Board Lifeskills Health Education Programme*, Galway, Centre for Health Promotion Studies.

Nic Gabhainn, S., C.C. Kelleher and the Irish Network of Health Promoting Schools Steering Committee, (1998), *Evaluation of the Irish Health Promoting Schools Network*, Dublin, Department of Health and Children

Nolan, Brian (1990), "Socioeconomic Mortality Differentials in Ireland", *Economic and Social Review*, Vol. 21, No. 2, 193-208

Nolan, Brian (1991), *The Utilisation and Financing of Health Services in Ireland*, Dublin, ESRI

O'Donovan, O., P McCarthy, C. Kelleher (1995), "Health Service Provision for the Travelling Community in Ireland", Appendix, *Report of the Task Force on the Travelling Community*, Dublin, Department of Health

O'Donovan, O. (forthcoming), "Re-theorising the Interactive State — Reflections on a Popular Participating Initiative in Ireland", *Community Development Journal*, Vol. 35, No. 3

O'Shea, E. (1997), "Male Mortality Differentials by Socioeconomic Group in Ireland", *Social Science and Medicine*, Vol. 45, No. 6, 803-809

Pappas, G., S. Queen, W. Hadden and G. Fisher (1993), "The Increasing Disparity in Mortality between Socioeconomic Groups in the United States, 1960 and 1986", *New England Journal of Medicine*, Vol. 329, 103-109

Pocock, S., A. Shaper, D. Cook, A. Phillips, and M. Walker (1987), "Social Class Differences in Ischaemic Heart Disease in British Men", *The Lancet*, Vol. 2, pp. 197-201.

Quick, A. and R.G. Wilkinson (1991), *Income and Health*, New York, Oxford University Press.

Rawls, J. (1971), *A Theory of Justice*, Cambridge, Mass., Harvard University Press

Robinson, D. and S. Pinch (1987), "A Geographical Analysis of the Relationship between Early Childhood Death and Socioeconomic Environment in an English City", *Social Science and Medicine*, Vol. 25, No. 1, 9-18

Rosengren, A., K. Orth-Gomer, H. Wedel, and L. Wilhelmsen (1993), "Stressful Life Events, Social Support and Mortality in Men Born in 1913", *British Medical Journal*, Vol. 307, 1102-1105

SAHRU, (1997), *A National Deprivation Index for Health and Health Services Research*, Technical Report No. 2, Small Area Health Research Unit, Trinity College, Dublin

Saxena, S., A. Majeed and M. Jones (1999), "Socioeconomic Differences in Childhood Consultation Rates in General Practice in England and Wales: Prospective Cohort Study", *British Medical Journal*, Vol. 318, 642-6

Schrijvers, C.T.M., J.P. Mackenbach, J-M Lutz, M.J. Quinn and M.P. Coleman (1995), "Deprivation and Survival from Breast Cancer", *British Journal of Cancer*, Vol. 72, 738-743

Sen, A. (1982), *Choice, Welfare and Measurement*, Cambridge, Mass., MIT Press

Smith, J.P. (1999), "Healthy Bodies and Thick Wallets: The Dual Relation between Health and Economic Status", *Journal of Economic Perspectives*, Vol. 13, No. 2, 145-66

Starrin, B., C. Hagquist, G. Larsson, and P. Gunnar Svensson (1993), "Community Types Socioeconomic Structure and IHD Mortality — A Contextual Analysis Based on Swedish Aggregate Data", *Social Science and Medicine*, Vol. 36, No. 12, 1569-1578

Tunstall-Pedoe, H., D. Vanuzzo, M. Hobbs, M. Mahonen, Z. Capaitis, K. Kuulasmaa, U. Keil for the WHO MONICA project, (2000), "Estimation of the Contribution of Changes in Coronary Care to Improving Survival, Event Rates and Coronary Heart Disease Mortality across the WHO MONICA Project Populations", *The Lancet*, 355, 688-700

Tussing, D. (1986), "Irish Medical Care Resources: An Economic Analysis", Dublin, ESRI Paper No. 126

Weich, S. and G. Lewis (1998), "Poverty, Unemployment, and Common Mental Disorders: Population-based Cohort Study", *British Medical Journal*, Vol. 317, 115-119

Whitehead, M. (1987), *The Health Divide: Inequalities in Health in the 1980s*, London, Health Education Council

Wiley, M.M. and R.B. Fetter (1990), "Measuring Activity and Costs in Irish Hospitals: A Study of Hospital Case Mix", ESRI Paper No. 147

Wilkinson, R.G. (1996), *Unhealthy Societies: The Afflictions of Inequalities,* London, Routledge

Wilkinson, R.G. (2000), "Inequality and the Social Environment: A Reply to Lynch et al.", *Journal of Epidemiology and Community Health*, Vol. 54, No. 6, 411-2

Wolfson, M., G. Kaplan, J. Lynch, N. Ross, and E. Backlund (1999), "Relation between Income Inequality and Mortality: Empirical Demonstration", *British Medical Journal*, Vol. 319, 953-957

World Health Organisation, (1986), *The Ottawa Charter for Health Promotion,* Copenhagen

Chapter 9

Towards More Robust
Equality Objectives

*Sara Cantillon, Carmel Corrigan,
Peadar Kirby and Joan O'Flynn*

9.1 INTRODUCTION

The origins of this study lie in the Combat Poverty Agency's
1999-2001 Strategic Plan one of the objectives of which is to
narrow "the gap between the rich and poor through promoting
a fairer distribution of resources, services and employment opportunities in favour of people living in poverty" (1999: 10). The
book has been written to stimulate and inform policy and public
debate on the links between inequality and poverty in Ireland.
In particular it considers how the unequal distribution of resources and opportunities impacts on patterns of poverty. Contributors have discussed theoretical and conceptual issues that
underlie distribution and redistribution patterns and they have
examined some of the reasons why inequality has been growing during a period of rapid economic growth. Particular attention is given to the role of public policy in addressing imbalances in the distribution of the economic and social goods that
result in one group of people being poor and another rich, or in
one group being "more equal" than another. This final chapter
draws together key conclusions from the preceding analyses,
advocates a more explicit policy commitment to reducing inequality and eliminating poverty and outlines approaches to realise this objective more effectively.

9.2 RECONSTITUTING DISTRIBUTIONAL OBJECTIVES: FROM POVERTY REDUCTION TO EQUALITY

In the opening chapter, Kirby charts the way in which poverty reduction replaced greater socioeconomic equality as the principal distributional objective of Irish social policy between the early 1980s and the 1990s. He links this to a shift in western thinking on inequality over recent decades as it has moved from the objective of equalising the distribution of income and wealth throughout society to the objective of equal opportunities for women and minority groups such as Travellers, people of different ethnic origins, people with disabilities or the gay and lesbian community. One practical consequence of this shift, highlighted in his chapter, is the absence in the National Anti-Poverty Strategy (NAPS) of any objective to reduce income inequality. He argues that there are important distinctions between the concepts of poverty and inequality, as an increase in one can be found alongside a decrease in the other, and he points out that inequality has increased as poverty has decreased in the Ireland of the Celtic Tiger.

A principal theme of this book has been to shift the focus back to what is often called inequality of condition, namely the growing gap in incomes and resources — and therefore the material conditions of life, and opportunities for choice and advancement — open to different groups and individuals. The theme is explored both theoretically and empirically. Chapter 1 argues the case that poverty reduction is a minimalist objective that neglects some essential dimensions of what constitutes well-being or quality of life for individuals and groups. Among the issues it neglects is people's ability, despite their income, to access equally such public goods as education or health care, and the complex question of how people's status, in their own eyes and in the eyes of society, is related to their material standard of living. Thus, being relatively poor in a wealthy society can be a major obstacle to equal participation in that society, even if one has an income sufficient to satisfy basic material needs. The chapter also goes on to argue that empirical evidence worldwide points to the fact that, as the World Bank's *World Development Report* for 2000-01 puts it: "Other things being the same, growth leads to less poverty reduction in unequal societies than in egalitarian ones" (2000: 55). Therefore, even if government opts for a minimalist goal of reducing poverty, it is likely to be less effective due to growing inequality.

In Chapter 2, O'Flynn and Murphy extend the analysis through examining links between the distribution of decision-making power in a society and the distribution of income, wealth and opportunities. They outline different ideologies which inform distributional objectives — from liberalism to the Third Way — and discuss their implications for the balance achieved between the objective of economic efficiency and that of social equality. Chapter 2 also examines the tools available for redistribution of income and wealth, such as the taxation system and the social welfare system, and it goes on to explore critically the potential for redistribution of some new approaches such as the NAPS, social partnership and a rights approach to social provision. In these ways, O'Flynn and Murphy further develop the distinction between poverty and inequality, linking them to the way power is distributed in society and to the ideologies which inform and legitimate this distribution.

Having drawn a clear theoretical distinction between poverty reduction and greater distributional equality in these opening chapters, Chapters 3 to 8 focus on the distribution of income and other resources (welfare, housing, education and health) and the impact that public policy has on this. In Chapter 4, O'Reardon illustrates the increase in relative income poverty, the growth in the poverty gap and the worsening inequality in income distribution. These outcomes he situates in the context of Ireland's recent rapid economic growth and the emergence of social partnership as the dominant political economy model. In Chapter 5, Fitzgerald addresses the role of social welfare and taxation in the redistribution of incomes. She concludes that, while the former directs income towards the poorest in society, the latter system directs it much more towards the better off. In addition, Fitzgerald draws attention to the unequal tax treatment of earned income and capital income, which also serves the interests of the better off. In Chapters 6 to 8, Archer, Drudy and Punch and O'Shea and Kelleher highlight the unequal distribution of opportunities, provision and outcomes in the areas of education, housing and health care, all of which currently serve the needs and interests of those who are higher up on the income ladder.

A conclusion that can be drawn from a number of contributors is that, operating within a liberal economic ideology, Irish policymakers have consistently prioritised the needs of the economy over social objectives. It is also made clear in these chapters that government policies play a key role in generating and sustaining existing patterns of inequality. Furthermore, the more minimalist distributional objective of poverty reduction rather than the more difficult challenge of reducing socioeconomic inequality has remained the focus of public policy. This will need to change if inequality in its broader sense is to be successfully addressed. As various contributors to this book have made clear, taking the challenge of equality seriously will require that policymakers formulate more demanding social objectives and more effective and broad-ranging mechanisms to achieve them.

9.3 SOCIAL SPENDING PATTERNS AND DISTRIBUTION

In Chapters 3 and 5, Cantillon and O'Shea and Fitzgerald, respectively, examine the role played by social spending and the taxation and welfare systems in the redistribution of resources and the impact these have on patterns of inequality. While offering a review and critique of the current welfare and tax systems, the two chapters also suggest improvements as to how the welfare and tax systems could redistribute resources and potentially alter notions of social expenditure and social assistance.

Policy debate regarding redistribution needs to be placed in a context where firstly, it is recognised that inequality of disposable income (and wealth) is relatively high in Ireland and secondly that the dispersion of earnings in Ireland is increasing. It is often claimed that significant redistribution is not feasible as increasing globalisation undermines high tax/high welfare systems. Even assuming that such an assertion is true, the claim needs to be placed in an Irish context. It is now generally known that Ireland has the lowest tax burden (taxation revenue as a percentage of GDP) in the EU and that social expenditures are also relatively low in Ireland. It is less generally realised that Ireland has never had a relatively high tax burden — the tax protests of 1979 and 1980 were as much caused by the distribution of the tax burden within Irish society as by the scale of the Irish tax burden. Further reductions in the tax burden in Ireland are therefore unnecessary for efficiency purposes and, if implemented, will almost inevitably have a negative impact on the extent of inequality, as the poorest 20 per cent in Irish society have little if any taxable income.

Both chapters indicate that the Irish tax system is broadly proportional. The income tax component is progressive, despite the presence of regressive tax expenditures, but this progressivity is offset by the regressive structure of PRSI contributions and the regressive impact of excise duties. Capital income and wealth in Ireland are treated very generously from a taxation perspective. Given these properties, it is not surprising that tax reductions, which focus on income tax reductions, are inevitably going to further increase income disparities. The recent introduction of tax credits (which is equivalent to the standard-rating of personal allowances) was potentially a very progressive move. However, the actual progressivity of this move is dependant upon income tax reductions being targeted almost exclusively on increasing these tax credits. Yet recent reductions in income tax through cutting tax rates and widening the standard rate tax band have taken precedence over increases in personal allowances/tax credits.

Other tax policy alterations are suggested in these chapters. The structure of PRSI contributions should be reformed - a lower rate should apply to a broader base. Indeed, this latter measure is capable of improving both efficiency and equity. Tax breaks, when justified, should only apply at the standard rate of tax as such breaks are particularly regressive; the poor cannot avail of tax breaks as they do not pay tax. Tax breaks accorded to pension contributions and the income of pension funds appear particularly regressive in this regard and warrant attention from a distributional perspective.

Given the tax system's characteristics and the apparent general unwillingness to accept higher taxes, there is a need to look beyond the tax system as a mechanism for redistribution. The Commission on Social Welfare focused attention on the welfare system as the key mechanism for addressing redistribution. Indeed, as the poorest 30 per cent in Irish society depend on welfare payments, the level of welfare payments is particularly crucial in tackling poverty. Social welfare expenditure in Ireland is among the most targeted but least generous in the EU (8.5 per cent of GNP in 1999). One disadvantage of targeting welfare payments so tightly is their inability to redistribute significantly. However, it should also be noted that the existence of well-targeted social expenditure offers the ability to increase welfare payments substantially without affecting economic incentives, i.e. there is no serious economic efficiency argument against increasing well-targeted welfare payments significantly. Even if work incentives placed an apparent restraint on increases in welfare payments, this issue can be addressed via increased child benefit and FIS (family income supplement). An increased uptake of FIS should be particularly encouraged. Increased welfare expenditures could be directed initially at increasing state pensions and unemployment payments as these mechanisms appear to have significant impacts on the distribution of income.

In terms of improving equity by pursuing a policy of redistribution, increasing welfare payments is the obvious policy instrument, followed by increasing tax credits, increasing the standard rate band, decreasing the standard tax rate and decreasing the higher tax rate. Given the superior ability of the welfare system to tackle redistribution, it is interesting to note that the ratio of tax reductions to increases in welfare expenditures has increased from about two in the early 1990s to about five by 2000. However, the most recent budget, Budget 2001 arrested this trend.

The process of social partnership in Ireland has served to reduce unemployment and increase economic growth and hence national income. Social partnership has involved pay moderation in return for significant tax reductions and some increases in social expenditures. Employers benefit in particular from this trade-off as they gain from both increased economic growth and pay moderation. However, from a distributional perspective, it is noteworthy that commitments on increased welfare expenditures tend to be rather non-specific whereas commitments on reduced taxation levels are often specific and almost inevitably exceeded greatly during the lifetime (if not the first year) of the agreement. With respect to actual tax packages, it appears that, when offered a choice, the social partners have in the past opted for the less redistributive package.

In the long term, reduced levels of taxation can restrict the amount of government spending. However, in Ireland in the short to medium term, reduced taxation levels have not been a constraint as economic buoyancy has increased tax receipts.

Home ownership is an asset that will greatly impact on the future distributions of wealth and education and is probably the most important mechanism for transmitting earning power to the next generation. These examples emphasise the need to look beyond the tax and welfare systems as potential mechanisms for redistribution. The NAPS recognises this through its focus on education and unemployment and the inclusion of health and housing in the current review of the Strategy. Indeed, redistribution is far from being an explicit goal of the tax system. Social expenditures, which can encompass much if not all of public expenditures, can be used for the purposes of addressing redistribution. However, over the course of economic cycles, Ireland is a relatively low spender in terms of both gross and net social expenditures.

Social expenditures also have disadvantages as a mechanism and measure of redistribution. For example, as a percentage of GDP/GNP narrowly defined social expenditures decrease in boom times and increase during a recession. They therefore tend to increase inequality in boom times and decrease inequality in times of recession. Social expenditures are also used for the purpose of efficiency as opposed to redistribution. There is a need for a broader concept of social equity, one that goes beyond income transfers and social provision. Social quality offers one such concept. It argues for the recognition and representation of people in the decision-making process. In relation to older people, social quality incorporates the need for adequate income but also highlights the need for health promotion, community-based health and social care, life-long learning and flexible retirement. More generally, increased participation in the information based service economy could serve to decrease, as opposed to increase, the dispersion of earnings.

9.4 STRATEGIES FOR CHANGE

Having identified weaknesses in the policy approaches to tackling poverty and inequality, which policy strategies can alter the structural nature of inequality in favour of more social, economic and political equality that could also advance the elimination of poverty? Drawing from, rather than repeating themes in the book, a number of ideas are proposed below. These are not a blueprint, but are offered as signposts to more effective policy and to actions that might prevent and eliminate poverty through advancing greater equality.

9.4.1 ALTERNATIVE SOCIAL, ECONOMIC AND POLITICAL PERSPECTIVES

The first two chapters of this book and the opening section to this chapter set a clear challenge to reweight the emphasis in recent policymaking towards greater concern with the material conditions of people and the growing gap between rich and poor in Ireland. Evidence in earlier chapters repeatedly shows the link between the outcomes of social and economic policy and the structure of distribution. It has been demonstrated that equality is not an explicit policy objective or else it is interpreted in a relatively weak way as equality of opportunity.

For those concerned with tackling poverty and creating a more equal society, the challenge is to devise and win public support for strategies in favour of more equal income and wealth redistribution that transform the inequalities resulting from an emphasis on wealth creation and a concern with efficiency over equity. The challenge includes informing and educating public opinion about the extent of inequality in Ireland and its implications. There must be public debate, involving all sectors, on what kind of society we wish for the future. At its simplest, is it a society that reflects and advocates strong social solidarity, support for greater equality and for government intervention to redress market imbalances or one where individual self-interest and market liberalisation dominate? A further strategy is for those advocating the former to build strong alliances and work together to transform dominant approaches to policy analysis and policy design and formulation. This latter should include democratic approaches to planning that draw on the experiences of community participation and notions of empowerment.

9.4.2 SOCIAL RIGHTS/CITIZENSHIP

A number of chapters (for example, Chapter 2 by O'Flynn and Murphy and Chapter 7 by Drudy and Punch) propose that a social rights approach provides the state with an active tool to correct unjust market outcomes in a collective way. For instance, it is proposed that housing needs to be conceptualised, not as a market commodity or as an investment, but as a fundamental right. The welfare state and a progressive tax system are cited as making social rights a constitutive dimension of citizenship. However, a minimalist rights approach focusing on the rights of the poorest is cautioned against. Social rights, informed by a commitment to economic, social and political equality of condition, are advocated. Our concept of social justice needs to include a concern with the distribution of important resources such as an adequate standard of living, housing, health, education and so on. A range of economic and social rights are already embodied in the Constitution, legislation, policies and programmes. What is advocated here is to build on this foundation by adopting a more explicit rights approach in policymaking. This can provide a framework for setting stronger equality objectives in policymaking, for target-setting and for making explicit the impact of policy through measuring the extent to which such rights are realised.

The above two strategies provide a framework for change. In addition, remedying data gaps, developing integrated approaches to policymaking and devising effective mechanisms to proof policy design and formulation for its impact on poverty and inequality are needed.

9.4.3 REMEDYING DATA GAPS

One of the necessary tools in achieving an improvement in public policy is the availability of appropriate and timely information and data on which policies can be based. The Living in Ireland Surveys (LIIS), undertaken by the Economic and Social Research Institute as part of a pan-European study, and a number of studies commissioned from this work by the Combat Poverty Agency, the Department of Social, Community and Family Affairs and others, have added considerably to our knowledge of household poverty and income distribution. However, the fact that these surveys relate to households means that they do not capture information in respect of some of the relevant populations in poverty. In particular, as they are excluded from household surveys, we have little information on the incomes of the very poorest, including the homeless, refugees and asylum seekers and Travellers. For different reasons, we have little information on the incomes of the most affluent among our population. This is due to the very significant gap in our knowledge relating to wealth in the form of savings and investment, property holdings, stock and share portfolios etc., as opposed to income from earnings. The lack of data in this area means that we have little information on the incomes of the rich and of the role played by such wealth in increasing inequality. While recognising that the collection of such data is fraught with difficulties, and may do little to change the overall distribution of incomes, by clearly identifying the extreme positions on the income scale, such information is important in informing policy on redistribution.

The issue of gender inequality in respect of income and resources is one that also arises in the context of household surveys. As the LIIS surveys do not, in the main, question partners within households separately, the findings are perceived to be "gender blind" by women's representative organisations (*The Irish Times*, 17 October 2000). While we know that the earned incomes of women are lower than those of their male counterparts (Nolan and Watson, 1998; ESRI 2000) and some research has been undertaken on the intra-household distribution of incomes and access to and consumption of material goods (Nolan and Watson 1999; Cantillon and Nolan 1998, and Rottman 1993, 1994), a more complete picture has yet to emerge. Data of both a quantitative and qualitative nature will be required for this. More broadly, the lack of qualitative data on the experience of poverty and inequality also represents a significant gap in our knowledge. While often considered the "softer" side of social research, properly conducted qualitative research has a valuable role to play in both identifying the needs of those experiencing inequality and poverty and in the design of policy responses to these situations.

Clearly other gaps have been identified in our information in relation to specific areas. For example, in the area of health status, O'Shea and Kelleher highlight in Chapter 8 the lack of research into health inequalities in Ireland and the relationship between these and life circumstances, including socioeconomic status. Archer asserts the need for more analysis on the nature of the relationship between educational attainment and socioeconomic status, as well as on the purpose of education and its relationship to society as a whole. It is clear from these and other references that further research and evaluation in the area of policy to address inequalities and poverty is required if we are to fill in some of the blanks. Sound information on which to base policies should be a priority for any government. However, recognition of the importance of such information in policy formulation, implementation and evaluation is also essential but to date has been slow to develop in Ireland. The emergence of a programme of research within the Equality Authority, as well as continuing policy and research work by the Combat Poverty Agency, the National Economic and Social Council and the National Economic and Social Forum may serve to address some of these gaps. However, greater resources and expertise than is available to these bodies is required to address them all.

9.4.4 INTEGRATING POLICY APPROACHES AND PROOFING POLICY

The theme of social policy integration is specifically raised by Archer in Chapter 6 where he argues that policy analysts should move beyond calling for the integration of educational strategies with other measures such as housing and taxation. There is a need to explain why such integration is important and to identify which measures in other social policy areas are important from an educational point of view. This view is clearly grounded in the analysis that any action to address educational inequality must be seen in the context of addressing structural inequality in society.

Proofing of policy can potentially be a tool that supports enhanced social policy integration. As discussed in Chapter 2, policy proofing is currently employed as a mechanism for ensuring that policy design and policy reviews are assessed for their impact on issues such as poverty and gender. In the case of poverty proofing, it is to operate in the preparation of government Departments' Strategic Management Initiative strategy statements, in annual business plans, in preparing memoranda to government on significant policy proposals, in preparing Estimates and annual Budget proposals, and in preparing legislation, the National Development Plan and relevant EU programmes. The unequal distributional outcomes of recent Budgets, as referred to by Fitzgerald in Chapter 5, raise questions about the effectiveness of poverty proofing in the budgetary process. Likewise, O'Flynn and Murphy suggest that there is little publicly available documentation on the application of poverty proofing (Combat Poverty Agency, 2000.) It seems that relying on voluntary and pro-active implementation of poverty proofing is an inadequate approach, even when there is already a government decision that this is a requirement of government Departments. This has clear implications for the commitment in the Programme for Prosperity and Fairness (Government of Ireland, 2000: 98) to develop equality proofing and to take account of the integration of "equality proofing with other proofing systems".

Statutory obligation to proof policy, appropriate training and support for public service staff, a requirement to publish poverty and/or equality proofing exercises and giving higher priority to allocate resources (both new and existing) to actions emanating from the proofing process should be considered as steps to build up institutional and policy implementation capacity for expanding equality and eliminating poverty. The NESC is currently reviewing poverty proofing and will assess how poverty proofing can be integrated with other proofing requirements such as equality proofing, rural proofing and eco-auditing. A joint study by the Combat Poverty Agency and the Equality Authority on the inequality focus of poverty proofing will also be relevant to future developments on this issue.

9.5 CONCLUSION

The overall aim of this study is to inform and stimulate debate on how social spending creates or reinforces inequality and poverty. This is an important study in the context of the government's NAPS and ongoing public debate about who benefits from our new-found wealth. This study argues for a more equal distribution of income, wealth and resources such as education, housing and health as essential requirements for tackling poverty and for a more sustainable, participative and just society. The evidence, from the various contributors, strongly supports the need for more robust action on poverty and inequality if the NAPS commitment to ensure that very rapid, economic, social and demographic change reduces social inequalities and social polarisation is to be realised.

References

Combat Poverty Agency (1999), *Strategic Plan 1999-2001*, Dublin, Combat Poverty Agency

Government of Ireland 2000, *A Programme for Prosperity and Fairness*, Dublin, Stationery Office

Johnston, Helen and Tracey O'Brien (2000), *Planning for an Inclusive Society: An Initial Assessment of the National Anti-Poverty Strategy*, Dublin, Oak Tree Press in association with the Combat Poverty Agency

Nolan, Brian and Dorothy Watson (1999), *Woman and Poverty in Ireland*, Dublin, Oak Tree Press in association with the Combat Poverty Agency

Rottman, David (1993), *Income Distribution with Irish Households: Allocating Resources within Irish Families*, Dublin, Combat Poverty Agency

Rottman, David (1994), *"Allocating Money within Households: Better off Poorer?"* in Brian Nolan and Tim Callan (eds), *Poverty and Policy in Ireland*, Dublin, Gill and Macmillan

World Bank (2000): *World Development Report 2000/2001: Attacking Poverty*, New York: Oxford University Press

Glossary

The list below is a brief guide to some of the terms used in this book. Fuller definitions will be found in the text.

Average tax rate refers to the fraction of a person's total income paid in taxes.

Contractarianism refers to a method of arriving at moral judgements, rather than a substantive moral theory, through establishing principles instead of choosing particular rules.

Crude death rate measures the mortality differences between different socioeconomic groups without taking account of age; it is not therefore totally accurate.

Egalitarianism is belief in the principle of equal rights and opportunities for all.

Equity relates to the most socially just allocation of any good or service and involves some concept of justice or fairness in their distribution. Equity may imply equality but does not necessarily do so.

Gini coefficient is a widely used international measure of income or wealth inequality. The closer the coefficient to 1, the greater the inequality.

Imputed income is the rent homeowners would have to pay if they were tenants. It therefore constitutes an effectual subsidy to homeowners.

Incentive distortion is that which discourages people taking a job or keeps them in low-paid employment in order to retain social welfare benefits.

Liberalism is an ideology concerned with individualism, the belief in a constitutional state, private property and a competitive market economy.

Marginal tax rate is the amount of tax paid on an extra unit of income.

Neoliberalism is an updated version of classic liberal ideology which favours a market-driven development model over a state-directed one.

Perfect competition is an extreme classification of a market with a large number of buyers and sellers. There are no entry or exit barriers to trade a homogenous good, no government intervention nor transport costs and an elastic supply of factors of production.

Poverty proofing is the process whereby government departments, agencies and local authorities assess policies and programmes at design and review stages to establish their likely impact on poverty and other inequalities.

Progressive taxation redistributes income by taking more from the rich than those on lower incomes. ***Neutral taxation*** takes an equal percentage from all income groups while ***regressive taxation*** takes more from the poorer sectors.

Rawls' theory of justice seeks to validate theories in terms of their following right procedures rather than promoting the best consequences. Rawls argued that impartial, rational actors making choices behind a veil of ignorance are best able to choose between different justice theories. He said that civil liberties must be available equally to all and where inequalities exist they must be to the benefit of the least advantaged.

Redistribution is the process of transferring income from the well-off to the less well off via income tax, social welfare and the use of other benefits.

Regulation is state intervention to control or legislate for payments to individuals received from the sale of their resources, skills or services.

Replacement ratio is the ratio between a person's welfare income when unemployed and after-tax take home pay when employed.

A *rights approach* is based on elaborating as rights such social goals as an adequate living standard and decent housing. It seeks to establish a claim or legal entitlement to a particular resource or opportunity.

Selectivity provides social transfers to the less well-off on a means-tested basis.

Social closure is a process whereby certain classes or specific status groups in society retain power and income.

Social expenditures are benefits provided from public and private sources in the form of cash, goods or services to those who need support when faced with social risks such as illness, old age, maternity, loss of a supporting spouse or unemployment.

Social housing in Ireland is housing provided on a non-market basis to those who cannot afford to buy their own home or to remain in the private rented sector. It includes housing

provided by local authorities, housing associations, housing
co-operatives etc.

Social partnership is a mechanism for reaching a national
agreement between the Irish government and the social partners: employers, trade unions, farmers and community and
voluntary groups. Pay, tax and social welfare as well as other
economic and social policy concerns are currently agreed
roughly every three years.

Social quality is the extent to which citizens can participate in
social and economic life in ways that enhance their potential
and individual well-being.

Social transfers are those redistributive transfers made by
the state in favour of people with a low standard of living. They
involve collecting income via taxation and giving income to
others through direct payments or subsidies.

Targeting is the policy of directing additional resources to
areas and groups whose need is greatest.

Tax wedge is the gap between the costs incurred by an employer to hire a worker and the actual take home pay of that
worker.

Third Way is an emerging political philosophy which seeks
a balance between the unrestrained free market and state
socialism or centrally planned economies. It accepts capitalism but seeks to humanise it through state intervention,
welfare supports, collective decision making and a mixed
economy without damaging the dynamism of the market.

Universalism is the general provision of state services and
transfers without reference to the means of the recipients.

Utilitarianism is a philosophy that equates well-being with
maximising the sum total of human happiness. The optimal

solution is seen as the sum total of individual utilities. This puts no value on equality but is prepared to consider the unlimited sacrificing of the individual's well-being in favour of the overall good.

INDEX